SCREENWRITING
INTO FILM

SCREENWRITING INTO FILM

Forgotten Methods and New Possibilities

~Revised & Expanded Edition~

ANDRÉ SEEWOOD

To order additional copies of this book, contact:
Xlibris Corporation
1-888-795-4274
www.Xlibris.com
Orders@Xlibris.com
33982

CONTENTS

This work is dedicated to my father
A.B. Redding and the film professor
who inspired me, Dennis Turner, both
of whom are watching the film of life
from the other side

ACKNOWLEDGEMENTS

This book would simply not have been possible without the generous support and tolerance of my parents, Daisy & A.B. Redding. I would also like to thank The Detroit Film Center, The Public Benefit Corporation and The Center for Creative Studies for allowing me a forum to teach and discuss my ideas with intelligent and stimulating students, filmmakers and faculty; many of whom found these ideas applicable to their own artistic development.

The countless conversations that always became 2-3 hour marathons, about film and other related subjects I've had with friends such as Dana Thomas, Andre Royster, Gordon Ison, Steve Douglas, Royce Davis and Hercules Stewart have, no doubt, contributed indelibly to this book. I'd also like to thank Reverend Dwight Evans for all of his support and encouragement throughout the years. And finally, were it not for the continuous encouragement and recognition from Professor Rayfield Waller, this book would have perhaps remained an incomplete manuscript covered in the dust of passions lost. I thank you, Ray—you're the coolest Bro I know. And I thank God for my faith, these ideas and these beliefs.

Introduction to the Revised Edition

Writing, in general, is often thought of as an intuitive process. The success or failure of writing a screenplay seems to have more to do with one's actual talent and creative intuition than one's preparation or observational and analytical skills. The Great Storyteller is one who makes it all up as he or she goes along as opposed to the calculating thinker who measures and assembles bits and pieces into a coherent whole. But in the opinion of this writer, the Great Storyteller is a calculating thinker who only makes it seem as if he or she has made it all up as they went along. It is true that writing is to a large extent, intuitive, but behind every intuition lay preparatory events and observational skills that push the writer along in the direction to complete and tell the story in a particular way. To put it simply, writing is a combination of creative intuition and analytical preparation.

The analogy of screenwriting to mountain climbing is not as far-fetched as it would seem. The mountain climber must be prepared: his picks, boots, ropes, pulleys, supplies and etc, are all part of his preparation to climb the mountain. But he must also rely on his creative intuition: the judgment of what lay out of sight by looking at what's in front of you and the quick reaction to sudden changes that confront you. (See the film: TOUCHING THE VOID—2004) The screenwriter faces a figurative mountain that is no less intimidating and formidable: the screenplay. Only careful preparation can increase the chances of successfully completing what lay ahead of you. It is my sole wish that the contents of this book are used as preparation for the screenwriter on the journey up that mountain.

The screenwriter must in the end rely upon his creative intuition, but having certain preparatory and analytical tools can only aid in the difficult process. When I was younger, brazen and more defiant I shunned all formulas and archetypes as they seemed to take all of the creativity and discovery out of writing; Carl Jung was a favorite whipping boy.

But that was the hubris of youth. The old archetypes only look original in current films because they are cloaked in hip clothing and talking into cell phones. The old formula doesn't seem like a formula at all when you identify so completely with the characters and you and your generation are only encountering the formula for the first time. This goes along way in explaining why so many of my generation identified with Coppola's APOCALYPSE NOW (1979), having never read Joseph Conrad's book Heart of Darkness and so many of today's young generation identify with Park Chanwook's OLD BOY (2004), having never read Alexandre Dumas' book The Count of Monte Cristo. Yet there is a certain depth added to films that borrow or re-work literary source material that will be discussed in later chapters.

Such observations would seem to make remakes easy to do, but as many of us have experienced the new version is usually no comparison, critically or commercially, to the old version. All of the remakes and movies created from comic books point not to the often heard conclusion that Hollywood has run out of ideas, but instead that Hollywood and its audiences have run out of ways to accept new ideas. Perhaps the formulas and archetypes that are gathered in this book are meant to help a screenwriter re-approach or reinterpret rather than remake and ruin. The great filmmakers from Orson Welles to Jean-Luc Godard broke all of these so-called formulas and eschewed such archetypes . . . or did they? Breaking the rules because you don't know the rules can make one a fool. Breaking the rules in spite of the fact that you know the rules can have you hailed as a genius. This has less to do with the fickle nature of critics as it does in knowing which rules to break and when.

The impetus for a revised edition of this work was motivated by an influx of new and daring films released after 1997, the proliferation of relatively inexpensive digital video cameras and affordable non-destructive computer based editing systems. Films like THE MATRIX Trilogy, Christopher Nolan's MEMENTO (2000), Gaspar Noe's IRREVERSIBLE (2003), and the screenplays of Charlie Kaufman made the original version of this book seem incomplete and premature in some of its pessimism. The maturity of digital video and computer based editing systems is again putting the cinema in the hands of the brazen youth. Yet I fear that without some perspective on the past the promise of the future is too easily squandered in 'this week's special effects' and the commercial trends that grow stale quicker than the design of the opening credits of SEVEN.

Although it is certainly not my intention to simply write about many of the films just mentioned, THE MATRIX trilogy does not need a word for or against it from this writer that would carry any weight upon the volumes that have already been written. I am not simply trying to play critical catch-up. I made a lot of discoveries since the first version of the book that I thought would be better incorporated into a revised edition. I cut out a lot of chapters to avoid repetition and some observational mistakes. For instance my elation over the Coen Brother's FARGO (1995) caused me to be suckered into their conceit that the film was based on true events, **which** had to go. But I still love the film because now I understand that those fictional events were truthfully written and I might re-approach FARGO with a specific chapter some time in the future. Also I made some disparaging comments about Gene Siskel and

Roger Ebert, but now that Siskel has departed us those comments just seemed ridiculous. American film criticism was sinking way before they came along and has fallen even deeper since their arrival without making either one of them the scapegoats.

What follows is not a book of rules or a set of irreproachable formulas and equations that through some kind of cinematic alchemy will bring forth a great screenplay. What follows are observations, notes and the readings and research from previous thinkers, gathered together from years of studying and attempting to make films. The chapters on the seven motivations of murder and the five archetypes of drama are not meant to be the final word or inarguable precepts. These are all starting points that are meant to inspire rather than constrict.

Although I must apologize now for often my rhetorical style slips into an unflattering mode of absolutism, when in fact I only mean to indicate new possibilities from my observations of the methods of others. So if the reader discovers more than seven motives for murder, then in that discovery is perhaps a groundbreaking film. The more character archetypes discovered or known to the screenwriter gives him or her greater cause to explore them in their own dramatic works. I'd like to also ask for the reader's forgiveness as I refer obsessively to Francis Coppola and Mario Puzo's THE GODFATHER films. But it must be said that THE GODFATHER and THE GODFATHER part 2 are the proverbial benchmarks of American cinema and any reference to these works only serves to underscore their significance, quality, and classic status.

Throughout the book the reader will encounter the concepts and theories of the poet\filmmaker Pier Paolo Pasolini; in fact much of his work is the foundation upon which this book was built. One does not have to agree with Pasolini's politics, lifestyle, or artistic style to appreciate how much of what he said related to the process of filmmaking as a legitimate art form in its own right. The theories of other noted filmmakers are also included, from Russian filmmakers Sergi Eisenstein, Andrei Tarkovsky and French filmmaker Robert Bresson. But more often than not, it is the theoretical work of Pasolini that encourages the filmmaker to find his or her own personal voice in the cinema, by respecting the peculiar aspects of cinema that separate it from the other arts. It is also significant that unlike many other film theorists, from Christian Metz to Gilles Deleuze, the theorists I draw from are filmmakers themselves—so what they have to say can have an immediate practical impact as opposed to that of an academician.

As much as we'd like to think that great writing is wrought from intuition, it is just as often wrought from disagreement; disagreement that forces us to find our own way once we feel trapped by another's way. In fact it is the disagreement with a film professor I had many years ago that would subsequently become the point of departure for the creation of this book. So disagreement can be good so long as that disagreement is backed up with passion, curiosity and discovery. Intuition might be just the psychological conceit needed to cover the artist's egoism and absolutism. So with this said, I hope that the reader can find some use for this book in their preparation to climb the mountain of writing a screenplay.

SCREENWRITING: Practical Realities

E ach writer has his or her own personal approach to the act of writing for the screen. The disorganized writer may only be able to pull things together the day before the deadline. The organized writer may need to begin the first of many drafts well in advance of the deadline. Complicating matters, is the fact that no book, system, instructor, or guru can substitute for talent. So much of what has been written about screenwriting is ultimately academic. Yet many writers, myself included, continue to try to explain, suggest or map out new ways of approaching what is ultimately a subjective field where each surprising success in screenwriting further mystifies any attempt to systematize an approach. Most attempts at standardizing the screenplay deal solely with the mechanics of the screenplay format. There are many software programs that allow the writer to effectively write following these mechanical guidelines, but the machine cannot supplant talent, it can only be an aid to it.

My concern with this first chapter is the content, the story, for it is my sincere belief that the story must be grasped before the process of writing a screenplay can earnestly begin. It might seem unnecessary to have to say such a thing, that the story must be grasped first before writing the screenplay, but so many screenplays are started and left incomplete for this single reason that I had to mention this problem first. I should qualify my statement by saying that there is a greater propensity for a successful completion of a screenplay if the story is grasped before the actual writing of the screenplay. We must run the bath water and fill the tub before we put the baby in it, so to speak.

GRASPING THE STORY: The Simplification Process

One method for grasping a story uses several steps that involve the simplification of the story idea and its gradual expansion which helps plot the course of *what* is being told and can help determine *how* the story will be told. Writing is a discipline and if one respects it as a discipline the greater respect that discipline will garner for the writer.

The first simplification is *The One Sentence Premise*. Summarize your entire story into a one-sentence premise, almost as if it were a pitch to a prospective producer or investor.

E.g.: **Wasteland is the story of a delinquent teenager, with a dark secret, who is held hostage in an abandoned building, after he witnesses a murder by a young vicious killer.**

No plot twists, no elaborate explanations, keep this as simple as possible. There are two reasons for this initial simplification:

1) You're able to articulate your proposed story idea with great simplicity and confidence. This saves you the embarrassment of trying to remember every minute detail and plot twist when you're pitching your idea. And believe me you'll always be pitching your idea to actors, producers, crew-members, etc.

2) It gives you a simplified narrative starting point that you can refer to as you're writing your screenplay. This is very helpful in allowing you to determine the narrative approach and keeping you focused as your subsequent script expands with characters, motivations, and plot twists.

The second simplification is to write out a one to three paragraph *synopsis* of your story idea. This is not a treatment, nor is it a final summary that you cannot deviate from. This synopsis is just what it is, a short statement of what your story is about, where it will take place, who is in it and what will happen.

Example Synopsis of WASTELAND

A delinquent boy witnesses a brutal murder. The killer chases the boy through abandoned streets. The boy hides in a vacant building. The killer finds and confronts the boy. They discuss the crime with a nonchalant candor: over a shared forty-ounce of malt liquor and a blunt (or marijuana filled cigar). The boy reveals that he has been hiding the body of his girlfriend, whom he murdered the previous night, in this abandoned building. The boy and the killer grow hostile towards one another and fight. Only one emerges from the abandoned building alive.

This synopsis may or may not follow the actual presentation and structure of the events within the script and subsequent film. The synopsis gives us a slightly expanded view of what the story will concern. From this synopsis one must do the most important simplification:

Identification of Theme(s)

In one or two sentences identify the theme or themes you want to pursue or explore in the story. This is the most important part of the narrative simplification process. Without a theme, no story is of any lasting interest. Theme will be the organizing principle of the presentation of all events and characters within the story. A theme can be found within a story (for instance the theme of "family" legal and illegal as in Puzo's novel THE GODFATHER) or a theme can be applied to a story externally by the director or screenwriter. For example, the theme of professional integrity imbued within the films of Michael Mann, particularly HEAT (1995) and THE INSIDER (1997). Whether a theme or set of themes is found within the story or applied by the director/screenwriter one should never confuse story context with theme. Writer, T. Birch tells us that," the story context of FORREST GUMP (1994) is," a slow witted man makes his way in the world." The theme of the film, on the other hand, is a profound metaphysical issue: do we live in a world guided by chance or does God's grace influence or control certain events? The theme is introduced at the beginning of the film as a feather floats through the air (obeying chance and the laws of physics) and finally lands (by chance) near the hero." (T. Birch, Films and Popular Culture: Mistakes in Criticism)

See here how theme is the organizing principle in the presentation of events. The decision to create an opening shot with the floating feather which lands by chance at the Hero's feet is a pictorial illustration of a thematic concept that will organize the entire film. So one must find the theme within the story or find certain thematic obsessions that drive one throughout life and apply these obsessions to the stories one encounters or constructs. In actuality, if one's thematic obsessions are strong enough one will select only the stories that explore those obsessions; they will be the only stories that interest you.

Recognition of Story Archetype

Author Christopher Booker gives us seven basic story archetypes that inform the thematic structure of stories told throughout history all over the world in his expansive and insightful work, THE SEVEN BASIC PLOTS: Why We Tell Stories (Continuum Books, London, 2004). Although it seems counter-intuitive to limit all creative possibilities to seven "basic" certainties, as I mentioned before in the introduction; what often keeps us from noticing these seven basic story archetypes are the variety and uniqueness of the characters as well as the peculiarity of a story's context (circumstances, time period, setting and genre). Character and story context cloak an age old story archetype from our immediate comprehension and contribute to our cultural expectations and understandings of the conventions that distinguish one genre from another. Booker notes seven basic plots which I will list below:

1) Overcoming The Monster (Stories where an unlikely hero or heroine is called to protect the community or a loved one from a dark evil other. E.g., David & Goliath, The Epic of Gilgamesh, PREDATOR)

2) Rags to Riches (Stories where a poor and denigrated orphan receives a treasure or sudden wealth, but must grow internally to appreciate what is truly valuable in life. E.g., Jane Eyre, CITIZEN KANE)

3) The Quest (Stories where the hero or heroine is called to search for a fantastic treasure or distant valuable goal, but each station along the journey brings them perilously close to death while revealing something more about themselves in the process. E.g., The Odyssey, APOCALYPSE NOW)

4) Voyage and Return (Stories where a hero, heroine, or group of characters unexpectedly travel out of their normal everyday surroundings and into another 'abnormal' world that eventually becomes life threatening and they must make a 'thrilling escape' to return to their normal world. E.g., Alice in Wonderland, LORD OF THE RINGS)

5) Comedy (Stories of confusion and misunderstanding among characters who have disguised themselves, swapped identities, cross-dressed, or are mistaken for someone or something else which are initiated by the self-righteousness and/or hardness of heart of a character who must finally recognize their delusion to set things right. E.g., Much Ado About Nothing, ANCHORMAN: The Legend of Ron Burgundy)

6) Tragedy (Stories where a hero or heroine is tempted by a dark obsession to sever or destroy all bonds of loyalty, friendship, family and love by becoming a monster to others which leads to their own destruction or imprisonment. E.g., Macbeth, THE NINTH GATE, IRREVERSIBLE)

7) Rebirth (Stories where a hero or heroine fall under a dark spell that traps them in a state of living death until a miraculous act of redemption by another character liberates them. E.g., Sleeping Beauty, ALPHAVILLE, BLADERUNNER)

He says that these seven plots," are so fundamental to the way we tell stories that it is virtually impossible for any storyteller to ever entirely break away from them."[1] For instance, the Overcoming the Monster story archetype can be seen in films as disparate in style and circumstance as James Cameron's ALIENS (1986) to Martin Scorsese's CAPE FEAR (1991). The inhuman monster in ALIENS was originally designed by artist H.R. Giger and the human monster in CAPE FEAR was characterized by actor Robert DeNiro as ex-convict Max Cady. Clearly, the same archetype was cloaked by the different story context and genre of each film, but both films use this same story archetype to support a similar thematic structure.

Suffice it to say, that integral to each of the seven basic stories is the inner transformation of a character or set of characters from moral darkness to light or from ignorance to knowledge. Without this inner transformation none of the stories would work, so to speak, on our collective consciousness or hold our immediate individual interest. Booker links this internal transformation of a character to a deeper collective psychological disposition in all humans and I am inclined to agree with him. Although it is not my intention to summarize each of these story archetypes; I must encourage the reader to seek out Booker's rewarding work. He gives an exhaustive and detailed discussion of each story archetype, or plot as he calls it, that can aid the screenwriter tremendously by helping him or her identify which archetype best describes their story and what specific points of the plot must be addressed in that story to contribute emphatically to its demonstration without destroying the uniqueness of the character and peculiarities of the story's context.

For instance, in Jim Sheridan's film, GET RICH OR DIE TRYIN' (2005), written by Terence Winter, we can readily see the Rags to Riches story archetype of a recently orphaned child who learns to deal drugs on the streets of New York to survive and later grows up to realize his dream of becoming a rap superstar. The Rags to Riches story archetype has its literary antecedents in stories like, Aladdin and His Enchanted Lamp and Charles Dickens' David Copperfield, but the urban setting as well as the "thug" rap persona of rap music star Curtis "50 Cent" Jackson as the lead actor in GET RICH OR DIE TRYIN', obscures the archetype from our immediate comprehension. Moreover, this film attempts to splice another story archetype, that of Overcoming the Monster, into its story with limited dramatic success in the form of a gangster kingpin who'll stop at nothing to fulfill his evil desires for power and control.

So if we take these seven basic stories and factor in the idea of reversing them (e.g. Riches to Rags) or splicing them together for added complexity (e.g. Quest/Voyage and Return) it becomes apparent that rather than limiting ourselves with seven basic certainties, we are actually opening up our creative possibilities. And we may open these creative possibilities even further through our presentation of these basic story archetypes. It is the presentation of a story that is referred to in this book as a narrative or the way the tale has been told. If it is true that legendary French filmmaker Jean-Luc Godard said that," a story has a beginning, middle, and end, although not necessarily in that order," then we can be equally certain that true cinematic narration begins with the order of the story; its presentation to us.

The significance of recognizing which of the seven basic story archetypes best describes your own is that it helps you to develop your story properly by encouraging a thorough understanding of what specific plot points must be made to bring that particular story archetype to a satisfactory resolution. Far from turning a story idea into a formula, the recognition and adaptation of a story archetype helps to focus the theme and purpose of the material by discouraging misguided attempts at originality that can ultimately dilute the dramatic power and emotional impact of the story. If we are indeed telling the same seven basic stories over and over again, then our originality (after establishing the uniqueness of character and context) must come from the way we tell the tale and not simply the tale itself. Later chapters in this book will discuss in exhaustive detail the difference between story and narrative, but until then we will concern ourselves with the elements of story, character, motives, and the simplification process.

Writing the Treatment

The final simplification process is the writing of the treatment or as writer Michael Rabinger in DIRECTING: Film Techniques and Aesthetics calls it," The step outline."

"Here the writer summarizes in short story, third person, present tense form only what the audience will see and hear from the screen, allotting one numbered paragraph per sequence. It should read as a brief, stream-of-consciousness summation that never digresses into production details or the author's thoughts. It should include only the bare essentials, seldom dialogue, only summaries of each conversation's subject and development. Here is the beginning of something I have been working on:

Step Outline for THE OARSMAN

1. At night between the high walls of an Amsterdam canal a murky figure in black tails and top hat rows an ornate coffin in a strange, high boat. In a shaft of light we see that MORRIE is a man in his late thirties whose expression is set, serene, and distant.

2. Looking down on the city at night, we see a panoramic view over black canals glittering with lights and reflections, bridges busy with pedestrian and bike traffic, and streetcars snaking between crooked, leaning seventeenth-century buildings. As the view comes to rest on a street, we hear a noisy bar atmosphere where, in the foreground, a Canadian woman and a Dutch man are arguing fiercely."

(Excerpt from DIRECTING: Film Techniques and Aesthetics, by Michael Rabinger 2nd ed. pg. 143)

The importance of a step outline is multifold:

1) It allows you to concentrate on telling your story through images and sounds the basic and fundamental attributes of the cinematic language.

2) One can begin to build the lead and supporting characters.

3) It allows you, during the screenwriting and even the production process, to examine and re-examine your story, guiding you through the re-writing or re-thinking process. The key to all writing is re-writing.

4) In adapting novels or conceptual narratives the writer can determine with greater clarity what to keep and what to throw away by constructing the step outline as closely as possible to the theme(s) within the story or within the artist.

The simplification process is a formulaic method that should allow a writer/filmmaker to grasp his or her story with clarity and certainty. The grand and profound ideas that can be illuminated through a narrative—need not be present as one begins shaping the narrative. The potential for narrative confusion, creative fatigue or outright failure is higher when a writer cannot build his or her script from a clearly defined, simply articulated story. By completing the simplification process and defining theme(s) one can have a story that has a beginning, middle, and end. Having a complete story is half of the work of a complete screenplay. Having a strong theme or set of themes is the only way to get to a dramatically satisfying ending. Without a theme the entire script or story will be weakened. It is theme that guides you towards your ending (by illuminating the major conflicts and allowing you to pick which conflicts to resolve and which conflicts to leave open). Theme is the organizing principle of the characters and events presented in the narrative and subsequent film.

So by the end of the simplification process one should have:

1) A one sentence premise
2) A one or two paragraph synopsis
3) A theme or set of themes to be explored
4) Recognition of Story Archetype
5) A step outline or treatment of the story

These are the essential elements to grasping the story before beginning the screenplay that can increase the propensity for successfully completing the screenplay.

I must urge here that the simplification process does not mean that one cannot or should not deviate from what one has written. Ideas, depending upon the writer, take time to develop fully and are often scrapped, rewritten, or re-approached over and over again. I believe I re-wrote my screenplay for my film, WASTELAND, twelve times. The screenplay for my latest work, WHAT THE MAN WITH NO SHOES SAID TO THE MAN WITH NO FEET, underwent multiple re-writes, even down to very last hour of shooting—BUT, I had my story together years before I ever thought we would be shooting it as a film. Having my story before the screenplay allowed me to know my ending as well as how my re-writing would affect my ending. It helps to have a strong intuition about where you are going, even though you might not know exactly how you are going to get there.

FINDING THE THEME(s)

The theme is the underlying question or concept that your story ultimately asks, answers or explores. A story can have a single theme or multiple themes. The complexity of the story itself is not determined by the *quantity* of its themes, but instead by the *richness* of its theme(s). If a story has multiple themes it is best to divide them into major and minor themes (major, being the ones you feel most passionate about, minor being those held by supporting characters). It is the major theme(s) that your ending will demonstrate (See: Towards a Thematically Justified Ending).

The simplest way to identify themes is through the goals and wants of your characters. For instance, in a horror film your main character might just want to survive through the night. Thus, your immediate theme can be identified as survival. With this theme of survival you can now design ingenious events and circumstances that your character must overcome to demonstrate the theme of survival. The more ingenious the events or circumstances the richer the demonstration of the theme.

How you demonstrate your theme is a matter of your own creativity and originality, but you must have a theme to demonstrate or else your entire story will remain in the dark. In a later chapter we will examine the final film by Robert Bresson, L'ARGENT (Money, 1983) which has as its theme, borrowed from Tolstoy," How evil is spread." Bresson uses various cinematic editorial strategies to focus the audience's attention upon this single theme throughout the film. The events, actions and behaviors of your characters must illuminate your theme(s). If you don't illuminate your themes through the events, actions and behaviors of your characters then your story will be weakened, your characters will be flat and finally you'll have to rely solely upon CGI (Computer Generated Images) and other special effects to try and distract your audience from the purposelessness of your weak story.

Unfortunately, when one is putting together a story intuitively it is difficult to grasp the theme of the story without losing the thread of intuition that was guiding you. The loss of intuition while grasping the theme is really a consequence of inexperience rather than talent and one should not let it destroy one's will to complete the work. An alternate strategy is to complete the story and then search for the themes that are pregnant within it. A theme can be identified by careful observation of the actions and/or circumstances that reoccur throughout a story. It is the reoccurring action and/or circumstance that usually demonstrate the theme(s).

In the following chapters we will explore the building blocks of storytelling from character, theme, to ending. So it is of the utmost importance that we understand now that theme is what ultimately determines which narrative form should be used to best demonstrate it.[2]

NOTES

[1]   Pg. 6, THE SEVEN BASIC PLOTS: Why We Tell Stories, Christopher Booker, Continuum Books, London 2004.

[2]   For a more in-depth discussion on theme, drama and first draft revisions see Chapter: How to Dramatize: Perspective\Dialectic\and Thematic Node

BUILDING THE CHARACTER

"I obtain my first information concerning a man from the language of his physiognomy, of his behavior, of his apparel, of his rituals, of his body language, of his actions, and also, finally, from his written-spoken language. It is in this way that, in the final analysis, reality is reproduced in cinema."

-Pier Paolo Pasolini, 'The Written Language of Reality,' from HERETICAL EMPIRICISM, Indiana University Press, 1988, Trans. B. Lawton & L.K. Barnett.

To build a character one must think of that character first as a real living, breathing individual existing in the real world and not simply as a tool to highlight the vanities or cover up the frailties of one's ego. An individual's character is judged primarily in two ways: by what we see them do and what we hear them say. [1] Often there is always a discrepancy between the two modes; sometimes people don't do what they say or say what they don't actually do. It is within this discrepancy, between what a person says or doesn't say and what a person does or doesn't do, that is the dramatic crucible wherein an individual's character is judged. But we will return to this judgment of character later, first we must look at how a character is built in the cinema.

Most of us are already aware of how apparel or costuming defines a character from the superhero to the Mafioso; clothing is the first outward expression of character. More than this, clothing can also signify or obscure the class, education, age, race, and of course gender of an individual. Bernardo Bertolucci's first feature film, LA COMMARE SECCA (The Grim Reaper, 1962) based on a short story by Paolo Pasolini," is essentially a police enquiry into the murder of a prostitute, whose abandoned body by a Roman highway is revealed in the opening shots. An off screen police officer interrogates a series of men present in the park where the prostitute was waiting for a client—a petty thief trying his luck in the city, a smug pimp under the thumb of his aggressive fiancé, a smooth talking waiter from Milan, and a couple of awkward boys looking for money to buy food for a dinner with their would-be girlfriends. As each of them tells his version of events, we see the truth behind (and often in contradiction to) their verbal testimonies through extended flashbacks covering the day and night of the murder." [2] Far from being a simple murder mystery, LA COMMARE SECCA, in the tradition of the best Italian Neo-realist films, is almost an anthropological study of the various characters and circumstances of post-war Italian life. The guilty character, Natalino (Renato Troiani), speaks with a Northern Italian accent and wears wooden clogs that clack mercilessly against pavement and floor alike. His oddness, against the Southern Italian location of the film and the differences of the clothing and situations of the other characters mark him with a fatalism that outwardly expresses his guilt even before we ever see what he is accused of having done. Yet it is more enriching to have spent the day with these characters than to solve the murder itself which is revealed to be a vicious new form of class struggle and a post-war reevaluation of the sanctity of human life understood through the cries of Natalino when he is captured," She was just a whore."[3]

An individual's character is also judged by how they *respond* to their environment or milieu. Response to environment contributes to the building of a character by soliciting an audience's identification with the main character by how that character finds a solution to the problems within a particular situation or circumstance. In completed stories, the most important component of this solicitation is: The Introductory Circumstance. When a character is first introduced via a circumstance or situation, however slight or life threatening, he or she is judged by the audience; judged by what the individual audience members intuitively believe they would do in a similar situation or circumstance vis-à-vis the actual actions/decisions of the character. As audience members, we cannot help but to contemplate our own possible solutions before judging how the main character has responded; it is in this way that we are all involved, intuitively, with the logistics of a story.

The introductory circumstance is therefore pivotal to the audience's relationship to the main character and their understanding of the story. If the character appears smarter, more cunning, decisive, or physically skilled in solving the problems within the circumstance, he or she appeals immediately to the audience's idealized self. (i.e., that part of the individual audience member's psyche that sees itself as "better than most".) We might call this the "heroic self" of the audience.

If the character must rely on the help of donor or auxiliary characters in solving the problems of a particular circumstance, then he or she appeals to the audience's cooperative or "social self". (i.e., the ethics of team work, equity and fairness) If the character questions the rules, the authority, or the very legitimacy of the circumstance or situation itself whether through irreverence, rebuke, or direct challenge- he or she appeals to the audience's "rebel self"; the outsider, the joker, the villain, the agnostic or independent thinker. And finally, the character can acquiesce, submit or be coerced into satisfying the demands requested by the problems within the circumstance or situation and appear as a victim. In this case, an audience's identification with the main character is solicited through sympathy and its corollary of revenge or justice by appealing to the audience's "victimized self". So we have the four categories of an audience's collective intuition: 1) The Heroic Self, 2) The Social Self, 3) The Rebel Self and 4) The Victimized Self. The purpose of the introductory circumstance is to allow an audience a way to identify or empathize with the main character or characters as a way of defining the character(s) and eventually understanding the story.

In a deceptively complex film like the Coen Brothers' FARGO (1996) we are given no less than three introductory circumstances that directly relate to our judgment of the main character and the rich machinations of the film's story. The first introductory circumstance features a meeting with the main character, Jerry Lundegaard (William H. Macy), and his hired kidnappers, Carl Showalter (Steve Buscemi) and Gaear Grimsrud (Peter Stormare). Besides providing the audience with the relevant information concerning

24

the proposed kidnapping of Jerry's wife, this first introductory circumstance reveals to us the mix-up in scheduling between Jerry and his hired kidnappers which foreshadows later more unfortunate mishaps and mistakes in scheduling in the botched kidnap and ransom plot. Secondly, it reveals that Jerry has a sense of cunning, but lacks the physical skill and other abilities to get what he wants out of life directly. He must rely on auxiliary characters and a spirit of obsequious cooperation to solve this circumstance.

The second introductory circumstance presents Jerry's wife Jean (Kristin Rudrud), his son Scotty (Tony Denman), and his father-in-law Wade Gustafson (Harve Presnell) at his home just before dinner. This second circumstance reveals the emasculating situation of Jerry's domestic life in that his wealthy father-in-law looks down on him with contempt while belittling any of Jerry's attempts to get a loan from him to start a business of his own. Here we see Jerry as a victim of circumstance, so to speak, in that he has obviously married into a well-to-do family, but receives very little respect as a man for having done so. He also shows himself to be a bit of a rebel when he questions the hierarchy of Wade's company business structure by presenting his own business idea directly to Wade instead of following the usual protocol and presenting it to Wade's second in command. And finally, the third introductory circumstance reveals Jerry at work as an auto salesman for his father-in-law's auto dealership. Here he is seen attempting with great subterfuge, cunning, and trickery to swindle a customer into paying for a service he doesn't want on his new vehicle; further revealing that Jerry's rebellion has a villainous motive.

These three introductory circumstances appeal directly to the dark side of the audience's intuitions about the character by carefully building a portrait of Jerry Lundegaard that distinguishes him from us while simultaneously allowing him to become our gateway into the sardonic mayhem and murder that unfolds within the story. We have a complex character whose responses to his environment are alternately cooperative, deceptive, and victimized; all are responses that are important elements within the overall story. An introductory circumstance which reveals a main character's response to his environment helps the audience judge what kind of person the main character appears to be. Of course, as the story progresses the character can reveal other actions and responses that betray our initial intuitions that were gathered from costuming, ritual, physique, and their dialogue with other characters and in doing so enrich the character and the story.

We look at the behavior of an individual, his or her physical, mental and/or spiritual response to their environment; then we look at his or her apparel (not only what he or she is wearing, but also why we think they might be wearing such apparel in a given environment or milieu). The physique of an individual is also very significant. Psychologist William H. Sheldon revealed to us in his ATLAS OF MEN (1954), the three basic physiques of the male and by extension the female:

The Endomorphic—Roundness, centered on the abdomen as the physique of Clemenza (Richard Castellano) in Coppola and Puzo's THE GODFATHER or Kathy Bates in MISERY illustrate.

The Mesomorphic—Muscular, centered on the muscles and circulatory system as the physique of Santino (James Caan) in THE GODFATHER or Sarah Conner (Linda Hamilton) in James Cameron's TERMINATOR II illustrate.

The Ectomorphic—Angular/Skinny, related to the brain and the nervous system as the physique of Travis Bickle (Robert DeNiro) in TAXI DRIVER or Shelly Duvall in Stanley Kubrick's THE SHINING (1980) illustrate.

Sheldon also gives a detailed portrait of the temperaments of individuals that can be cross-referenced to these body types:

Endotonia—a love of relaxation, comfort, food, and fondness for people
Mesotonia—assertive, loves action
Ectotonia—private, restrained, very self aware

Sheldon, himself, was very aware that the degree of body type and temperament can overlap within an individual, so it was important to observe a person very carefully before determining the degree of body type and temperament.

In fact, these physiques and temperaments can be mixed and matched to create challenging and unique characters by the dramatist. For instance, an extreme endomorph (fat) can have the temperament of extreme ectotonia (private/self aware) as author Robert Bloch's original portrait of Norman Bates in his novel PSYCHO. In the book, Norman Bates was a fat, balding, middle aged man with a private (psychotic) temperament. Screenwriter, Joseph Stephano (with Alfred Hitchcock and his wife Alma's blessing) changed the Norman Bates character to an extreme ectomorph (angular/skinny) with an extreme ectotonic (private/psychosis) temperament. The key to the building of the Norman Bates character in Hitchcock's film of PSYCHO (1960) was this matching of extremes in temperament and physique.

The screenwriter, filmmaker, and casting director must give great thought to this aspect of character either intuitively or by intense people watching. No doubt the great appeal of the film NAPOLEON DYNAMITE is based on the physique, temperament, and apparel of its eponymous lead character. Dr. Sheldon, himself," was a keen observer of animals and birds as a child, and he turned this talent to good effect by becoming an avid people-watcher, and out of his observations he gradually elaborated his typology." (pg.88, TRACKING THE ELUSIVE HUMAN, Tyra & James Arraj, 1988) Sheldon gives us some fundamental keys to interpreting the character of an individual in normative circumstances. The physique and temperament, whether matched or mixed, are good places to start when building a character.

But how a character responds to the dramatic extremes of their fictional environment is usually distinguished by how the writer plays these normal assumptions of body type and temperament against each other to reveal an inner spiritual strength or frailty. A classic film like Stuart Rosenberg's COOL HAND LUKE (1967) written by Donn Pearce and

Frank R. Pierson reveals how the spirit of a character can withstand the crushing physical punishment and mental stress of imprisonment by creatively and continually striving to be free. A horror film, like the recent SAW (2004), plays against our assumptions of body type and temperament, particularly if not incredibly, with the body of the mastermind of the plot.

Another great example of a writer/filmmaker playing against our normal assumptions of body type, temperament and spirit is in Andrei Tarkovsky's film MY NAME IS IVAN (1962—Ivanono Detstvo) from a Vladimir Bogomolov short story. In this film, a steely eyed young boy is engaged by the Soviet army to perform reconnaissance missions during the Second World War. All of our assumptions about childhood and the extreme circumstances of war are challenged by this film. As Tarkovsky recounts," A third thing that moved me to the bottom of my heart: the personality of the young boy. He immediately struck me as a character that had been destroyed, shifted off its axis by the war. Something incalculable, indeed, all the attributes of childhood, had gone irretrievably out of his life. And the thing he had acquired, like an evil gift from the war, in place of what had been his own, was concentrated and heightened within him."[4] So we can conclude that body type and temperament can be the external 'cloaks' that a writer can use to reveal an internal strength or frailty of a character's spirit. It is by usurping our assumptions about a character placed in extreme environments and circumstances that the internal, spiritual, nature of a character is revealed.

Pasolini also describes another important key to building character, if not the most important: Rituals. Because ritual is such an inherent part of our day to day lifestyle, it often becomes the most oblivious aspect of character that is overlooked by the screenwriter. The reason for this oblivion is simple, we often only associate with others whose rituals match or blend well with our own and in matching and blending with others our rituals remain oblivious to us, unless there is a deviation.

Ritual is just what the word implies: repeated actions or behaviors that support an individual or group's well being and cohesion. Martin Scorsese gives us a dynamic presentation of ritual in GOODFELLAS. Henry Hill begins a sequence of the film by saying," Saturday nights were for wives, but Friday nights at the Copa was for the girlfriends." While he is giving this verbal information we see Tommy (Joe Pesci) and Henry (Ray Liotta) shaking hands and kissing the cheeks of their male peers and acquaintances. This gives us a view into the ritualistic actions and behaviors that define the characters that inhabit this world, this milieu.

These actions and behaviors reoccur and reaffirm the spiritual, material, and mental belief systems that galvanize the group by validating the membership of the individual. The implication is not only that certain nights at the Copa are designated for certain female companions, but also that each one of these nights that Tommy and/or Henry came to the Copa the shaking of hands and the kissing of cheeks must be performed with all the male members of their mafia family. Ritual is performance ad infinitum. Far

27

from being expressions of homosexuality, these kisses and hand shakes are expressions of fraternal affection within a brotherhood of men who are cheating on their wives and can be counted on to keep the secret. These behaviors and actions define them from all of us who did not take our wives or girlfriends to the Copa or shake hands and kiss the cheeks of our male acquaintances.

But another director whose keen sense of ritual becomes the penultimate definition of the humanity and individuality of his characters is the often-neglected Jacques Becker (1906-1960). This overlooked genius whose major works and life were completed at the beginning of the French cinema's Nouvelle Vague (French New Wave 1959-1968), produced several films in different genres that bear his remarkable talent to individuate and humanize his characters in spite of the genre.

In the elegant and elegiac gangster film, TOUCHEZ PAS AU GRISBI (Don't Touch The Loot, 1954), aging gangster Max Le Menteur (Jean Gabin) finds his retirement plans rudely interrupted by the kidnapping of his hapless partner and best friend, Riton (Rene Dary). After pulling off the heist of a lifetime (50 million in gold bullion) in near total anonymity, Riton lets word slip out through his insecurity with his young, two-timing, lay Josy (Jeanne Moreau). To get Riton back alive, Max must turn over the loot to the up and coming hoodlums now acting as kidnappers. Almost all is lost for love, for friendship, but most importantly to continue a ritualized way of life that has a dignity and a charm soon to be lost also.

Clothing, food, drink, music, and the different kinds of women become ritualistic actions and behaviors that define these characters and their milieu. All of this, most importantly, is what defines the character of Max. While watching the film one gets the deliberate impression that every word, every gesture, every mannerism, every want and wish has been expressed before—so much so that the lives being lived within the film have become ritualized. This is made absolutely and dramatically clear in the first scene of the film that takes place at Madame Bouche's restaurant at night in Pigalle (a notorious section of Paris).

Here Max and Riton sit at a table with their respective ladies: Lola and Josy, where both have been trying to convince Max to come see the new floor show the two of them will be performing at Pierrot's night club that evening. A song is playing on the jukebox. A man at a neighboring table hands Max a newspaper with the headline," 50 Million in Orly gold bullion robbery . . . still missing." Max hands the paper back to the man. The girls say," Max you have to come, Lola's a mermaid in the second number. It'll give the johns heart failure." The song ends and Max gets up to play his favorite tune. Outsiders enter the restaurant, but are turned away by Madame Bouche. Max's tune, which is the theme music of the film, plays. The insiders of the restaurant mock and laugh at the outsiders who tried to enter. Marco, a youthful hoodlum arrives, greeting all those who know his name and sits at the table with Max, Riton, and the others. The girls continue asking Max to come to the show. Max gives Marco a piece of cake that he eats silently. Riton tells Max that he can go to the show and then leave when he's ready. Lola looks at Max and says," No one is forced to stay." At this statement Max looks up and directly at Lola and knowing that she has spoken too strongly (a gauche) averts her eyes down to the table. Max agrees to go but can't promise to stay. Max also invites Marco. He notices Marco's sullen demeanor and asks him what is the problem," You owe some dough here?" Marco says," 9000." Max says," Relax, I'll take care of it." As Max leaves the table Marco says," Why should you?" Max pats him on the back as he leaves. He goes to the bar and pays Marco tab, with extra credit to spare, as well as his own tab; then all leave *'ensemble'* (together) for the club.

This introductory circumstance establishes the ritualistic behavior and actions that will ultimately constitute the entire film and appeals directly to the collective social self of the audience. The milieu is closed to outsiders. The control of women exercised with the eyes and facial expressions of Max reveals both the familiarities that Max has with them as well as the limits and boundaries of their relationship to him. The way Max read the demeanor of Marco and answered the question before Marco could explain his demeanor, again establishes ritual as the defining characteristic for understanding the close inter-personal relationships these insiders have with one another.

Max's reluctance to go to the show is confirmed in the third scene as he explains to Riton that he is too old to be waiting to take showgirls to a hotel when 10 years earlier he would have been waiting for the girl," to come home with the bread." Max has been around and around the block and he knows its time to retire from the rigors of this lifestyle. Moreover, the playing of his tune, his favorite melancholy yet whimsical melody is a ritual that defines his soul, the yearning for joy in a place where one has known both sorrow and happiness is the most effective presentation of ritual as repeated performance.

So we build the character by what he or she wears,

1) Costume

How they respond to the interruptions and circumstances of their environment,

2) Response to environment or milieu

How they are built

3) Physique (which includes gait, body language, gesture)

The repeated behaviors, actions, and performances

4) Ritual

And finally, their speech (idiom, accent, rhythm, vocabulary and tone)

5) Dialogue, or quite simply the ways in which they express themselves and understand others.

THE INFINITE POSSIBILITIES OF WHAT WE DISAPPROVE

The attentive screenwriter will do his or her best to build their characters, using these impressions of reality or im-signs as Pasolini described them, because this is one of the many ways the cinema communicates to us. Whether celluloid or digital, it reproduces reality with reality but what makes it an art is the subjective emphasis the filmmaker gives these impressions through sound and image. "The cinema author has no dictionary but infinite possibilities."[5] Yet to fully appreciate these infinite possibilities we should defer to a discovery by French filmmakers Alain Resnais and Marguerite Duras," that a character becomes a real character when he begins to do things we don't approve."[6]

Some of us use our characters as simple mirrors of our own narcissism which inhibits us from allowing the characters (or the actors portraying the characters) to become more than mere caricatures. Resnais and Duras' discovery reveals that when we release a character from our inhibitions—when a character is finally freed from our own vanities and frailties—the writer/filmmaker can allow the character and the film to take a direction that can challenge and fascinate us. Admittedly, it is not easy to allow your character(s) to do things that you don't approve, but often all it takes is one gesture, line or glance and this can free up the writer to follow his or her intuition towards rich goals and powerful conflicts and resolutions. The disapproved of act is a form of what Aristotle called *hamartia* or," errors made in ignorance or through misjudgment; but it will also include moral errors of a kind which do not imply wickedness."[7] For it is intentional wickedness that would make the character irredeemable in the eyes of the audience. The disapproved of act must be a moral error made through ignorance or misjudgment so that it can ultimately be forgiven and/or redeemed. I'd like to "return to the well" of cinema history and give some interesting illustrations of disapproval as dramatic possibility and juxtapose those achievements with a contemporary film that fails to open itself up to these wonderful possibilities because of the inhibitions of the filmmakers.

PUZO'S CONCERN

Let us encounter a fact that has become legend: Mario Puzo and Francis Coppola were in great disagreement with each other during the construction of the screenplay for THE GODFATHER PART II. Coppola was adamant in his desire that Michael Corleone have his brother Fredo (John Cazale) murdered, if for no other reason than to," destroy the Corleone family, and make it clear that Michael was a cold-hearted bastard murderer."[8] Coppola was not simply being hubristic, he was being a moralist. His need to debase the character of Michael Corleone was a reaction to the 'gap' between what he thought he had done in THE GODFATHER PART I: "I felt I had presented [Michael] as a monster at the end," and the public," thought I had romanticized Michael."[9] Now, Puzo, on the other hand, was just as adamant about not wanting Michael to murder his brother. This disapproved of action would, no doubt, kill some of the box office and thwart the chances of another lucrative sequel.

Yet it was Puzo, the man who says he wrote The Godfather novel because he wanted to make some money, that came up with the most artful and profound compromise: Michael could have Fredo killed, but only after their mother dies. He knew intuitively," that if Michael killed his brother while his mother was still alive the audience would never forgive him."[10] The genius of Mario Puzo is often obscured by his explicit statements about the financial incentives for writing the novel. Puzo's true concern was with the presentation of plausible characters whose actions and behaviors would ring true to the audience in spite of their criminal activities.

Although Puzo did not approve of Fredo being killed at the behest of his brother, Michael, he allowed the act to occur—after the mother's death—thus expanding the dramatic possibilities concerning the inter-relationships of the Corleone family. These expanded inter-relationships come together in the magnificently rendered scenes of Michael's sister, Connie Corleone-Rizzi (Talia Shire) discreetly begging him to see Fredo at their mother's funeral. (We should note that previously Connie and Michael were estranged from each other.) When Michael does come to see Fredo, while their mother's body lay in its casket behind them, he gives him a duplicitous "Machiavellian" embrace with both arms. As Fredo weeps in his arms, believing that they are reconciled, Michael coldly glances at his henchman, Al Neri (Richard Bright); a hidden code, signaling that Michael's order to kill Fredo had not been changed despite this appearance to the contrary. The entire scene evokes an observation by Machiavelli," the great majority of mankind are satisfied with appearances, as though they were realities, and are often more influenced by the things that seem than by those that are."[11] Because of Puzo's reluctant acceptance of an action he disapproved of for the character of Michael and the fate of Fredo, new dramatic possibilities were expanded between Connie and Michael as well as many of the other supporting characters.

IN PURSUIT OF REDEMPTION

In Pier Paolo Pasolini's debut film, ACCATTONE (1961), we follow the struggles and tribulations of a lowly street hustler\pimp whose life alternates between the tragically comic and the pitifully tragic as Accattone (Franco Citti) tries to achieve everything he can in life without having to work for it. The very name Accattone is Italian slang for beggar, thief and scrounger. There is a pivotal scene in the film where Accattone steals a locket from around the neck of the son he has fathered out of wedlock, whom he rarely ever sees, so that he can buy food to eat. This is a moment that both condemns and exalts Accattone. His actions are reprehensible in the eyes of the audience and yet this action humanizes the character, divorcing him from a simple narcissistic presentation of Italian post-war life; he is given a kind of 'cardinal' flaw that is so necessary for man to survive in a world that is less than heaven.

"This is a moment that both condemns and exalts Accattone." (Franco Citti) Photo courtesy of Norman MacAfee Collection

It is a disapproved of action that begs for the character to redeem himself. Pasolini moves his Accattone character into pure tragedy and an almost saintly demise as he tries to pursue his redemption. Acts that we disapprove of can have the effect of giving the character a goal to achieve and conflicts to overcome that audiences can ultimately identify with and empathize. In both THE GODFATHER PART II and ACCATTONE, characters perform acts that are disapproved of either by the audience or the authors, but they are necessary actions that expand the story and dramatic possibilities inherent in the material that would have otherwise remained dormant.

Having a character express an opinion or perform an act that you yourself would not do and that you don't approve of, removes the narcissism (or vanity) that imprisons your characters as reflections of your own ego. When the character does something that we disapprove, it has the effect of intensifying the inter-relationships among supporting characters (like Connie and Michael) or adding an urgency of redemption to the story which increases the richness of the material. It is really only by intentionally creating the 'disapproved act' that the writer can begin to explore the truth in the fiction.

IT'S HARD OUT HERE FOR A FILMMAKER

In Craig Brewer's film, HUSTLE & FLOW (2005), we have the story of a hustler\ pimp, Djay (Terrence Howard), who wants to get out of the 'street game' and become a rap artist. The film, produced by filmmaker John Singleton and Stephanie Allain, was a modest success, with its signature rap song," Whoop Dat Trick," receiving an Oscar for best song in 2006. Strong performances and Oscar award winning song aside, the story itself suffers severely from the inhibitions (or prohibitions) of its creators. The reason the film suffers is that to bring the story of a pimp who wants to be a rap star to the screen, the filmmakers had to neutralize the violent and unforgiving misogyny (hatred and degradation of women) that is at the core of a pimp's (any pimp's) character.

The best selling literary authors on the topic of African-American pimping, Donald Goines and Iceberg Slim, have at the center of their pimp characters, a vicious hatred and disrespect for women typified by violence, a soul crushing authority, and a perverse loyalty (that allows the pimp to pursue his pleasures unfettered with the profits of the women who sell their bodies for him). The proverbial bitch slap," was a display of dominance, both to the recipient and any observers. A pimp had to have it known at all times that he was in charge of his shit."[12] The sheer cruelty, avarice and two-faced nature of the pimp (who seduces and abuses, drugs and denigrates his women to keep them in line) was removed from the pimp character of Djay in HUSTLE & FLOW.

In fact, the relationship between Djay and his working girls is one of mutual agreement rather than the bare-fisted dominance and control so typical of the 'real' participants in the street sex trade. The "charm" of the pimp (and I use that word ironically) has been surgically removed from the pimp character in HUSTLE & FLOW; thus neutralizing a truthful and uncompromising portrayal and weakening the inter-relationships among the characters. Let's face it, couldn't the White girl, Nola (Tarlyn Manning) turn tricks just as easily and with more success without Djay watching her back and taking her earnings? These teenage runaway White girls are often called 'snow bunnies' in the street slang of Black pimps and are ruled with an iron fist. A pimp doesn't necessarily provide protection for his prostitutes (that's part of the game that they play on their women). How can he? He's not in the room, backseat, alley, or bush where such acts actually take place between a prostitute and her john. A real pimp controls the mind of his woman and he does this with a cult-like discipline that necessitates violence, verbal denigration, humiliation, fear and in some cases physical torture.

HUSTLE & FLOW suffers greatly from this weakness of dramatic possibilities if simply because neither the filmmakers nor the actor wanted to allow the character to do what they (and the naïve viewing audience and critics) ultimately would have disapproved of: Djay beating and berating his women unmercifully for total domination and control over their minds and bodies. Even Pasolini's ACCATTONE, made over 45 years ago, revealed the pimp's misogyny towards his woman, Maddalena (Silvana Corsini). After she was beat up and had her leg broken by a gang as revenge for Accattone snitching to the police on one of their members, Accattone forced her back out onto the streets, with a cast on her leg, to make him some money so that he could eat. Many readers may object to what I am suggesting if simply because today's audience would probably not tolerate such behavior on screen, but I ask," Why make a film about a despicable character and not show what makes us despise him?"

Moreover, had the filmmakers decided (or resolved) to include this vicious misogyny in the form of a disapproved set of actions against women, it would have increased the dramatic potential of the supporting characters; particularly the recording engineer, Key (Anthony Anderson), a married and church-going man who would have certainly objected to such behaviors. (One wonders how he could have tolerated what little he did see or suspect was going on in the first place?) Because the film lacks an explicitly disapproved of act, it does not have the redemptive force that would give its story the significant moral urgency it sorely needed and it leaves its supporting characters with little to do.

If we are going to tackle difficult subjects (pimping, mafia, drug dealing, prostitution, bi-sexuality, etc.) we cannot be timid and narcissistic in our telling of these subjects; compromising or neutralizing the matter, makes the issues even more conspicuous for not having been fully explored. Although Terrence Howard gave an admirable performance, the danger of what the filmmakers were playing with—misogyny—proved to be too much for their cautious spirits to bear. An Act or opinion of which we disapprove is the best way to reveal new dramatic possibilities that were dormant in the material and\or hidden from our narcissistic view. The act or opinion can expand the involvement of supporting characters and\or create stories of redemption that move an audience. In many instances, the disapproved of act is what precipitates a character's inner transformation from darkness to light or from egocentricity to selflessness. If a writer cannot 'divorce' him or herself from their fictional character they may never see the beautiful possibilities that lay in what they disapprove of.

NOTES

[1]   Alternately, in reality we are also judged by how we smell, but the effect of hygiene can be mimicked on screen.

[2]   David Thompson, LA COMMARE SECCA, DVD Liner Notes, Criterion Collection (2005)

[3]   Perhaps we should contemplate the woman who is a prostitute. She is not particularly attractive and looks about 8 or 9 years past her prime. From her angular and aging physique it looks as if she started prostituting herself during or just after the war as a means of survival that has now become a ritual. Her erotic twitches to entice her john seem more like rehearsed movements that play on the domineering aspirations of the male ego. Moreover, her ritual of waking in the afternoon, no matter what the weather, seems to imply an empty life whose only affirmation is found in brief, cheaply purchased, nocturnal encounters. If we somehow feel sorrow for her murder as a human being, then we should feel it for her as a part of society also. Far from

34

being socially worthless, even the prostitute has a necessary function in society that moral obstinacy and class prejudice cannot totally obscure.

(4)   Page 17, SCULPTING IN TIME, Andrei Tarkovsky, trans, Kitty Hunter-Blair, University of Texas Press, Austin 1986.

(5)   Pg 545, Cinema as Poetry by Pier Paolo Pasolini in MOVIES & METHODS Vol 1, ed. By Bill Nichols, University of California Press, Berkeley, 1970.

(6)   Pg.32, ALAIN RESNAIS by James Monaco, Oxford University Press, New York, 1979.

(7)   Pg. xxxiii, Introduction to Aristotle's POETICS by Malcolm Heath. Penguin Books. New York. 1996.

(8)   Pg. 86, GODFATHER II: A Deal Coppola Couldn't Refuse by John Hess in MOVIES AND METHODS Vol.1, Ibid.

(9)   Pg.83, Ibid.

(10)   Transcribed from Mario Puzo interview on THE GODFATHER Collection DVD. Paramount Pictures 2001.

(11)   Niccolo Machiavelli, DISCOURSES. Book 1, 25.

(12)   Pg.55, LOW ROAD: The Life and Legacy of Donald Goines by Eddie B. Allen, Jr. New York. St. Martin's Press. 2004.

FIVE CHARACTER ARCHETYPES OF DRAMA

Archetypes	Defined by	Narrative Placement	Narrative Destiny
The Hero	The Selfless Act	Anywhere in story	Either survives physically or His/her acts survive in the admiration of others
The Villain	The Selfish Act	Anywhere in story	Is killed/mortally wounded or defeated by the hero or the acts of others directly inspired by the hero
The Trickster	Reveals or changes the destiny or fate Of the hero	At the crossroads or turning point	Can return to receive gratitude or acknowledge-ment from hero
The Pragmatist	Peacemaker/keeper Interdependence Fairness, sympathy Loyalty	Matched with Hero or Nihilist	Dies a violent or unjust death First half of story For the hero Second half of story for Nihilist
The Nihilist	Self-gratification Independence Lack of sympathy Sociopathic cunning Detests hypocrisy	Matched only with Pragmatist	Dies in a hailstorm of Bullets or violent death

Each of these archetypes and the narrative paradigms most usually associated them will be discussed in the following pages.

THE PARADIGM of the HERO and the VILLAIN

Vladimir Propp identified for us the dramatic paradigm of the hero and the villain in his work,' MORPHOLOGY of The FOLKTALE'. After careful analysis of a compendium of Russian folktales Propp enumerated the functions of the dramatis personae found in the tales. He revealed an underlying structure of the folktale that can be found even in the folktales of ancient and diverse cultures. In our modern culture Propp's enumeration and detail of the Hero and the Villain forms a dramatic paradigm that can be seen in the most popular blockbuster films to the most obscure Japanese anime or graphic novel. In his list of functions he identifies one of the most important distinctions in the character of the hero. He identifies that there are two types: the seeker hero and the victimized hero. Within his list of functions, we find a paradigm that suggests that the villain must perform some selfish act. An act that either harms the hero or his/her family (a victimized hero) or the villain takes or destroys something that causes the hero to go on a search to seek a goal or object that is lacking (a seeker hero). In the following, we will look at how a hero and a villain are defined and how the creative dramatist can modify or enhance these definitions by looking at how other dramatists have achieved these modifications.

THE SELFLESS ACT

Much has been written about the hero and the villain archetypes, so much that we turn our attention to what defines these archetypes and where these archetypes can be placed in the narrative. For instance, if the hero is defined by his selfless act(s)—acts committed where in which he has no ulterior motive, financial gain, or concern for his own self preservation—this archetype does not have to be revealed at the beginning of the narrative. The hero can be revealed anywhere in the story. For example, Travis Bickle (Robert DeNiro) is not perceived as a hero until the final third of Scorsese and Schrader's TAXI DRIVER (1975). His actions during the beginning and middle of the narrative are disturbing, even threatening. His first selfless act comes when he kills an armed robber and saves a storeowner. This act begins the transition of this disturbed individual towards the full heroic nature of his destiny that was buried underneath his growing nihilism and despair. So it is conceivable that a villainous or disturbed character can be transformed into a hero later in a narrative via selfless acts that are redemptive in the eyes of the audience.

A film like, THE SHAWSHANK REDEMPTION (1996) features a victimized hero first presented as a villainous character. The character is later disproved of the murder of his wife and ennobled by a selfless act. This observation begs the question: Can a hero be revealed as a villain later in a narrative? The answer is yes, of course, but there must be some external force to change the selfless character into a selfish character. Say, for instance, in Shakespeare's MACBETH (1971) as filmed by Roman Polanski, we see a character first as hero then as villain. Macbeth is hailed as a hero at the start of the narrative for fighting selflessly on the behalf of the King, but once his mind is poisoned with selfish ambition from the (trickster) witches and that ambition is goaded by his wife, Macbeth turns villainous. This is why I concluded that the hero or the villain archetypes could be placed anywhere within the narrative. Since the revelation of the hero or the villain through selfish or selfless acts can be thematically justified even at the last moment of the story as in TAXI DRIVER or the first moments as in MACBETH.

THE TRICKSTER

More often than not it is a trickster character that changes the destiny or fate of the hero, for good or ill. The trickster, whether magic creature, cunning sage, sexual tempter, is there at the crossroads of the narrative: the threshold of destiny. "All tricksters like to hang around the doorway, that being one of the places where deep-change accidents occur." (The Trickster Makes This World, Lewis Hyde pg.124) Most of us can identify the oracle in THE MATRIX series as a trickster character. Trickster characters can divine the destiny of their heroic or villainous inquirers. In THE MATRIX (1999), the oracle/trickster told Neo (Keanu Reeves) exactly what he," needed to hear," to guide him towards his heroic destiny. As Lewis Hyde mentions," Tricksters are masters of reversal," and the oracle's use of reverse psychology to allow Neo to accept his destiny was just the 'truth' that was needed to inspire his selfless act of saving Morpheus (Laurence Fishburne).

Returning to our earlier example of TAXI DRIVER, we can identify the character of Wizard (Peter Boyle) as the Trickster archetype whose hackneyed advice to Travis Bickle neither inspires nor detracts Travis from his fate. What is important is that Travis sought Wizard out and his words," You do a thing and that's what you are . . . I mean, we're all fucked more or less," act as a commentary for the audience about Travis's place as a cynical everyman in this increasingly pragmatic society and ultimately his heroic destiny.

The trickster is always found at the crossroads of the character's destiny. He or she stands in the doorway of what was and what is to come. We should also remember the Voodoo diviner that changes Lil' Dice to Lil' Ze in Meirelles' CITY OF GOD (2003). It was in this change, this divination that Lil Ze came to menace the world he inhabited as a vicious drug lord and later a raving nihilist. This trickster archetype is not always a magical creature, shaman, psychological expert or mystic, the trickster archetype has a thousand faces. In Native American folklore the trickster is the coyote and in West African Yoruba religion the trickster is called Eshu. In Greek mythology the trickster is Hermes and of course in Norse mythology the trickster is Loki. The trickster is a character of many disguises who sets, divines, or modifies the fate of the hero and/or villain.

But we should also be receptive to the concept of the trickster being an inanimate object as opposed to always thinking that the trickster is a person or magical creature. In Peter Jackson's LORD OF THE RINGS series the trickster is the ring of Sauron itself: ". . . forged in secret, a master ring to control all the others . . ." This inanimate object changes the fate and destiny of whomever possesses it. Thus, the trickster to the creative dramatist does not always have to be a person or a magical being it can be an object that causes the hero or the villain to change their destiny or fate to acquire it or destroy it.

THE SELFISH ACT

We know that what divides the hero from the villain is the selfish nature of the villain's actions. Self interest, while not a vice in and of itself, separates and defines the villain from the hero in that the villain acts solely upon what will gratify his own predilections. He will stop at nothing and loses all decorum, moral judgment, and respect to acquire what he or she wants. Villainy can also be disguised in the form of Tempter and Temptress characters who inflame the passions of heroes and heroines, but for their own selfish gain. But we must be very careful as we construct our villains; for although the villain is selfish, the reasoning, the justification for his actions should not be silly or implausible. That is to say, the villain has his or her reasons for these actions and those reasons are usually sound if we take into consideration the self-interest that guides their judgments. Without sound reasoning underpinning the selfish acts of the villain, the character can too easily slip into caricature.

What often weakens, so many dramatic attempts, is a weak or implausible villain. Yes the hero can fly through the air, dodge bullets, bend light and steel, but the villain must have a valid reason for his or her selfish acts or the force of the drama will always appear weak and circumspect. Perhaps the cumulative effect of television news reports that summarize crimes as 'drug related', 'gang related', or 'the result of a domestic violence situation,' has contributed to the new dramatist's inattention to the reasoning of the villain. Saying a murder was committed because of an outstanding debt or giving the villain the most obvious actions that will have him or her judged as bad is not enough to support a full dramatization of the villain archetype and/or drive the narrative to a dramatically satisfying conclusion.

The selfish act has a myriad of dramatic manifestations. The motive of revenge, which can be used by hero and villain alike, has its only dividing line in the fact that the hero usually has a self-less interest in exacting revenge upon an injustice, whereas the villain has a personal vendetta or score to settle. That selfless interest is usually found in the need to set things right, a moral urgency that concerns and affects the community at large and not just the hero alone. Murder as a form of Erasure or Removal usually stems from the selfish actions that can benefit or protect the villain. Outside of Rage (crimes of passion or psychosis) villainy is fueled by self-interest and protected by the absolute power it wields to corrupt others. The chapter, Seven Motives of Murder, explores these and other dramatic manifestations of selfless and selfish acts in greater detail with illuminating examples.

THE GHOST DOG SYNDROME

For example, although many, myself included, admire and respect the work of maverick independent filmmaker Jim Jarmusch, the weakness of his film GHOST DOG: THE WAY OF THE SAMURAI (1999) is found within the weak motivations given to the Mafia hoods within the story. After Ghost Dog (Forest Whittaker) successfully completes a hit that was contracted by Mafia boss, Frank (Henry Silva), he does not shoot the only witness to the crime, Frank's daughter. Although it is clear that Frank did not want his daughter killed, he inexplicably orders his cronies to kill Ghost Dog. The rest of the narrative rests on this premise, the killing of Ghost Dog, but there is no plausible reason for this order and the entire film suffers as a result.

It is unclear and never explained why this Mafia boss or even Ghost Dog's Mafia contact would want to kill an untraceable, professional hit man that did his job successfully. The motivation to kill a hit man could only stem from a botched job that could somehow allow law enforcement or rivals to trace the hit back to the boss who ordered it. Moreover, the only witness was the Mafia Don's daughter who seemed quite unaffected by the whole affair.

The fault is solely Jarmusch's in attempting to satirize the Mafia (which he otherwise succeeded in doing) he allows his initial implausibility in villainous motivation to stand as an emblem of the weakness of the mob. But the lack of a villainous motivation is really a weakness in the dramatist's reasoning about what motivates mob hits and violence. The point here is that the dramatist must approach the actions of villains with just as much sincerity, clarity, and rationality as he or she does their heroic characters. The attempt to make a caricature of the Italian mob to uphold an ancient form of Japanese mercenary allegiance with an African-American as the Samurai is more like the punch line to a bad racial and cultural joke. It's not the stereotype that hurts it's the non sequitur.

Many people like the movie for very different reasons: some like the musical score by hip-hop wunderkind RZA, others like the wise Samurai sayings spread throughout the film; still others enjoy the odd comedic aspects of the work which cannot be denied. Who could ever forget the Mafia hood who dances and recites the lyrics to rap group Public Enemy's song,' Cold Lampin'?" Yet if we look beyond the veneer of the hip-hop music, comedy, and ancient Japanese sayings we find a story that does not take the motivations of the Mafia seriously and as a result calls into question its very own thematic underpinnings.

THE PRAGMATIST & THE NIHILIST

My discussion of the pragmatist/nihilist archetype will be brief, as I have already written at length about these archetypes in another chapter. You will note that the pragmatist archetype can appear beside the hero or the nihilist because it is the reaction to the demise of this character that separates the hero from the nihilist. The hero, whether victimized by the demise of the pragmatist or seeking the killer of the pragmatist, has in his or her heart the need to rectify a wrong. It is a moral imperative, whether articulated or not, that guides the selflessness of the hero's actions.

Let us define the pragmatist before we go any further. The pragmatist is the character whose sense of fairness, sympathy, duty, and self-control acts as a moral compass for another character not yet revealed to be the hero of the tale. In Vladimir Propp's terminology a pragmatist character would be called an auxiliary character. The pragmatist is level headed and is usually determined to find a harmony among men because of man's interdependent circumstances. In most cases, the pragmatist appears to be the hero of the tale until he or she meets their sudden demise.

Typically, in a standard police drama, the pragmatist was the older, wiser partner who was killed before or just as the drama began. In William Friedkin's TO LIVE AND DIE IN LA (1985), the pragmatist, Jimmy Hart (Michael Greene), is viscously killed early in the film, which sets up the determination of his partner, Federal agent, Richard Chance (William L. Peterson) to get revenge. Of course, the surprise here is that Chance does not survive his own revenge plot, but his new partner, John Vukavich (John Pankow) does and fulfills the duty with selfless aplomb.

Yet, the pragmatist in a hero's tale need not be solely dramatized as a singular character. The pragmatist archetype could be rendered as a pragmatic situation, like a family, a domicile, or a political position. Any situation or circumstance that requires an individual to compromise or maintain moderate positions relative to the views, situations or circumstances of others, is a pragmatic situation.

For clarity, the pragmatic situation is a situation that persuades a person to be tolerant; to hold, defend, and accept antithetical or compromised views or perspectives. For instance, in Roland Emmerich's THE PATRIOT (2000), Benjamin Martin's (Mel Gibson) initial refusal to vote for the impending American revolutionary war was founded upon his need to protect his family, home, slaves and materials. Benjamin had a heroic background in the previous French and Indian war, but his current pragmatic situation as a widowed father made him tolerant of the community's decision to go to war, but unwilling to sacrifice himself or any member of his family for the war.

Only when the conflict is brought to his home and his eldest son, Gabriel (Heath Ledger) joins the army and is captured and his middle son, Thomas is killed in front of him; only then does Benjamin Martin lose the value of his pragmatic situation and tolerant stance to take up arms and fulfill his heroic destiny. So here we have not simply a pragmatic character that is murdered to launch a hero's journey, but the destruction of a pragmatic circumstance. The creative dramatist can imagine many modifications to this paradigm, but it will only bear fruit if the narrative destiny is adhered to: the pragmatist must die unjustly/violently or a pragmatic situation or circumstance must be disturbed or destroyed.

And so we have identified five archetypes of drama as well as two of the most important narrative paradigms: the hero/villain and the hero/pragmatist. A great debt is owed to Vladimir Propp, Joseph Campbell, and Claude Levi-Strauss for investigating the structure of mythology and the folktale. There may be many more archetypes, but I've noted the ones to which I am most sensitive. This was not meant to be an exhaustive discussion. The last archetype and paradigm must be approached with caution and great scrutiny, for the nihilist/pragmatist paradigm is really an investigation into the hypocrisy that lies underneath a society or community. We will discuss the nihilist/pragmatist paradigm in great detail in a later chapter.

SEVEN MOTIVES OF MURDER

The trivialization of why people kill other people—or the motives of murder—is perhaps a consequence of several influences: second and third rate films and television movies, badly conceived first person shooter video games, local news media that simplify the causes of violent crimes in order to be first with breaking news, and even comic books that simplify motives in an effort to present a Manichean "good vs. evil" dramatic context for its superheroes. Bad scripts and the bad movies that are born from these examples usually have as a distinguishing feature: a trivialization of the motives of murder (more like an unquestioned acceptance of man's need to slaughter other men) that allows gun fire to replace reason and body counts to replace drama. But perhaps the most significant contributing factor to the trivialization of murder in fiction is the frequency of murder in real life; we have become inured of it.

There is, of course, a deep seated psychological need to trivialize the motives of murder based on what psychologists Jonathan Haidt and Roy Baumeister called 'the myth of pure evil'. "Of this myth's many parts, the most important are that evildoers are pure in their evil motives (they have no motives for their actions beyond sadism and greed); victims are pure in their victim hood (they did nothing to bring about their victimization."[1] But Baumeister, in his book EVIL: Inside Human Violence and Cruelty," found that people who do things we see as evil, from spousal abuse all the way to genocide, rarely think they are doing anything wrong. They almost always see themselves as responding to attacks and provocations in ways that are justified. They often think that they themselves are victims."[2] The myth of pure evil is a powerful psychological mechanism that encourages an audience's identification with the hero (the good guy) and allows entertainment to perpetuate the myth for maximum profit with minimum insight.

The purpose of this chapter is to explore the reasoning for murder as a response or reaction to certain contingencies that motivate or mitigate human behavior for good or evil. It is no secret that the screenwriter\filmmaker who better understands the motives of their characters can construct better villainous or heroic characters and as a consequence construct richer stories. Although murder itself seems a dark side of human nature to contemplate, as we shall see, murder has heroic motivations as well. It is perhaps by giving greater scrutiny to these different motivations that we can present the matter without trivializing the act or those characters that commit it.

Below is a list of motives that I have identified as the criminal motives of murder. This list is by no means exhaustive, but for the sake and scope of the argument it has been limited to these general categories:

1) **ERASURE:** To keep someone from talking and/or cover up one's participation in a crime
2) **REMOVAL:** To remove an obstacle to one's advancement: actual or perceived
3) **JUDGMENT:** Vengeance or Revenge for a perceived or actual injustice

4) **RAGE**: As a result of passion and/or psychosis
5) **COERCION**: To force a person, group, community or country to comply with the expressed or implicit political, social, criminal or religious beliefs of another.

The criminal motives for murder are fairly simple to digest. The first motive for murder is to keep someone from talking. Mob hits, the dishonor among thieves, witnesses, others who know the truth of someone's criminal actions, are all part of the first motive. The murder of Stacks (Samuel L. Jackson) in Scorsese and Pileggi's GOODFELLAS (1990) was an attempt to forestall this character's eventual capture and subsequent snitching to the police concerning the multi-million dollar Luftansa Heist. Stacks had to be erased to keep law enforcement from following a trail of evidence that would have led them to an accomplice who could be turned into a witness. Even when we look at rape victims who are murdered the concept of erasure, to keep someone from talking—telling—is still a viable interpretation. When the victim is also the witness, erasure is a final alternative to forestall a criminal's exposure.

We also see murder used to "erase" the fact of a criminal's participation in a crime dramatized in the Coen Brothers film, MILLER'S CROSSING (1990). During the finale, Johnny Casper (Jon Polito) is killed by Bernie (John Turturro) as he came to Tom Regan's apartment. Tom Regan (Gabriel Byrne) comes home and uses the gun from the dead man's pocket to kill Bernie. By placing the gun in the dead man's hand, Tom Regan's own participation in the murder is erased. He has effectively re-staged the crime scene to suggest a shoot out where both victims killed each other, covering up or 'erasing' his own involvement. There are many other dramatic examples, but these will suffice for our understanding of the first motive for murder.

The second motive for murder is to remove an obstacle to one's advancement (actual or perceived). The real life murder of Paul Castellano at the behest of John Gotti and associates allowed Gotti to ascend to the status of Don in the New York Gambino crime family. The," it's not personal, it's business," mantra of THE GODFATHER reveals how this motive for murder, whether actual or perceived, is powerful enough to cause conspiracies for murder to be born. The qualification, actual or perceived, is used to allow theoretical room for Hate crimes to be included. If we remember the horrific murder of an African-American man named Robert Byrd in Jasper Texas that was perpetrated by two White ex-cons who were members of the Aryan Nation, the perceived obstacle to the advancement of these two White males were African-American males. Robert Byrd was singled out as a symbol of the obstacle to the advancement of the perpetrators White race. Of course the reasoning was unsound, but the motive was certain.

The motives of Vengeance and Revenge are grouped under the umbrella of Judgment. This judgment is particularly striking in the case of murders committed as acts of Vengeance. The assailant(s) or the suborned agent(s) are acting from an assessment of the previous actions of their intended victim(s). For instance, the murder of convicted child molester and Ex-priest John Geoghan in prison by fellow inmate Joseph L. Druce in August 2003 was an act of vengeance against a person judged as despicable for his previous actions. The same could of course be said for the jailhouse slayings of serial killers Jeffery Dahmer and Albert DeSalvo (the alleged Boston Stranger). Indeed, one wonders if the jailhouse slayings of individuals whose crimes are considered so immoral as to be seen as irredeemable are tacitly allowed to occur by guards and officials who turn a blind eye, knowing that society will do the same. So we might say that vengeance itself must be justified by a severe moral judgment against a person's previous actions.

Revenge, on the other hand, differs from vengeance in that the morally repugnant acts have happened directly to the victim who now returns the offense (often in the greatest degree of murder) to his or her assailant. If vengeance is a judgment against a person for their actions upon others, then revenge is a judgment against a person for their direct actions upon an individual. To put it simply, vengeance is a judgment delivered by the witnesses, but revenge is a judgment delivered by the victims or those who loved them. For instance," in 1215 the jilting of an Amidei girl was avenged by the murder of the offending member of the Buondelmonti family," which touched off a ferocious and decades long feud among the Italians of Florence in the poet Dante's time.[3]

This tit-for-tat revenge for the insult or death of another from one's faction plays itself out in the modern day slayings of gang members whose actions are used to get revenge upon those who have harmed or insulted their members. Revenge can also be pursued by the loved ones of the victim if the victim is not present or unable due to death to participate. "Revenge is based on some concept of equity. An eye for an eye, a tooth for a tooth; the wrongdoer should suffer to the same extent that he or she has hurt the victim."[4] It is ironic that love (whether familial, romantic, or fraternal) can be a motivation for murders committed as acts of revenge.

The fourth motive of Rage is predicated upon interpersonal dynamics for crimes of passion and internal mental disturbances for crimes of psychosis. Crimes of passion are usually wrought from the need to annihilate the emotional, mental, financial or physical distress that someone else is causing another. The jealous rage, intense power struggles, fears of abandonment or imprisonment within one's interpersonal relationship with others can become powerful enough to become a motive for murder. The recent trial and conviction of School teacher Nancy Seaman for the murder and dismemberment of her husband Robert Seaman in Michigan is a horrific example of the intense and violent rage crimes of passion invoke in their assailants.

Enraged and distressed over the imminent divorce between her and her husband the prosecutor, Lisa Ortlieb argued that," Seaman bought [a] hatchet on Mother's Day for the expressed purpose of killing her husband," (WDIV-NEWS, Detroit). The hateful and rage-filled arguments between Nancy Seaman and her husband that led to his eventual murder and dismemberment often culminate, unfortunately, into a common motive for murder in crimes of passion. And let us not forget the disturbing statistic that over half of the females murdered are victims of the murderous rage of their spouses or boyfriends.

It is common knowledge that the severity and repetitive nature of the victim's wounds are often easily discerned as crimes of passion by investigators.

The psychosis of an individual can lead to murders of a most heinous and disturbing nature. These individuals are entangled within the fictions of the mind that often result in their committing crimes that shock and appall even the most hardened veteran cop or investigator. The heinous actions of Andrea Yates, who was convicted of murdering her five young children in 2001, was clearly a result of her increasing psychosis and her declining mental condition that was overlooked by her doctors. And in Detroit the sudden spate of murderous violence against whole families by deranged boyfriends and husbands from 2000 to 2002 was as perplexing as it was perverse.

The Minnesota Street massacre where a mother and her five children were slaughtered, the Patton street slayings where two mothers and two children were slaughtered were all committed by the boyfriends and fathers of the victims within the span of two years. These mental disturbances, often caused by the overwhelming increase in emotional and economic stress exacerbated by drug or alcohol abuse, result in a rage against something in the mind that results in the killing of others. The complete reasoning that fuels the psychosis motive is often known only to the assailant and can usually only be deciphered by mental health professionals or extraordinarily empathic individuals who are willing to look into the background of these individuals and discern how their own behaviors and the stresses they encountered help to debilitate their mental health.

The act of murder itself can be used to force others to comply with expressed or implicit political, social, criminal, or religious beliefs. I call this motive of murder, Coercion. Human history is filled with examples of mass murder committed to force the conversion or complicity of others. The Crusades, The Middle Passage of African slaves, The Native American's Trail of Tears, The Salem Witch Trials, the list of murder used as a coercive act is clearly an attempt to force the survivors and/or the witnesses into accepting some form of indoctrination or complicity in their own destruction.

Terry George's film HOTEL RWANDA (2004) dramatized the genocidal ethnic civil war between the Rwandian Hutu and Tutsi ethnic groups and gives us a fresh illustration of murder as coercion. The mass murder of Tutsis by Hutu Militia was a form of coercion for other Hutu's who either refused to comply with the ethnic hatred or sympathized with the Tutsi victims. In the case of Paul Rusesabagina (Don Cheadle), he was married to a Tutsi woman and the ethnic genocide was clearly an act of political coercion to which he refused to submit. More than any other motive, it is the motive of coercion that reveals to us that acts of murder are not as careless, random or insouciant as the news media or poorly talented writers and filmmakers would lead us to believe.

These motives may seem to be simplistic generalizations to complex social and inter-personal issues, but the seemingly wide variety of reasons why someone kills another person are often just obscured versions of these motives. People murdered during robbery attempts are killed either because they are perceived to be obstacles to one's financial advancement (not giving up the money or materials) or to keep them from talking. Print

45

and television news often mischaracterize murder as random (victims don't know their assailants) or without reason (senseless) for ratings as these mischaracterizations play into our general notions of a myth of pure evil. In actuality, many murders are wrought from the escalation of mutual violence and abuse in altercations between friends, lovers, family members and acquaintances. Even if one concedes that random or senseless violence does exist, it is far less common than we are led to believe. We should not let our notion of pure evil keep us from engaging in the dramatic insight necessary to understand our villains and create richer and more rewarding stories. Yet there is an interesting question begged here: Are there any heroic or 'good' motives for murder?

The previous motives we might deem solely the villainous motives for murder, but there are three more motives that are listed below that complete our categories:

6) **DEFENSIVE:** Protection of one's life or the lives of others, materials, property and/or the preservation of a community or a way of life.
7) **SACRIFICIAL:** For the protection, maintenance or establishment of a moral or religious ideal.
8) **JUDGMENT:** Vengeance or Revenge (See previous definition)

These three motives we might call the 'heroic' motives for murder.

We should immediately note that Judgment as a motive for murder occurs twice on our list. Both a criminal and a hero, as a justification for murder, can utilize judgment (vengeance or revenge). "Revenge is the flip side of the Golden Rule of doing unto others as you would have them do unto you. Revenge does unto someone what he has already done unto you."[5] For instance, we might see the return of a young 'Don' Vito Corleone to his hometown in Sicily to murder the aging and half blind Don Ciccio as a belated act of revenge in Coppola and Puzo's GODFATHER II. We know that when Vito was a young boy his father, brother Paolo and his mother were all murdered at the behest of this Mafia chieftain. The revenge is justified in the eyes of Don Vito Corleone because of the injustice that was reckoned against his family.

It would seem that the only thing that separates the hero from the criminal is the degree of self-interest that fuels the motive of revenge or vengeance. If the judgment has the greater goal of "ridding the world" of a despicable person, a person who could not be served with revenge by legal or fair jurisprudence, then it falls on the side of the hero. This is of course not an unequivocal interpretation, but Vito Corleone's interest in getting revenge upon Don Ciccio (a despicable character) was certainly more personally motivated that it was socially motivated. But as writer Georges Polti has told us," the most satisfying of spectacles is still that of an individual capable of executing a legitimate, although illegal, justice."[6]

Clearly, defensive motives for murder are usually very easily discerned: a rape victim who kills her or his attacker, self-defense, etc. In many states, homeowners have the right to shoot and kill unwanted home intruders in defense of their property. Finally, murder to protect a community or a way of life can take us anywhere from the violent suppression of a riot to the political motives for war between countries as lucid examples. This is not to say that all defensive motives are heroic, as cases of police brutality that end with fatalities reveal, but more often than not society and the legal system views defensive homicide as justifiable and under many circumstances the people who commit it as heroes.

At first blush, sacrificial motives for murders appear solely the domain of heroes, but upon deeper inspection this domain becomes unavoidably tenuous. What are sacrificial motives for murder? When is murder seen as a sacrifice? Do we turn our attention to the finale of Milos Forman's film of Ken Kesey's ONE FLEW OVER THE CUCKOO'S NEST, where Chief Bromden suffocates a lobotomized and unresponsive Randall P. McMurphy? Perhaps sacrificial motives that concern euthanasia, assisted suicide, and the medical circumstances of brain dead or vegetative individuals are about quality of life ideals that can no longer be maintained given the circumstances. The dire circumstances and bleak future of a paralyzed individual and the person who cared for her the most was dramatized to academy award winning perfection by Clint Eastwood in MILLION DOLLAR BABY (2004). The recent film by Mike Leigh, VERA DRAKE (2004), which has an ordinary cleaning woman who doubles as an abortionist, casts her in a heroic light, even though many might see her activities as murder. The sacrificing of unborn children for the happiness or contentment of adults makes sacrificial motives the most controversial of the heroic motives for murder.

An example of murder with a sacrificial motive over an ideal sends us into history. As late as the Nineteenth century the duel was fought over points of honor between men with swords, guns, knives, chains, and fists. Yet is one really a hero because one has killed another over an ideal, be it honor, love of country, or dignity? The seppuku of the Samurai warrior or the suicides of disgraced Roman senators are interesting examples of suicide (the murder of oneself) with sacrificial motives. Such suicides are not seen today as heroic, but if in ancient cultures these actions were viewed as final acts of heroism in the face of shameful defeat, then perhaps we must consider this interpretation as viable.

To return briefly to the motive of judgment as a heroic motive for murder, we should look at the finale of Scorsese and Schrader's TAXI DRIVER. After Travis Bickle (Robert DeNiro) has killed a pimp and his hustlers, and ironically runs out of bullets to kill himself, he is written about as a hero for his murders which resulted in the return of a runaway teenager to her family. This ending, with the disturbed Travis Bickle viewed as a calculating hero, is justified by his lack of self-interest in the commission of the violent acts. Specifically, he was not trying to benefit from the murders, the people he killed were of a despicable nature, and there was no existing relationship between himself and his victims that would reveal a personal vendetta. To the police and the media his vengeance was justified by his lack of self-interest and his judgment upon those despicable characters he killed; that Travis was first plotting to assassinate a presidential candidate was only known to the audience and himself. Moreover, that Travis was intending to kill himself (as evident from his bloody finger placed against his temple), reveals that he never intended to be considered a hero—his violent actions were truly selfless.

And so we have the seven motives of murder divided by the criminal and the heroic:

1) Erasure
2) Removal
3) Judgment*
4) Rage
5) Coercion

Criminal
_____

Heroic
6) Defensive
7) Sacrificial
8) Judgment*

By isolating and interpreting these motives our intention is not to feel safe in an increasingly hostile world nor is it to lay the rhetorical groundwork for some kind of criminological panacea. Instead, this catalog is a matter of simplifying what we often like to view as too complex or rationalize as superfluous for the dramatist. The richer the reasoning behind the motivations for murder the better the characterizations and the overall script. All this is not to say that there are no other motives for murder or that separate motives cannot be divided into primary and secondary motivations.

More importantly, there are also just as many murders committed from miss-reading the motives or others. But miss-reading the actions and intentions of another person usually falls among one of the four criminal motives. MILLER'S CROSSING is a full exploration of the mounting intricacies and violent consequences of such miss-readings. As Gabriel Byrne's character says," Nobody knows anybody, not that well." Because there is a corruption in the heart of man and," since men are a sorry lot," to quote a favorite refrain of Machiavelli, there will always be a rich variety and variation of motives of murder for the dramatist to draw on. [7] So as society changes in complexity, density and striations then perhaps more and more motives for murder might be found, but then if this speculation comes true perhaps only a vengeance from someone greater could save us from ourselves.

NOTES

[1] Pg. 74-75, THE HAPPINESS HYPOTHESIS by Jonathan Haidt, New York. Basic Books, 2006.

[2] Ibid.

[3] Pg. xvi, THE INFERNO, Dante, trans. John Ciardi, Mentor Books, New York, 1954.

[4] Pg.156, EVIL: Inside Human Violence and Cruelty by Roy F. Baumeister. New York. W.H. Freeman and Company. 1997.

[5] Pg.157, Ibid.

(6)   Pg. 19, THE THIRTY-SIX DRAMATIC SITUATIONS by Georges Polti, The Writer's Inc., Boston. 1921.

(7)   Pg. 134, THE PORTABLE MACHIAVELLI, ed. Peter Bondanella & Mark Musa, Penguin Books, New York, 1979.

THE FOLLOWING ARE THREE SCENARIO QUESTIONS THAT REQUIRE YOU TO DETERMINE WHICH MOTIVE OF MURDER BEST FITS THE SCENARIO.

1) A jealous and angry man shoots his wife's lover in the face. Later he removes all immediate identification from the body and brings the corpse to his home. He meticulously stages the scene to make it look like he killed a burglar. Once the wife finds out that it was her lover who was killed, she pretends to continue her affair to spite the husband and force him to either confess or slowly drive him insane. **Which Motive of Murder best fits this scenario?**

A) Defensive
B) Sacrificial
C) Removal
D) Rage

2) A man hears a thief break into his home. He grabs his gun and kills the thief. In a panic, because of an impending court case, he removes the body and buries it deep in the woods, far from his home. Everyday he begins to believe that he sees the dead man: at his job, on the jury and in his bedroom as he makes love to his girlfriend. Eventually, he suffers a nervous breakdown and must be involuntarily committed for treatment. Because of his odd behavior, he loses his court case. **Which Motive of Murder best fits this scenario?**

A) Defensive
B) Sacrificial
C) Removal
D) Rage

3) A villainous drug dealer's mother is killed unintentionally in a car accident by a corrupt police officer. The drug dealer puts out a $100,000 hit on the corrupt police officer's life. He is eventually killed by another corrupt police officer who needed the money to pay off the mounting debts from his gambling addiction. **Which Motive of Murder best fits this scenario?**

A) Defensive
B) Removal
C) Judgment
D) Erasure

The Answers are located at the end of the filmography section of this book.

HOW TO DRAMATIZE
Perspective\Dialectic\and Thematic Node

I n the most simplistic explanation: to dramatize is to give at least two different and opposing perspectives on a single situation, character, or circumstance and then bring those two perspectives into conflict with one another. Like the proverbial military concept of '*kill or be killed*' simplifies the perspectives of comrades towards their enemies; war itself is a dramatized conflict of differing political perspectives—albeit with deadly consequences. You've, no doubt, often heard the phrase," There are two sides to every story," when first hearing why two lovers are quarreling. Well, to dramatize a situation or circumstance is to give two plausible perspectives about a situation or circumstance and then bring those perspectives into conflict with one another. **How you bring the two perspectives into conflict with one another as well as how you resolve the conflict is decided by the theme(s) you have chosen to pursue within the story.**

Most early drafts of our scripts fail because we have failed to give a certain depth, a palpable truth or declarative honesty to one perspective because we—as writers—solely believe in the other. In short, we side with one perspective and lack the creative empathy to see it from the other point of view. This is particularly noticeable when men who lack a certain maturity approach dialogue for female characters or when youthful writers of crime films fail to take into earnest account, the perspective of those who want law and order. This kind of 'dramatic chauvinism' is most often the culprit that shortchanges the dramatic potential of first drafts and causes many writers to bristle at input from those who might see the situation or circumstance differently from the way they have tried to present things.

I'm sure a perceptive reader might be inclined to say that the different perspectives correspond directly to the dramatic personae of The Protagonist and The Antagonist. But to dramatize creatively is to reveal the contradictory perspectives as they develop into conflict and not just to suddenly and without thought assume characters as ready made labels. Examples of contradictory perspectives are those held by Peter Parker (Tobey Maguire) and his best friend Harry Osborn (James Franco) concerning Mary Jane (Kristen Dunst) and the true nature of Spiderman in Sam Rammi's blockbuster films of the comic book superhero.

So drama is a question of perspective in as much as it is created by the conflict of contradictory perspectives about a situation, character, or circumstance. But the key to this seemingly simplistic paradigm I am trying to explain is the plausibility of a particular perspective. What often ruins the first draft of a script is the dramatic chauvinism that causes the writer to weaken the plausibility of one character's perspective in favor or allegiance to another's perspective. Returning to SPIDERMAN (2002), there was a genuine and palpable tension and conflict generated between Harry and Peter's perception of Mary Jane. It is this conflict that anchors the first film because it is plausible that a person's best friend would 'covet' or be in love with his best friend's woman. The richness of this film concerning both its box office receipts and its story is tied to that increasing conflict generated by a human drama (unrequited love and destructive jealousy) we can easily identify with and respond towards.

The more truthful, the more honest, and the more significant we can present our character's perspective on a situation, character, or circumstance the richer, more complex, and more dramatic we can make the conflict(s) with in the script. To put it simply, a writer must say to him or herself if my character looks at things this way," *Have I given the audience an opportunity to see or hear why my character looks at things this way?"* But note, that we don't ask ourselves this question to simply place the answers matter-of-factly in the script, but instead to help broaden our own perspective on our characters and distinguish these contradictory perspectives within the script. If we want to mature as writers then our own perspectives have to mature and broaden and this is how we will make our own scripts and films richer. The difficulty is in seeing the other side of things and making a contradictory, if not problematic or offensive—perspective plausible (but not necessarily palatable) until the conflict is resolved and/or the theme is revealed.

A DIALECTICAL APPROACH TO DRAMATIC FORM

In truth what I am suggesting here is a dialectical approach to drama that is founded upon the film theory of Russian director, Sergei Eisenstein (1898-1948). In his 1929 essay, "A Dialectical Approach to Film Form," Eisenstein outlines a modern editorial strategy that is summarized concisely by film historian David A. Cook as," a way of looking at human history and experience as a perpetual conflict in which a force (thesis) collides with a counterforce (antithesis) to produce from their collision a wholly new phenomenon (synthesis) which is not the sum of the two forces but something greater and different from them both" [1] Where Eisenstein's theory relates specifically to the juxtaposition of shots to make film narration dynamic, a dialectical approach to drama isolates two contradictory perspectives (the thesis and antithesis) as personified by a character or a group of characters and brings those two perspectives into conflict with one another through the action, dialogue and circumstances within the film. After the conflict there is something greater and different from both perspectives that I believe is derived from the theme(s) of the story.

All of the great dramatic and comedic films proceed by establishing a conflict of perspectives about a character, circumstance, or a past, present or future action or event. In a drama like THE GODFATHER it was Vito Corleone's negative view of Drug peddling contra the positive view of Drug peddling held by the other five mafia families. The conflict of the two perspectives was the catalyst for the assassination attempt on Vito Corleone and the savage murder of Sonny Corleone. The synthesis of the two contradictory perspectives is found in the rise of the youngest son, Michael Corleone (Smarter than Vito and yet more ruthless than Sonny) and the eventual destruction of the family. In a comedy like DR. STRANGELOVE (1963), it was the insane perspective of Commander Jack D. Ripper (Sterling Hayden) contra the rational perspective of Captain Mandrake (Peter Sellers) concerning the irrevocable deployment of nuclear armed B-52 bombers headed to Russia to drop their bombs and," protect our precious bodily fluids." The synthesis of the rational fear of man's self destruction and the irrational fear of man's political indoctrination are found in chance; the chance or random probability that a mistake or sheer happenstance could guide man to his doom as revealed by the one plane that was not recalled in Kubrick's DR. STRANGELOVE.

These are just broad and simplified examples because most films contain multiple conflicts of perspectives about a situation, character or circumstance that are synthesized (resolved) and become the thesis for another conflict and so on and so forth until the end of the film; this we should call a dialectical progression of dramatic form and it is a particularly useful approach for epic or historical dramas that cover a large time period with spectacular events. (See: Fig. 1) Bernardo Bertolucci's epic 1900 (NOVECENTO—1976) proceeds in this dialectical progression as it presents the contradictory views of early twentieth century Italian peasants as personified by Olmo (Gerard Depardieu) and the landowners who conspired to begin the fascist movement as personified by Alfredo (Robert DeNiro). "Bertolucci's vision of Italian history has been attacked as either too ideological in its praise of his beloved peasants or as too softhearted in his portrait of Alfredo Berlinghieri, a weak-willed bourgeois whose friendship for Olmo does not prevent him from being used by . . . fascist bullyboys, who eventually terrorize and murder a number of the peasants."[2] Despite these shortsighted criticisms, 1900 presents a dialectical progression of dramatic form in its dialectical approach to history. It is only by seeing the issue from both sides can we see the contingent, conspiratorial and contradictory forces at work in reality. As Olmo asks of Alfredo when they are both children looking out upon a city far away in the distance," Do they have a view of us—just like we have a view of them, would you say?" 1900 presents a dialectical perspective upon a transitional moment in Italian history: the movement from peasant to industrial society.

Complex dramas can be created by the misjudgment of perspectives or by multiplying the perspectives for dramatic or comic effect as the screenplays of Charlie Kaufman attest. (E.g. THE ENTERNAL SUNSHINE OF THE SPOTLESS MIND—2004, BEING JOHN MALCOVICH—2000) Again, how the conflict is synthesized is controlled by the theme of the overall film. The dialectical progression of dramatic form proceeds thusly:

Fig.1

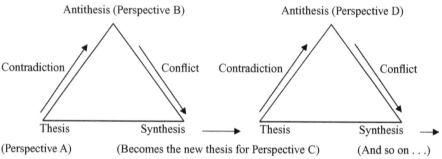

Figure 1 shows us the familiar dialectical pattern established by philosopher Hegel, adopted by Karl Marx and his followers and developed by filmmaker and theorist Sergei Eisenstein in his conceptualization of montage or film editing. It is important for us to note that the presentation of contradictory perspectives need not always involve explicit historical or political dramas, but also personal dramas for it is only in finding the personal in the historical and the historical in the personal that we can present perspective (A) and make the drama dynamic by introducing the antithesis: perspective (B).

The dialectical progression of dramatic form is not a formula, but a structure that lay beneath ancient and modern dramatic narration. It is a structure we can see from Homer's The Iliad to Ridley Scott's KINGDOM OF HEAVEN (2005). What often keeps us from perceiving this dialectical structure is our exclusive identification with only one of the two perspectives. The so-called "suspension of disbelief" that is so crucial for narration to seduce a spectator is founded upon how deeply we can identify with either perspective (thesis or antithesis) as presented within the story. Once we have identified with the (hero or heroine) the dialectical progression of drama is hidden from us as we "root" for the good guys or the bad guys.

Returning to the previously cited criticism of Bertolucci's 1900, his alternating presentation of the contradictory perspectives of peasant and landowner is what actually caused the critical outrage against the film. The reason is simple: those who identified with the landowners found the presentation of the peasants to be overly romantic and those who identified with the peasants found the presentation of the landowners to be too sympathetic. Author Robert Burgoyne in his penetrating analysis of the film has noted that," This discrepancy produces multiple perspectives within any given scene, creating what might be called a polyphonic text, wherein different, competing voices make the assignment of a simple, unitary ideological position impossible."[3] But the artist must concentrate all of his powers, his talent, his intuition and his vision upon the synthesis of the two perspectives for his work to transcend the propaganda of the "left" or the "right"; this is usually done by either terminating the dialectic in myth or terminating the myth by critiquing the contradictions it does not in truth resolve. We will examine both approaches below.

A prominent characteristic of American Cinema is found in the use of the dialectic to create synthesized myths that resolves the conflict of the two perspectives in a way that insures the profitability of the film. If synthesis is supposed to be the collision of perspective A and perspective B into something greater and different from either of the two, then the American blockbuster achieves its blockbuster status by terminating the dialectic in a profit-motivated myth or at the very least, palpable beliefs that distract attention from real, concrete unresolved conflicts in ordinary life. D.W. Griffith's THE BIRTH OF A NATION (1918), one of the first true blockbusters of cinematic history, was also the first film to capitalize on the profit-motivated synthesis of myth in historical drama with its White men in Black face and its overtly racist perception of African-Americans before and after the Civil War. GONE WITH THE WIND (1939) and even STAR WARS (1977) also presents a profit-motivated synthesis of myth that is really the simplistic triumph of one perspective over the other, i.e. good vs. evil and good wins.

The perspective discarded is almost always the perspective of the minority for reasons of ideology, race, religion and/or capital. This is a different use of myth, a modern use of myth that is distinguished from the ancient myths of Native Americans, Greeks, Kushites, etc. Ancient myths were used to resolve the contradictions between man and nature whereas modern myths attempt to resolve the trenchant and often irreconcilable contradictions among men. This discarding or triumph over a "minority" perspective is what gave American cinema the Western genre because by discarding the minority perspective (Native Americans, African-Americans) these films could support the perspective of the majority through the dominant myths believed by the majority and reap the profits that such beliefs and myths could attract.

DIALECTICAL PROGRESSION OF DRAMATIC FORM: A SPECIFIC ANALYSIS

ROCCO & HIS BROTHERS (Rocco E I Soui Fratelli—1960) by Luchino Visconti

A poor Southern Italian family moves North in search of prosperity, but instead finds disillusionment, crime, humiliation, and personal sacrifice. "The story of Rocco and His Brothers unfolds as a series of episodes, merging into each other, in which each of Rosaria Parondi's five sons moves in turn to occupy the centre of the stage. Each brother in a crude sense represents a certain kind of solution to the problems facing a Southern immigrant in a Northern urban environment. These solutions are not abstractly conceived, but evolve dialectically, each in response to the contradictions and inadequacies discovered in the last." [4] Luchino Visconti's film ROCCO & HIS BROTHERS contains the two most important elements that are required for a dialectical progression of dramatic form: 1) it covers a real historical time period where Southern Italians were immigrating to the

North after World War II and 2) it makes the historical events personal by ascribing certain perspectives to particular groups of characters or individuals. In fact, author Geoffrey Nowell-Smith in summarizing Visconti's own theory of "anthropomorphic cinema" says," . . . that the totality of a historical situation, both its static form and the process of its evolution, is crystallized in certain human figurations and in the development of a human drama." [5]

This human drama of a historical situation, if it is to be captured in its totality, is best delivered via a dialectic which gives either side or at least two contradictory perspectives, on a particular situation. This is why the film itself is a tragedy: it used recent historical circumstances to explain the present condition (circa 1960) of Italian society. The loss of innocence, identity and a longing for home are part of a grand mea culpa Visconti constructed as if it were an opera about what was being destroyed in the "new" Italy after WW II. I have composed a brief schematic of the opening sequences of Rocco & His Brothers that should reveal the dialectical progression of dramatic form in fig 2, below:

Fig.2 Dialectical Progression of Drama—Rocco & His Brothers.

Sequence: Vincenzo—Event: Arrival of Parondi family.

Perspective A	Perspective B
Arrival of Parondi family in Milan. Rosaria, the mother believes her son Vincenzo will help support the family now that the father has died.	Engagement party for Vincenzo and Ginetta. Ginetta's mother thinks that Vincenzo's family has come to celebrate the engagement, but when she finds out otherwise she suddenly insists that the Parondi's want to be a burden to them all.

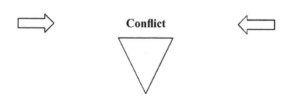

Conflict

Synthesis
Vincenzo loses his apartment
and his fiancé to take care of
the family. He rents a basement
apartment, in a housing scheme,
to support his family. No one has
a steady job.

Event: Introduction of Nadia (a wayward prostitute)

Perspective C

Nadia mentions Boxing as a way
to make money. Vincenzo doesn't
box anymore and doesn't think his
brothers should start.

Perspective D

Simone thinks it's a good idea.
Rosaria overhears the idea and agrees.
She encourages Rocco and Simone.
Rosaria doesn't like Nadia.

 Conflict

Synthesis

Simone starts Boxing. Rocco half
heartedly trains, takes a job at a laundry.
Simone wins his first fight.
Nadia and Simone begin an affair.

Event: Introduction of Morini, a boxing promoter.

Perspective E

Simone engages in petty theft while
borrowing money from Rocco at his
job. Simone starts an affair with
Rocco's female boss while stealing
jewels to give to Nadia.

Perspective F

Rocco's boss and co-workers suspect
him of being a thief. Nadia returns
a brooch that Simone stole from
Rocco's boss. She also tells him that
she is leaving Simone and going away.

 Conflict

Synthesis

Rocco quits his job and
goes into the Army.
Before he leaves he
delivers Nadia's message
to Simone who rejects her in anger.

This brief schematic overview of the first third of ROCCO & HIS BROTHERS should clearly reveal the dialectical structure of the film. We should note that each synthesis brings with it either the introduction of a new character (Nadia, Morini) or a new circumstance (The Parondi's basement apartment or Rocco's Army service). The perspective is split according the characters who view the new character, event, or circumstance differently; this split is what drives the conflict and leads to a new synthesis. This is particularly acute in this film and is strongly underscored by the first conflict between the mothers in the opening sequence of the film. The simple misunderstanding between the two mothers about why the Parondi's have come to Milan causes a deep rift between the two families that affects the entire film.

The second conflict between the brothers, Simone and Rocco, reoccurs later in the film over their perspectives concerning Nadia. When Rocco and Nadia begin an affair, Simone still considers her his possession and this leads to a powerful scene of rape and humiliation and leads the film to its tragic conclusion. Fig. 2 was simply a bare bones illustration of the elements of the dialectical paradigm that gives dynamic force (progression) to the drama within ROCCO & HIS BROTHERS. Let us look briefly at some of the key elements of this structure.

KEY ELEMENTS of DIALECTICAL PROGESSION

The first key to the dialectical progression of drama is the selection of a historical event, character, or circumstance that polarizes the audience watching the film as well as the characters within the film. From D.W. Griffith's THE BIRTH OF A NATION (1915, alternately titled: THE CLANSMEN) which incorporated the American Civil War to Sergei Eisenstein's BATTLESHIP POTEMKIN (Bronenosets Potoymkin, 1925) which was based on real historical incidents in the Soviet Union, it is essential that a dialectically progressing drama have as its catalyst a polarizing event, character, or circumstance from history. "The Parondi family is not this specific family but representative of all Southern families, of an entire Southern experience (more than nine million Southern Italians made the journey to the North between 1955 and 1971) . . ." [6] The real historical circumstance is what gives the dialectically progressing film its emotive power as viewers are able to identify with the characters as presented in their circumstances or through the historical events that happen to them. If the catalyst cannot be drawn from real historical events due to the political temperaments or ideological constraints of the day, the filmmakers can create fictional representations that function as allegories, such as the Charles Foster Kane/William Randolph Hearst character in Orson Welles' CITIZEN KANE (1941), the fictional Sampan boat massacre/the historical Vietnam My Lai village massacre in Coppola's APOCALYPSE NOW (1979) or the political allegory in George A. Romero's LAND OF THE DEAD (2005).

The second key to a dialectical progression of drama is the development and distinction of split perspectives; otherwise known as a polemical configuration. The polarizing event, character, or circumstance allows the perspective to be split in two so that a contradiction and conflict can be generated. Whether the contradiction is good vs. evil, confederate vs. yankee, or Black vs. White, the split of two perspectives is what begins the dialectic and seduces the audience into identifying with which ever perspective the filmmakers glamorize as the most attractive physically, intellectually, or spiritually. This is usually how a dialectical progression of drama becomes viewed as political or cultural propaganda in that an alternate perspective is diminished or "de-glamorized' to such an extent as to obscure its motivations or its raison d'etre. So it was easy for American critics to call Eisenstien's BATTLESHIP POTEMKIN a piece of communist propaganda but difficult for those same critics to call Griffith's THE BIRTH OF A NATION a piece of racist propaganda. The opposing polemical perspectives in a dialectical narrative structure allows a character or group of characters to become easily identifiable symbols of a particular state of mind, being or circumstance that an audience can respond for or against in the story.

The third key to a dialectical progression of drama is clearly found in how the synthesis is distinguished and presented. It takes a keen and objective mind to look back at a historical event and find a synthesis, a something greater and different, from the two perspectives that claim the events as their own. Moreover, the dialectical progression of drama is such that one could continue to move the drama forward with no termination in sight. But it is the theme that determines both the ending and points towards the conditions of synthesis; those conditions being something different and greater than the two perspectives. "For Levi-Strauss, myth is an intellectual means for resolving a conceptual contradiction or duality in a particular society." [7] A dialectically progressing drama most often terminates as a myth, but as we shall see the theme can determine whether the film critiques the myth or celebrates it.

The critique of a myth is found in the final moments of John Ford's great film, THE MAN WHO SHOT LIBERTY VALANCE (1962). The young journalist, after hearing the great tale and learning about who had really killed the outlaw Liberty Valance, turns to his publisher for permission to print this revelation. But the publisher answers," When the legend becomes fact, print the legend." The legend being that the well-educated but non-violent lawyer from the east, Ransom Stoddard (Jimmy Stewart) killed the violent and illiterate Liberty Valance (Lee Marvin) before he became a senator and brought statehood to the region and civilization to the tiny town of Shinbone. So a profit-motivated synthesis is found in the legend, the myth of law, righteousness, civilization and man's humanity as opposed to the damning and brutal truth. Such a synthesis might not hold up to great scrutiny but it reveals more about inner nature of those who might believe such a myth in spite of the contradictions it does not adequately resolve. But it is THE MAN WHO SHOT LIBERTY VALANCE that actually reveals how a dialectical progression of drama that terminates in myth can actually be used to challenge, even subvert a myth.

If we follow the trajectory of the work of structural anthropologist Claude Levi-Strauss as it was reinterpreted by sociologist Will Wright we find that myth," relates the past to the present," by mapping the present *onto* the past.[8] We note that a dialectical progression of drama is usually historical and it ends by terminating the dialectic in myth. But even though the dialectical progression of drama into myth allows us to," resolve a conceptual contradiction," in our present society, its use in film remains a symbolic gesture that can either celebrate or challenge the dominate myths of our society.

For instance, it is clear that John Ford was using the Wild West story of THE MAN WHO SHOT LIBERTY VALANCE as a commentary upon the experiences of contemporary American society in 1962. The civil rights movement was gaining ground, schools were being desegregated and Ford includes a multi-racial school and an American civics lesson in this drama of the civilization of the Wild West. If it is true that myths sustain their meaning by analogy, then Ford's film is analogous to the events of contemporary times that are dressed up as a historical Western drama. Although he terminates the film in myth or legend to be specific, THE MAN WHO SHOT LIBERTY VALANCE prints the facts that myth itself obscures: the brutal, yet heroic efforts of its tragic Irish figure, Tom Doniphon (John Wayne) and his African-American friend Pompey (Woody Strode) in the civilization of the West and the ideals of present day America. The film itself reveals how the media and those who write history deliberately censor the truth by showing that," American civilization has passed over the Tom Doniphons just as it passed over the blacks and the Indians."[9] So the dialectical progression of THE MAN WHO SHOT LIBERTY VALANCE terminates the myth instead of terminating in myth and we see that a dialectical progression need not always uphold the status quo or the profit motivated myths of the society it critiques.

COERCIVE MYTHS

The true force of a myth comes not solely from its symbolic content or its dialectical structure, but also from its seductive qualities that make an individual want to believe in the power of said myth to resolve the intransigent conflicts of modern society. Indeed, an individual must be deeply alienated to resist the seductive power of many of the myths that constitute and control modern society. Whether this alienation is racial, sexual, economic, or religious it is an alienation of such profundity that the dialectical process of synthesis is held in critical abeyance.

Myths are ultimately coercive in that they help focus and politicize those who believe in them to oppose those who do not. Unlike ancient myths that mediated between man and nature (thus, having an intellectual, spiritual, nutritional, and medicinal function) modern myths attempt to mediate the inequities and injustices among men (with democracy, law, wages, police, religions and doctors). But as I have shown, a dialectically progressing narrative can be critical of myth, if it reveals the conflict of the two historical perspectives as real experienced conflicts that are analogous to the myths we believe in today.

THE THEMATIC NODE: Demonstrating the Theme

A bothersome characteristic of unsatisfactory first drafts has to do with the writer's inability to fully demonstrate the theme of the story. Whether this theme is demonstrated through action, dialogue or both, the theme must be demonstrated; it must be integrated into the script and realized in the subsequent film. My standard definition of theme bears repeating here: the theme is the underlying question or concept that your story ultimately asks, answers or explores. A good screenwriter usually has at least one scene that demonstrates the theme as explicitly as possible without explaining it directly. (Please note: to explain is not to demonstrate and to demonstrate is not to explain.) The scene that demonstrates the theme(s) in a film I will call: A Thematic Node. A thematic node is the scene that most explicitly demonstrates the theme(s) of the film—that question or concept that your story ultimately asks, answers or explores.

One might note that the thematic node is similar to Stanislavsky's idea of the spine of the play," a formula that attempts to express the unified movement of purpose that presumably informs a play, some common thrust underlying the projects or dominant motivations of its characters."[10] But the spine of a play is quite different from the thematic node or nodes of a film. For one point, the spine of a play is often found in an infinitive phrase that," guarantees that what is described will be action, purposive movement, a dynamic experiential texture rather than a theme or idea." [11] By contrast, a thematic node in a film is a scene, an action or series of actions and circumstances or observations (by character, camera, or microphone) that expresses a theme or idea as a "living reality" or a real "experienced" moment. Moreover, the thematic node can be put forth through the form of the film, through how a scene is presented by the camera, sound and editing. In short, the thematic node in film is more dynamic than the spine of the play, particularly in the fact that the thematic node can be presented in a wide variety of ways and juxtapositions (sound, image, dialogue, action, editing, etc.), whereas, the so-called spine of the play is most often an infinitive verbalized phrase. One need only to think of the static—quotidian—shots that punctuate the films of Japanese director Yashiro Ozu to see that a thematic node can even be an isolated image emptied out of drama, but filled with the underlying concept of the film to see the infinite creative possibilities.

For instance, if we examine an action film like Robert Clouse's fully restored version of ENTER THE DRAGON (1973) a "spine" is given at the beginning of the film as Bruce Lee discusses a warrior's vision with his Shaolin Master:

Bruce Lee: A good fight should be like a small play, but played seriously. **A good martial artist does not become tense, but ready; not thinking, yet not dreaming—ready for whatever may come.** When the opponent expands I contract, when he contracts, I expand—and when there is an opportunity I do not hit—It hits all by itself. [12]

In this restored opening sequence that was not shown theatrically in the United States, we have a "spine" or what I would like to call a master theme, which is unusual for an action film that has been stated explicitly in an opening dialogue scene. The subsequent relevance of this master thematic statement is demonstrated in virtually every fight sequence involving Bruce Lee. What was discussed as dialogue," . . . ready for whatever may come," was translated in multiple variations throughout the physical action scenes.

In the beautifully choreographed "Cobra" sequence, where Bruce Lee sneaks into Mr. Han's underground opium production facility, he must "be ready" for any and every obstacle, challenge, and threat. This sequence is the greatest demonstration of the master theme and becomes in my opinion the film's most fully realized thematic node. The sequence opens with Bruce Lee moving in absolute stealth to the secret opening into Han's facility, but it is blocked by a black cobra that he promptly captures and places into a knapsack for use later in the scene. The choice of widescreen allows most of Mr. Lee's violent actions to occur off screen and causes him to recapitulate the force of his violent actions upon the emotional contortions of his face and his primal shrieks. Mr. Lee moves breathlessly from fists, to feet, from feet to long sticks, to short batons, to the famous nung chucks in a total physical demonstration of the master theme stated in the beginning of the film.

Anywhere the theme is most powerfully demonstrated through action, circumstance, dialogue or a combination and variation of all three elements, we can define that scene as a thematic node. In a previous chapter of this book we cited the opening credits of Robert Zemeckis' FORREST GUMP, with its feather blown by chance as a visual demonstration of what we can now identify as a thematic node. Every screenwriter and filmmaker must often fight to protect the thematic nodes of their work. In many instances, the thematic node is not in the script and must be added by the filmmaker during production or while in post-production. In truth, some may believe I am just restating what I have already identified as a breakthrough scene, but the breakthrough scene has a greater purpose, that of breaking through to a heightened realism, whereas a thematic node is simply the demonstration of a theme.

OPENING SHOT/FINAL SHOT as Thematic Node

Another significant step that can help a screenwriter and filmmaker in the preparation of their screenplay is the construction of an opening shot and final shot (or sequence) that demonstrates the theme or theme(s) inherent within their story. An opening shot or sequence has the double purpose of establishing the filmmaker's thematic conception of the story and distinguishing the filmmaker's thematic obsessions from others. Whether the opening shot is mundane or startlingly bold, the filmmaker usually introduces this opening shot of the film with the theme of the story as a guidepost and not just an attempt at empty virtuosity. In keeping with our idea of a thematic node, the opening shot of a film—depending on the filmmaker's style and desire—can be the perfect place to establish his or her approach to the story. Let us consider briefly two examples of an opening shot as thematic node.

First let us consider, as an example of a thematic node as an opening shot\scene, the opening sequence of Roman Polanski's film, KNIFE IN THE WATER (Noz W Wodzie, 1962). A wife and her husband are driving along a country road, through sharply choreographed gestures, glances and unheard dialogue (drowned out by the sound of the car's engine) Polanski delivers a major thematic node of the film: the power struggle between husband and wife. This power struggle is at once delivered as the wife drives and we can see the husband's verbal admonishments. His complaints finally culminate with him pulling the steering wheel and his wife stopping the car and switching places with him.

Their bodies collide with each other (due to the tightness of the space or on purpose?) as he begins driving and after looking over at his wife's face, the husband quickly puts his arm around her neck and kisses her apologetically. Polanski cuts to a close up of the wife's face expressionless and unmoved by the sudden affection because she knows from whence it has come: she has given in to his ego yet another time. This is a demonstration of the theme of the film mercilessly choreographed with the fine attention to human detail that is the hallmark of Polanski's personal vision.

The second example of an opening shot\scene as a thematic node comes from another favorite reference, Pier Paolo Pasolini. The opening shot of his film Il DECAMERONE (The Decameron—1971), an adaptation of Giovanni Boccaccio's bawdy tales, captures a murderer in 'flagrante delicto'. The murderer (Franco Citti) strikes violent blows against an unseen victim whose cry diminishes and suddenly stops indicating his incapacity. But to make sure that he is dead, the murderer picks up a large rock and hurls it down upon the victim to finish the job. After this, he picks up the victim, who had been bound and placed in a large knapsack, and carries him to a cliff and dumps the body. The murderer looks down at his work and then spits in contempt.

This murder foreshadows the other deaths that punctuate an otherwise comic film, but it also encompasses Pasolini's major thematic preoccupation that we can see in all of his films: Death. So this opening scene functions as a thematic node that announces and distinguishes the thematic concern of the film author; it is like a signature stroke of Pasolini. The brutal abruptness of the presentation of the act of murder, there is a 'violent' cut from the festive music of the opening credits to the violent blows of the murderer, and the fact that the victim is off-screen suggests, metaphorically, for a brief moment that the audience is being pummeled. It has been said by writer Lino Micciche that Il DECAMERONE, I RACCONTI DI CANTERBURY (The Canterbury Tales—1972) and IL FIORE DELLE MILLE E UNA NOTTE (Arabian Nights—1974) form less a trilogy of life, than a quartet of death when one looks at Pasolini's final film SALO (1975).[13]

Just as an opening shot can be a thematic node establishing the thematic preoccupations of the filmmaker or the theme within the story, many filmmakers opt to hold their thematic nodes until the finale of the film. In doing so, they put their thematic statement in a place where it will have a maximum impact—something for the spectator to think about as they leave the theatre. Two examples of this kind of final shot\sequence thematic nodes will be examined below.

The final sequence in Alfred Hitchcock's PSYCHO with Norman Bates sitting alone in a room with a blanket draped around his shoulders staring directly at the camera (audience) is one of the most chilling thematic nodes in cinema history. "In this flat, stark, clinical, modernistic composition, Norman's appearance is pure American Gothic—smirking like a gargoyle, enswathed and yet spire-like. He's not just Mummy, he's Mummy Mummy, self embalmed in immobility."[14] This shot has a voice-over of the mother talking about her son," He was always bad," as if there has been a mythic 'incestuous' binding together of two consciousnesses: male\female—mother\son. It is a demonstration of the often misunderstood analysis of the psychologist from the preceding scene: that the son has become the mother. This 'twinning' of two separate consciousnesses in one mind was the actual theme being explored in the entire film (even in Marion Crane's 'thought bubble' voice-overs as she is escaping with the $40,000, she's thinking of what someone else would be thinking) and Hitchcock found a way to deliver the theme as a final thematic node that the audience would have to think about as they left the theatre: Can one mind house the conscious of two?

The elaborate final shot\sequence of Michelangelo Antonioni's film THE PASSENGER (1975)," is seven minutes long and took eleven days to set up and complete. The shot—this is a bare description—begins as a track from inside the hotel room towards the window facing the square at the Hotel de la Gloria where Locke/Robertson (Jack Nicholson) is lying on the bed. The shot moves to the bars on the exterior side of the window, seems to pass through the bars, and then pans 180 degrees around the square until it returns to the window looking inside from the outside through the bars at Locke/Robertson, now dead, murdered, during the time the camera accomplished its itinerary around the square." [15]

Here, in defiance of the critics who might have thought that Antonioni was offering this shot as some kind of an exercise in empty virtuosity, he was simply demonstrating in the most emphatic and explicit style possible his major thematic preoccupation: freedom. The shot seems to suggest the soul of a man escaping (transcending) into pure freedom, beyond the confines of the body and the physical identification. THE PASSENGER is ostensibly about a man, a journalist named Locke, who exchanges identity with another man whom he has found dead in a hotel room, named Robertson. In an effort to escape the romantic trivialities of his private life and the political ineffectualness of his professional life, Locke unwittingly gets himself 'locked' into even more dangerous circumstances. He has taken the identity of an underground arms dealer involved in the political in-fighting of several African regimes. This final thematic node is Antonioni's most emphatic statement about man's distracted pursuit of freedom from the chains of his own inflexible political positions and relationships in modern society.

After grasping the story, the screenwriter\filmmaker should give serious consideration to how the film will start and end—not simply for the obvious reasons—but also as a way to prepare how best to demonstrate the theme of the story within the film and assert one's creative identity and thematic pre-occupations. It is only in this way that one can hope to find one's own personal voice in the cinema—especially in a cinema that is growing exponentially due to inexpensive digital video cameras and computer based editing. One must consider how best to render one's thematic nodes so that your cinematic voice is heard no matter what the subject matter, genre or actors you use as tools to construct that expression.

It is imperative that the screenwriter look over his or her script and identify a thematic node and if one cannot be found then the construction of one might be the most important step to building a better second draft of the screenplay. It is also important that the writer make the effort to decide whether or not his or her theme could be better demonstrated with or without dialogue, through action or circumstance or a variation and combination of all three. This decision is circumscribed by the theme being pursued, but it is also intimately connected with the writer/filmmaker's personal vision. In fact, the establishment of a personal vision begins with the intuitive discernment of what will ultimately be a thematic node within the screenplay or final film.

NOTES

[1]   Page 171, A HISTORY OF NARRATIVE CINEMA, David A. Cook, 1st Edition, New York, W.W. Norton & Company, Inc. 1981.

[2]   Page 312, ITALIAN CINEMA: From Neo-Realism to the Present, Peter Bondanella. New York, Frederick Unger Publishing, 1983.

[3]   Pg.123, BERTOLUCCI'S 1900: A Narrative and Historical Analysis, Robert Burgoyne. Detroit. Wayne State University Press, 1991.

[4]   Page 128, 129. LUCHINO VISCONTI, Geoffrey Nowell-Smith. London. BFI Printing, 2003.

[5]   Page 124. Ibid.

[6]   Page 30, ROCCO AND HIS BROTHERS, Sam Rohdie, London. BFI Printing, 1992.

[7]   Page 203, SIX GUNS & SOCIETY: A Structural Study of the Western, Will Wright. Berkeley. University of California Press, 1975.

[8]   Page 211, Ibid.

[9]   Page 187, JOHN FORD, Joseph McBride and Michael Wilmington. New York. Da Capo Press, 1975.

[10]   Page 16, IBSEN: The Dramaturgy of Fear by Michael Goldman, New York, Columbia University Press, 1999.

[11]   Ibid.

[12]   Transcribed from the 25th Anniversary edition of ENTER THE DRAGON.

[13]   Pg.192, PIER PAOLO PASOLINI: CINEMA AS HERESY by Naomi Greene, Princeton University Press, 1990.

[14]   Pg. 218, A LONG HARD LOOK AT 'PSYCHO', by Raymond Durgnat, 2002, BFI Publishing

[15]   Pgs. 146-47, ANTONIONI by Sam Rohdie, 1990, BFI Publishing.

CONFLICT & GOAL:
The Substructure of Dramaturgy

"What I want, what's most important to me is that I have a guarantee, no more attempts on my father's life."

-Michael Corleone (Al Pacino) THE GODFATHER

At the bottom of all dramaturgy, whether comedy or drama, is conflict; conflict expressed as the blockage, manipulation, or dissolution of a character's or group of characters wants and needs. Let us simplify even further: X wants Y, but someone or something is blocking X from getting Y by selfish (villainous) acts. The only way X can get Y is through a selfless (heroic) act. [See: Fig.3] Whether it was the dresses worn by Tony Curtis and Jack Lemmon in Billy Wilder's SOME LIKE IT HOT (1959) or the answer Othello wanted from his wife Desdemona, all dramaturgy begins with the conflict of wants and needs. The only way to ignite a drama or comedy is to know exactly what each individual character wants at all times during the course of writing the screenplay. Only by keeping a definitive point of reference in one's head can one construct a screenplay that dramatizes the blockage, manipulations, or dissolution of these wants and needs.

Now, I have simplified the concept of conflict only to better reveal its substructure. This, of course, does not mean that a character's wants and needs have to be immediately on display from the moment the narrative begins or that a character cannot have multiple conflicts, multiple wants, and multiple blockages impeding him or her. Theme is what will guide the writer to the final resolution or dissolution of the conflict(s).

For instance, a character can slowly discover what he or she wants as the narrative progresses. Napoleon (Jon Heder) of NAPOLEON DYNAMITE (2004) stated near the end of the first act of the film that he wanted to ask a particular girl to a High School dance. Perhaps, this is what is meant by the cliché, coming of age: the character is coming to know what he or she really wants out of life and how to get it. There were several obstacles in his way that threatened to permanently block his access to Deb (Tina Majorino):

1) His profound Nerd Status
2) His clothing
3) His only friend Pedro (Efren Ramirez) who asked her to the dance first
4) Her lack of interest
5) His Uncle Rico's sleazy and selfish 'Bust Must+' business

The conflict of this comedy is found within the fact that the friendship between Napoleon and Pedro was blocking Napoleon's access to what he really wanted. Yet, through performing a selfless act (the riotous solo dance number) on the behalf of his friend Pedro (who wanted to be school president to attain a goal of respect) Napoleon was allowed to access what he wanted: a girlfriend. In getting what he wanted he also attained his ultimate goal: the affirmation of his normality through the dissolution of his nerd status. We must note that his selfless act served a dual function beyond simply establishing him as the hero of the tale: it helped to get Pedro elected and elicited the interest in Deb for Napoleon.

Sometimes when what our characters want is an idea or an abstract concept, we become confused as to how to create a conflict to dramatize the story. The simplest answer to this difficulty is that you must *personify* this abstract concept or idea in another character or group of characters. For instance, even though the Maltese Falcon was," the stuff that dreams are made of," this object magnifies the greed and perfidy within men. The abstract concepts of greed and perfidy are personified through the Joel Cairo (Peter Lorre), Brigid O'Shaughnessy (Mary Astor), and Kasper Gutman (Sidney Greenstreet) characters, who would stop at nothing (selfish acts) to get it. THE MALTESE FALCON (1941) reveals the depth of complexity characters can play against each other (through ruse, blocking, and other deceptions) to try to get what they want.

Another example of a character personifying an abstract concept is the character of the HAL 9000 computer in Stanley Kubrick and Arthur C. Clark's film 2001: A Space Odyssey (1968). During a top secret space voyage to Jupiter to make contact with sentient extraterrestrial beings, the HAL 9000 computer runs amok with a calm and patronizing voice detailing the absolute logic of its artificial intelligence. The supercomputer murders all the hibernating members of the crew and kills yet another who was sent on a fool's errand to fix an allegedly malfunctioning piece of equipment on the exterior of the ship.

The computer's reasoning for the murders is that humans are," imperfect," beings and cannot be allowed to jeopardize such an important mission. What the computer wanted was very simple: to eliminate all humans from its perfect logic and perfect mission. What the human wanted was also very simple: Astronaut Dave Bowman (Keir Dullea) wanted to stay alive and ultimately kill the perfect logic that was threatening his existence. We can see the selfish act of the computer and the selfless act of Dave (who went outside of the ship without his helmet to try and recapture the lifeless body of his fellow crewman) very clearly. Yet, 2001 is a very complex and ambitious film; much more is suggested in the conceptualization of the work. But no matter how ambitious and far-reaching the concept, underpinning the most profound cinematic narratives is the simplicity of conflict: X wants Y, but is blocked from getting it directly.

THE SOCIOLOGY OF DRAMATURGY

There are sociological foundations to this dramaturgical perspective of characters and their wants and needs as presented within a narrative that are illustrated in the two competing theories of social stratification. These are explained by sociologist Gerhard E. Lenski as:

1) FUNCTIONALIST THEORIES: which postulate that the inequality or stratification of society is based on the needs of societies, not out of the needs or desires of individuals.
2) CONFLICT THEORIES: that view social inequality or stratification as arising out of the struggle for valued goods and services in short supply by self interested individuals.

It may help us to look at this using Coppola and Puzo's THE GODFATHER as a dramatic illustration of both stratification theories.

The phrase," Its business, not personal," first spoken by the cunning Sollozzo (Al Letteri) character and repeated in turn by Tom Hagen (Robert Duvall) and Santino Corleone (James Caan) is the dramatic expression of this functionalist theory. Organized crime is not portrayed as an illegal enterprise with selfish interests, but instead as a selfless (non-personal) enterprise with a legitimate social interest. Certain classes and ethnicities need a Mafia to insure that they receive the goods and services they are entitled to but are otherwise kept from having. The treatment of Italian immigrants in the early 1900's, dramatized in THE GODFATHER II, gives the Italian Mafia a functional sociological underpinning. Thus, the Mafia itself is a consequence of the inherent and unavoidable stratification of society.

Yet after the murders of Sollozzo, the corrupt police captain McCluskey (Sterling Hayden) and finally, Santino Corleone, the conflict theory of sociology is revealed as the real dramaturgical underpinning behind the attempted murder of Don Vito Corleone and all of the subsequent violence. At a meeting of all the five families with a freshly healed Vito Corleone in attendance, Don Barzini says," Don Corleone had all the judges and politicians in New York [in his pocket] then he must share them or let others use them. He must let us draw the water from the well. Certainly he can present a bill for such services; after all we are not communists." So the true basis for the violent infighting among the Mafia families was a struggle over the limited supply of services (political influence) that left some families in an unequal position relative to the Corleones.

Perhaps the large scale narratives like the recent sword and sandal epics (TROY, ALEXANDER, GLADIATOR) or fantasy works like the LOTR trilogy and THE MATRIX trilogy require that the fighting between clans, groups, tribes, and machines begin as functionally orientated, but as the story begins to define its heroes and villains, the conflict theory begins to drive the narrative to its dramatic conclusion. This supports my assertion that dramaturgy must have conflict as its motivating dynamic and even though a story might have an allegorical or metaphorical intention—the paradigms of drama demand that these allegories, metaphors, or messages (ideological or moral) be personified in a character or group of characters whose competing self interests create conflict.

THE GOAL OF THE CHARACTER

"I never wanted this for you . . . I thought that when it was your turn, that you would be the one who'd hold the strings. Senator Corleone, Governor Corleone, something . . ."

-Vito Corleone (Marlon Brando) THE GODFATHER

When constructing the conflicts of a story, it is important that we look beyond immediate simplistic assumptions to effectively create complex characters. For instance, a villainous character might simply want money and the only way to get that is to steal it from a bank or person(s). This is an obvious and facile approach to conflict. "In and of itself money has little power to satisfy normal human desires, but as a medium of exchange, it can be used to attain creature comforts, improved health, status, and even survival itself." (Lenski, POWER & PRIVILEGE: A Theory of Social Stratification, pg. 39) You must think beyond the medium of exchange and towards the ultimate goal of the character.

What kind of lifestyle will that money finance for the character, or better still, what lifestyle or dream will this money ultimately continue to finance for the character? The character wants the money to maintain a lifestyle, a status, something that the money will enable him or her to continue to do. By sharing the rituals of the character with the audience as in Jacques Becker's TOUCHEZ PAS AU GRISBI or Scorsese's GOODFELLAS, one can understand why stolen money was so much more important than its face value. The money was needed to support a lifestyle that would have been otherwise unattainable under the current stratification of society.

The screenwriter must be careful not to oversimplify the goal of the character. The want is the expressed desire that ultimately leads to the goal of the character. If conflict is wrought from what the character wants, then the goal is *why* the character wants it. Whether it is a fulfilling and substantive life, as in AMERICAN BEAUTY (1999) or the continuation of an illusion of control as expressed by Ordell Robbie (Samuel L. Jackson) in JACKIE BROWN, the goal is the big picture possessed by the character. The want is a step or a series of steps that are needed to attain or sustain the ultimate goal.

The criminal wants money, but he or she wants it to maintain a lifestyle or an illusion. Writer/Director, Patty Jenkins' film MONSTER (2003) dramatizes the serial murders of Aileen Wuornos (Charlize Theron) as robberies that enabled her to maintain her ultimate goal of being loved and living with and providing for her lesbian lover. The goal here is an illusion, perhaps the goal is always an illusion in crime films, but it is clear that Aileen wanted money and that want brought her into conflict when she tried to stop prostituting herself to get it. She did it for love, but it was love that ultimately turned her in and destroyed her.

CONCLUSION

All this has been delivered to note that if the writer keeps the wants and desires of the characters as a reference point and the *goal* of the characters as a terminal point, a story can be brought to a very dramatically satisfying conclusion. The drama between what the character wants, how he or she goes about getting it and the goal is what is typically called a character arc. Conflict can be generated by the other characters who personify the blocking, manipulation, or dissolution of the wants of the main character through their selfish acts. Whether the goal is an illusion or a certainty—and whether the character actually attains that goal is a matter of thematic intention. One is reminded of Sterling Hayden's character of Johnny Clay at the end of Stanley Kubrick's THE KILLING (1956) as he watches his entire stolen loot blow away across an airfield. He wanted the money for sure, but he wanted the goal that that money would have enabled him to attain even more: independence. So a good drama has the options of having the character(s) attain the ultimate goal, maintain the ultimate goal, or reflect upon the loss of the goal.

Fig.3 Simplified Dramaturgical Formula

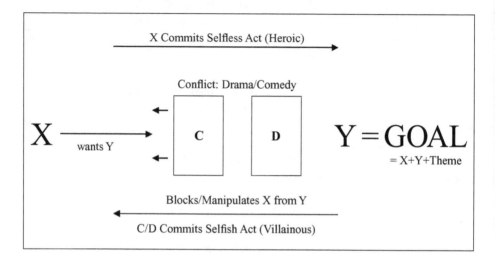

—I am indebted to Thomas Elsaeser's breakdown of the formal structure of the films of Rainer Werner Fassbinder in his article, A Cinema of Vicious Circles, found in the Museum of Modern Art book, RAINER WERNER FASSBINDER (1997) for this simplified dramaturgical formula. Also for an alternate version of this formula one could simply replace the heroic selfless act of X with a disapproved of selfish act that in turn makes redemption the ultimate goal of the character.

TOWARDS A THEMATICALLY JUSTIFIED ENDING

If we recognize and accept the assertion that the goal is not what the character wants but why the character wants it, then finding one's way to a thematically justified ending can be an exciting creative adventure rather than a point arrived at from sheer creative exhaustion. In my humble opinion, if one contemplates the goal of the character(s), one can often have an intuition, if not a certainty about the way the story should end before ever beginning to write the actual screenplay. It's the intuition that illuminates the journey of writing; it's the certainty that keeps one determined to enjoy the mystery of that journey. Again, having a notion of an ending before starting a screenplay—depending on one's writing style and spirit—increases the likelihood for a successful completion. The following discusses the three important terminal points that can help determine the thematic justification for how the story might end.

THE RIGHT of the FILM AUTEUR:
Modern Narration and Ancient Narration

If there is any flaw in Peter Jackson's LOTR trilogy that cannot be dismissed as nit picking, it is the generally acknowledged fact that the final installment, RETURN OF THE

KING, had too many endings. I would be the first to admit that this flaw had little to do with Jackson's brilliant storytelling abilities and more to do with his psychological/spiritual attachment to the material. Having worked on all three installments continuously for several years, it was no doubt an emotionally wrenching experience to have to let it go.

Moreover, the filmmaker's reverence for the J.R.R. Tolkien's literary material must have exerted a tremendous influence to veto any decision to end the filmed narrative anywhere before the actual ending of the literary narrative. Thus, the several opportunities to end the film on a thematic point as opposed to a narrative point is what extended the film nearly beyond the point of dramatic interest. The practical obsession with giving the trilogy a definitive sense of finality threatened to obscure the thematic concept of the material and led the filmmakers down the primrose path of answering all the questions concerned with each character's destiny.

Yet the end of the literary story should not simply determine the ending of the filmed adaptation of that story. Pasolini has taught us that images are much more expressive than words, that an image cannot be reduced to a single sign, but instead always contains multiple signs within a single image.* Like the word 'tree' isolates the idea of a tree in our minds but the image of a tree usually has the earth, the sky, the sunlight and other signs (historical and immediate) surrounding it and thus is more expressive in its recorded physical context than an isolated word on a page.

In lieu of this 'multi-leveled' aspect of the image, the ending of a filmed story should always be determined by the theme(s) that the filmmaker has chosen to explore or reveal. The canvas of the filmmaker is broader than the canvas of the literary artist or the theatrical artist. We know this to be relevant because if we look at the great film endings from the freeze-frames of Francois Truffaut's LES QUATRE CENT COUPS (The Four Hundred Blows—1959) and George Roy Hill's BUTCH CASSIDY & THE SUNDANCE KID (1969) to the elaborate final shots of Michelangelo Antonioni's THE PASSENGER (1975) or Jim Jarmusch's DEAD MAN (1995), the ending also tells us why the filmmaker chose to tell this story.

This is perhaps an essential difference between modern narration in the novel or film and ancient narration in the folktale or myth. In modern narration the author determines the ending from the themes he or she has chosen to explore. In the folktale or mythology the ending of a tale is determined by the needs of the culture that repeats the tale in its oral or ritualized traditions. In modern narration, the ending reveals the themes that were explored in the tale by the author and therefore the ending should not be thought of as a wrapping up of a character's life, activities, or all of a story's loose ends. The ending is the final demonstration of the theme—anything more is a bedtime story and anything less is a disaster.

THE ACCOMPLISHMENT

Returning to the concept of goal, why the character wants what he or she wants, we must look at the ideal: the perfect illusion from which all the character's actions, behaviors, and wants are pursued. This goal, whether it is attained, maintained, or lost is what should determine the ending of the tale. For it is within how the pursuit of that goal concludes that demonstrates the theme(s) within the tale. Let us look at these three terminal points (attainment, maintaining, and loss) individually using three classic films as illustration.

1) Attainment—an ending that has the attainment of the ultimate goal of the character is not solely reserved for Heroic films, although more often than not, the hero does attain his goal. But there are caveats to this attainment; something is lost as a result of something gained; attainment therefore always has its price. The classic film by Elia Kazan, ON THE WATERFRONT (1954) allows the character of Terry Malloy (Marlon Brando), an ex-prize fighter and long shoreman, to get what he wanted. But his ultimate goal to be a man, an equal among equals who chooses of his own will, comes with an expensive spiritual and physical price. The themes of manhood, fraternity, and fidelity are demonstrated in the choice to end the film with a beaten and battered Terry Malloy walking (as if carrying an invisible cross) into the doors of the dock with all the other workers behind him.

   Attainment, as an ending can be thematically justified as long as the price of that attainment is worn on the body and/or face of the hero. (See: the ending of Quentin Tarantino's JACKIE BROWN as an alternate example)

2) Maintaining—To maintain a goal is usually an ending reserved for narratives concerning war. From TORA, TORA, TORA (1970) to STARSHIP TROOPERS (1997), when heroes are battling with their villainous adversaries, the great speeches that inspire their fellows to sacrifice all are rooted in the maintaining of a goal that is culturally imbedded in their listeners. Those moments as rendered in Shakespeare's HENRY V, John Wayne's THE ALAMO (1960), or Mel Gibson's BRAVEHEART (1995), there is always a goal that is worth fighting for, worth maintaining, even if the participants don't live to see it themselves. We might look at John Carpenter's masterpiece, THE THING (1982), as a narrative that ends with the maintaining of goal that none of the participants will live to see or enjoy.

   Released as a remake of Howard Hawk's production of," THE THING (1951)," John Carpenter's film is really a bold rethinking of the original concept of a violent creature from another planet that unleashes terror upon a crew of scientists after it is dug up from a glacier in Antarctica. In Carpenter's version, the creature replicates living organisms (animal/human) by invading and absorbing the body on a cellular level. Once the few remaining members of the all male crew at an American base camp realize that they cannot let this creature loose into the populated world, their original goal of survival shifts towards the goal of maintaining a way of life that they themselves would never see again. The ending, where both RJ MaCready (Kurt Russell) and Childs (Keith David) share

74

a drink and await their certain death by freezing in the Antarctic hinterland, has poignancy beyond its horror film veneer.

This ending never directly answered the several questions: Exactly what happened to the two survivors? Whether anyone else will ever find out about the base camp? And because of a special effects flaw, the fate of one of the characters is never actually seen on screen. But this ending is thematically justified and far outweighs those unanswered questions and even the minor flaw of one character's sudden absence. The thematically justified ending is the modern film author's right and not just his or her privilege. We know there have been excesses, Andy Warhol's eight hour film EMPIRE (1964) comes to mind, but if a modern film author has a thematically justified ending then he or she has a right to end the film narrative at the point that best demonstrates the themes they were exploring.

For instance, the critical backlash at Michael Mann's film," ALI," was directed at the fact that he didn't tell more of Muhammad Ali's life story. Yet, Mann had determined where he was going to stop the narrative based on the themes he found within Muhammad Ali's life story that were compelling both dramatically and personally. Here in this film, the tension between Muhammad Ali the folk hero and Muhammad Ali the narrative character seemed to cancel out Mann's authorial right to end the narrative thematically as opposed to a culturally defined ending in the jaded eyes of some critics and spectators. The real challenge of the film ALI was in the nature of authorship between the folk tale (told by a people) and the modern telling of a tale (told by an author/auteur).

3) And now we can turn our attention to loss as a thematically justified ending. The loss of a character's goal seems like it is solely reserved for the bad guys in crime films. For instance Neil McCauley's (Robert DeNiro) death by the bullets from Detective Vincent Hanna's (Al Pacino) gun in Michael Mann's HEAT (1995) is a classic example of the criminal losing his goal. But in spite of this classic and typical example, loss is not solely reserved for the crime narrative, loss can be found in a wide variety of genres. From the empty handed gold prospectors of John Huston's THE TREASURE OF THE SIERRA MADRE (1947) to the unrequited and untimely expression of carnal love for a dead hit man in Rainer Werner Fassbinder's DER AMERIKANISCHE SOLDAT (The American Soldier, 1970), the loss of the goal is a bitter conclusion. Loss seems to signify the fatalism in what was promised at the end of the rainbow. And in the case of Fassbinder's ending for THE AMERICAN SOLDIER, loss is a persistent emotion held in dream-like futility that causes one to reflect upon the theme of the impotence of love given in a variety of thematic nodes of increasing severity and desperation throughout the film.

Loss gives us just as powerful an ending as attainment; if attainment allows a character to lose something before gaining something greater, then loss is a doubled inversion of attainment: you lose one thing and then you lose something greater than that one thing. Michael Cimino's THE DEER HUNTER (1978) gives us an incisive conceptualization of loss as a thematically justified ending. Seven friends living and working in the steel mills of Pennsylvania have their lives irreparably altered by the devastating events of the Vietnam War. Three of the friends enlist, Nick (Christopher Walken), Michael (Robert DeNiro), Steven (John Savage) and are shipped off to the front lines of the war. All three are captured, held captive and forced to gamble with their lives playing Russian roulette for the amusement and gain of their Vietnamese captors.

After a brilliant and daring escape from the enemy, the three soldiers are separated from each other. Nick goes AWOL from a military hospital in Vietnam and becomes a gambler addicted to heroin, playing Russian roulette in the Vietnamese underground for high stakes betting. Steven is a despondent amputee who refuses to go back home to his wife and child. But Michael tries to quietly return home decorated with medals and ignorant of the whereabouts and circumstances of his friends. While at home he furtively attempts to reveal his hidden feelings for his best friend Nick's girl.

When word reaches Michael about Steve, he visits him in the VA hospital and convinces him to come back home. Steve reveals to Michael that he has been receiving money from overseas all during his hospital stay and Michael realizes that this money is from Nick. He travels back to Vietnam during the fall of Saigon in a selfless act to find his friend and reunite them all. The loss of this goal, captured in the desperation and pitch of DeNiro's voice as he cries out Nick's name as the blood flows from an unlucky roll of the gun barrel, shows how loss of a goal is not solely reserved for criminals. Michael loses both his friend and his hope of ever reuniting them all together as it was before the war tore them apart. Heroes can also fail; perhaps redemption is found in the hope of having at least tried.

So whether the screenwriter/filmmaker decides to have an ending that suggests that his or her characters have attained the goal, maintained the goal, or lost the goal—it is an ending that must be thematically justified vis-à-vis the character's wants and the conflicts they've encountered in pursuit of that goal. Again, goal is why the character wants what he or she wants. Goal is the illusion, the ideal, and the perfection the character is seeking in trying to attain what he or she wants.

- "It is not true that the smallest unit in cinema is the image, when by image we mean that "view" which is the shot, or, in other words what one sees looking through the lens. All of us, Metz and I included, have always believed this. Instead: **the various real objects that compose a shot are the smallest unit of film language**. [My emphasis]"—Pier Paolo Pasolini, Heretical Empiricism, The Written Language of Reality, pg. 200

VISUALIZATION AS OPPOSED TO NOVELIZATION

It was filmmaker/film theorist Pier Paolo Pasolini who also informed us that a screenplay is a," structure that wants to be another structure." A screenplay is a text that constantly alludes to becoming a film. "In other words: the author of a screenplay asks his addressee for a particular collaboration: namely, that of lending to the text a "visual" completeness which it does not have, but at which it hints." (Pasolini, Heretical Empiricism, page 189) But all too often amateur screenwriters fall into an abyss of novelizing scene and/or character descriptions for the benefit of the reader in an attempt to fill in the inherent incompleteness of their screenplays. What seems like a courtesy for the reader becomes an obstacle for the filmmaker; for a novelized screenplay must be re-translated, rewritten, and adapted for the screen, in which case, the author has indeed written a novel which pretends to be a screenplay.

A genuine screenplay will always seem incomplete; in fact it is incomplete because it must be filmed: it must become what it hints at becoming. Scene descriptions or character descriptions should only contain the most pertinent production details, not flowery language, metaphors, similes, or the diversion of interior monologues. In most cases, an amateur screenwriter novelizes portions of his screenplay in an unconscious attempt to cheat the full dramatization of a scene.

To be more specific, because he or she does not know how to either visually or dramatically convey a mood, feeling, or exposition—a novelization of these details enter into the screenplay, making the text easier to *read*, but difficult to *film*. The novelist has a plethora of tools at his disposal to convey images into the reader's mind; the screenwriter can only hint at such things because the final images have not yet been created; they must be filmed. The grim reality that every screenwriter must confront is that all of his work will seem incomplete to an uniformed reader because he is not writing a novel—he is writing a screenplay which is a structure that wants to become another structure: that is a film.

The writer/director must write only the most calculated essence of his story because the novelization of the details he wants to convey are actually his own director's notes that he will eventually use to visualize his script and therefore should be kept to himself and shared with only his cast and crew during the production. In the following pages I will reprint the opening pages of two original screenplays by two authors whose permission has been graciously granted for analysis of the pesky problem I call novelization. The first example,' Detroit Stories,' by Royce Davis cheats a full dramatization, where as the second example,' Back To The Books,' by Steven Douglas relies on literary tools to give the reader a 'heads up' about what is going on, but would leave a viewer confused.

EXAMPLE #1

BEGIN MUSIC
ROLL OPENING CREDITS

NEW RENAISSANCE PRODUCTIONS

presents

Royce Davis's

DETROIT STORIES

FADE IN TITLE

THE BEGINNING

[1A]

INT: FILM MAGAZINE PARTY-NIGHT

The scene is a high society party being given by a film magazine. The room is filled with members of the magazine and film industry. *We get shots of people talking*. One special guest has just arrived and his name is ZACHARY.

Everyone crowds around him and is congratulating him on his recent film "THE WOMANIZER." A woman from across the room yells his name. She looks somewhat loose.

WOMAN

Hi Zachary!

Zachary waves back to her and smiles.

[2A]

Zachary is with his agent as they both flow through the people and make their way to the punch bowl. The publisher for the magazine comes over to them. His name is Daren and he has a very distinguished aura about himself.

DAREN

You looked great on the cover of the magazine. How about another for your next picture.

Zachary looks somewhat flattered. **[2B]**

ZACHARY

We'll see Daren. Maybe my agent Oliver can work something out.

Zachery takes a drink, then he sees a very attractive woman, somewhat broad, but still attractive.

When we read section **[1A]** of the scene description we have no problem visualizing in our minds the beginning of this film. The reader has superiority over how he completes the visual details of this scene. But major problems will arise when a filmmaker has assembled his cast and crew at a location to begin filming this opening scene: his actors and extra's will turn to him and say," What are we supposed to be talking about? We don't have any lines?" Now the writer/director will have to (1) have the actors improvise their lines which can be dramatically disappointing or (2) hold up the production while he or she writes dialogue to fill this gap, pushing the production schedule behind and costing valuable dollars. What was the problem in the first place? By novelizing the scene description [1A] the writer/director has *cheated the dialogue*, specifically with the troublesome sentence: **We get shots of people talking**. But what will the actors say? Moreover, the entire details of the scene description: A film magazine party, the director's name, and the title of the new film must be distributed within the dialogue of the '**shots of people talking**.' The mistake here is that the entire scene description is written for the *reader* of the script and not the *viewer* of the resulting film. Reading this script, everything seems okay, but to shoot it becomes a task wrought with difficulties due to the novelization of details thought inconsequential but they in fact provide an opportunity to orientate the viewer and make any exposition dynamic and interesting to present to the viewer.

In the section marked **[2A]** the character, Zachary, is walking with his agent, Oliver, and yet in section **[2B]** Zachary mentions his agent's name as if he's not there and continues to have a conversation with Daren whom we learn is the publisher of the film magazine in section **[2A]**. This is all severely problematic: 1) Because both Oliver and Daren have not been introduced to the viewing audience. The reader is given this information via the scene description **[2A]** but the resulting dialogue does not establish either supporting character's relationship to the lead character, Zachary. As it stands, only the reader will identify Oliver as Zachary's agent and Daren as the film magazine's publisher, but the viewer is left looking at two strangers. 2) Why introduce Oliver and Daren to the reader in the scene description **[2A]** and then turn around and not give Oliver any lines, but give Daren lines of dialogue that do not establish him as the publisher of the film magazine? This is dramatically incongruous. I believe this screenwriter was initially indecisive about which supporting characters would eventually be important within his overall story and this is what had contributed to the hackneyed introduction of the characters. This mistake emphasizes the necessity of having a treatment, story synopsis, and character description before sitting down to write a screenplay.

Example 1 shows us how novelizing scene descriptions and/or character descriptions causes the screenwriter to *cheat a full dramatization* and makes a script unnecessarily difficult to shoot. Moreover, example 1 shows us that the writer must have a concrete idea of which supporting characters are important enough within his overall story to be introduced to the viewing audience via dialogue, actions or rituals that define their relationship to the lead character(s).

EXAMPLE #2

TITLES—WHITE & BLACK ON MONTAGE

EXT—THE OPENING CREDITS FEATURE A PHOTO MONTAGE OF A JUNIOR HIGH GRADUATING CLASS AND IT'S [sic] CEREMONIES. IN THE BACKGROUND, YOU CAN HEAR THE FAREWELL SPEECH OF THE SCHOOL'S PRINCIPAL WHILE THE GRADUATION SONG, "POMP & CIRCUMSTANCE" PLAYS THROUGHOUT THE SEQUENCE.

FADE OUT.

CUT TO:

SEPTEMBER 1984
(burn in title)

EXT.—JOHN J. PERSHING HIGH SCHOOL
(first day of new school year)

CAMERA ANGLE PICKS UP different shots of school and morning activities:

1) CARS PULLING UP IN THE SCHOOL PARKING LOT.
2) LINES FORMING OUTSIDE THE DOOR.
3) SPRAY BOTTLES KEEPING JHERI CURLS STYLED.
4) OLD CLASSMATES BEING REUNITED.
5) FRESH BUBBLE-TOE ADIDAS STEPPING ONTO THE SCHOOL GROUNDS.

[3A]
It's the usual motions of black teens going back to school in the eighties revived for another year.

CUT TO:

EXT.—FRONT OF STEVE DUNCAN'S HOUSE: MORNING
[3B]
STEVE DUNCAN, a recent junior high graduate now entering his first year of high school at Pershing, pulls out a red, junked up moped out of his driveway. It's not a particularly great looking bike, but it gets up.

CUT TO:

ANGLE: HIS DRIVEWAY
Steve pulls out into the street and takes off for the new school.

CUT TO:

EXT—STREET: DAY

He cruises up a main avenue called Seven Mile Road and soon arrives to whip up into the school's faculty parking lot.

CUT TO:

EXT.—A DARK, SECLUDED SECTION OF PARKING LOT: DAY

[3C]
After pulling into this area of the parking lot. Steve hops off and quickly looks around to find a spot to "secretly" hide the bike and lock it. When he does, he opens a side panel on the rear and pulls a long, thick, chain out and wraps the wheels and handlebars to secure it. He notices the time his watch reads, 8:30AM, and looks around to see if the person who is suppose to meet him is coming. As he already figured . . . he isn't.

CLOSE: STEVE

> STEVE
> Damn, I knew he'd be late!

CUT TO:

INT.—J.D. DILES BEDROOM: DAY
[3D]
The person he's referring to as being late is his best friend and partner, J.D. Diles, who at this moment, 15 minutes before registration begins, is still in bed knocked out.

CAMERA descends down onto his face as WE SEE him slowly turn over.

'Back To The Books,' uses very colorful language to help the *reader* visualize the Eighties high school milieu with lengthy character descriptions that precede the actual character's dialogue. Based on our analysis of example #1 we should easily be able to see the problems inherent in Example #2. In section **[3A]**, a sentence like," *It's the usual motions of black teens going back to school in the eighties revived for another year*," is colorful and helps the reader, but the filmmaker may need more concrete descriptions of these 'usual' motions. Yet the major problem with 'Back To The Books,' is in the introduction of the characters and the establishment of a clear fictional time frame. Reading section **[3C]** of the scene description establishes the fact that the character, Steve, is looking at his watch and it is 8:30am. Later, reading section **[3D]** the reader is informed that the person Steve referred to in the dialogue as being late is co-lead character, J.D. Diles, who is still at home in bed. Immediately the filmmaker should become aware of the glaring flaws caused by the novelized scene descriptions which destroy the establishment of a fictional time frame upon which the two character introductions are based.

Section **[3C]** tells the reader that the fictional time is 8:30am and later section **[3D]** tells the reader that co-lead character, J.D. Diles, is 15 minutes late for school registration, but there is no shot that provides the *viewer* with any of this pertinent information. Indeed, how is the viewing audience ever to know that J.D. is late for registration if the actual time and definition of school registration are not set up on-screen in a previous scene? The entire intercutting between Steve Duncan and J.D. Diles is dramatically incongruous if the viewing audience isn't provided any clear fictional time frame with which to make any sense out of the on-screen events: 1) actual time of school registration, 2) A Close up shot of Steve Duncan's watch reading 8:30 and 3) complimentary dialogue or visual information indicating J.D. Diles awareness of his tardiness.

Another unnecessary aspect of the scene descriptions are the author's subjective descriptions of Steve's inner thoughts in section **[3B]**: "As he already figured . . . he isn't." Although such descriptions might make the script easier to read, such comments do little for the filmmaker who must film externally what is being thought internally by the character. It is a colorful detail best used by novelists to fill a reader's imagination and not a potential viewer's imagination. Such "novelized" details draw the reader and the filmmaker's attention away from the dynamism of film narration. For instance, after Steve says," Damn, I knew he'd be late." The simple cut to the sleeping character allows the audience watching the film to deduce that this was the person referred to, who would be late.

The knowledge of the power of film editing to alternate perspectives, settings, and situations must be foremost in the screenwriter's mind so that his pen does not rest upon literary conventions, but instead rests upon how the cinema can dynamically present and alternate perspectives, settings and situations," in the blink of an eye," to use the title of the book on editing by world renowned film editor, Walter Murch. Without an understanding of and a respect for the fundamental aspects of the cinematic language the screenwriter can too easily fall victim to his literary antecedents and vanities. (After all, most of us learn how to write before we learn how to film.)

The most concise and fundamental definition of the cinematic language was given by the late French filmmaker Robert Bresson in his book, NOTES ON THE CINEMATOGRAPHER:

"To set up a film is to bind persons
to each other and to objects by looks."[1]

Within this simple statement lay the keys to establishing point of view, directing actors, and the force and measure of editing or as it is called montage. The "binding" that Bresson speaks of is montage (the connection of one shot with another shot) and it is this ability to dynamically change location, fictional perspective, and expand or constrict fictional time that sets the cinema apart from the novel and from theatre.

To fully grasp what Bresson is suggesting we should look at the early montage experiments of Soviet filmmaker, Lev Kuleshov (1899-1970) and the discovery named after him called the "Kuleshov effect". "Kuleshov took unedited footage of a completely expressionless face (that of the pre-revolutionary matinee idol Ivan Mozhukhin, who had emigrated to Paris after the Revolution) and inter-cut it with shots of three highly motivated objects: a bowl of hot soup, a dead woman lying in a coffin, and a little girl playing with a teddy bear. When the film strips were shown to randomly selected audiences, they invariably responded as though the actor's face had accurately portrayed the emotion appropriate to the inter-cut object." [2] In each case the face was exactly the same and the audience reacted differently because of how the look of the actor was bound to the object or person as a consequence of montage. Kuleshov also did another experiment with the shot of a face of a smiling actor, a shot of a revolver, and a shot of the face of a frightened actor. Audiences alternately interpreted the sequences as fear and cowardice or menace depending upon where he placed the first actor's face in the sequence.

"Kuleshov concluded from these results, known today as the "Kuleshov effect," that the shot, or cinematic sign, has two distinct values: 1) that which it possesses in itself as a photographic image of reality and 2) that which it acquires when placed in relationship to other shots." [3] Kuleshov and the generations of international filmmakers that have followed have all realized that it is the second function, the meaning acquired after montage (editing) that best allows the filmmaker to communicate with the audience in a language that is fundamentally cinematic.

It is this fundamental language that must be understood and respected by the screenwriter *before* they begin writing their actual screenplay. The more a writer respects the fundamental aspects of the cinematic language and what it adds to the telling of a story the better, inevitably, a screenplay will become. The writer must not rely too heavily upon literary conventions and overdrawn scene descriptions for there is a danger that what has been described may pander to a reader's sensibility and not respect a viewer's intelligence. The reader has his eyes on the page; the viewer has his eyes upon the screen and his ears attentive to the audio accompanying it. The novelization of a scene in the scene descriptions, extra-fictional subjective comments, and external character introductions can make the writer a co-conspirator of his own self-deception in that the writer believes he has fully dramatized a scene when in fact he has not made the most important aspects of the scene self-evident.

In other chapters, particularly The Narrative Ellipsis and the chapter on Book Adaptations, I discuss in great detail the use of this fundamental aspect of the cinematic language in shaping a story or adapting a novel for the screen. To write for the screen one must understand that *in the cinema it is primarily editing that moves the story along* and not literary descriptions, metaphors, similes, and dialogue. It is this ability to bind objects and persons to each other by looks that sets the cinema apart and gives the film author his or her voice. Visualization instead of novelization is the most important technique that must be grasped to create screenplays that enrich the cinema as a whole and the viewer in particular.

WHO SHOULD LOOK AT MY FIRST DRAFT?

"Who are your friends? Do they believe in you? Or do they stunt your growth with ridicule and disbelief? If the latter, you haven't friends. Go find some."
Pg.47, Zen In The Art of Writing, Ray Bradbury

Knowing that a screenplay is an incomplete literary form: a written document that is less than a novel and even less than a film, how does a screenwriter get a competent critique of his work from lay readers? I sincerely believe that due to the inherent incompleteness of screenplays that are written to be shot, the lay reader is not the ideal critic for a screenwriter to solicit a critique of his work. For instance, for Steve Douglas' screenplay, BACK TO THE BOOKS, I suggested that he turn the subjective comments in his scene descriptions into voice-over narration for his characters. This voice-over narration would cut out a lot of unnecessary exposition and could be used to quickly establish the relationships among the characters and their circumstances. Moreover, he could even use this narration dynamically as Martin Scorsese did in CASINO (1995) where different characters picked up the voice-over narration and delivered multiple perspectives on their circumstances.

For Royce Davis' screenplay, DETROIT STORIES: The Beginning, I suggested that he use the film magazine party scene as Francis Coppola used the Wedding scene in THE GODFATHER; as a way to introduce the audience to the characters by way of the characters introducing themselves to each other and the main character, Zachary, commenting on others to his new female acquaintance. In this way he gets the most out of a single scene through dramatic economy. Since the screenplay is neither a novel nor a completed film, the lay reader may give the most damaging opinions and advice upon a work that does not allow his imagination to visualize specific details (as a novel) and contains technical cinematic terms beyond his grasp (tracking shot, V.O., CUT TO:, Off-Screen, etc.). The ideal critic of a screenwriter's work are other informed screenwriters and most importantly, other filmmakers who have completed at least one marginally successful project on their own. In these informed critics the amateur screenwriter must place his trust and seek their guidance, lest he will always novelize and never visualize the drama he has written and seeks to view. [4]

NOTES

(1) Pg. 12, NOTES ON THE CINEMATOGRAPHER, Robert Bresson, trans. by Jonathan Griffin, Quartet Books, London, 1986.

(2) Page 137, A HISTORY OF NARRATIVE FILM 3rd Ed., David A. Cook, W.W. Norton & Company, New York, 1996.

(3) Ibid.

(4) We might note that the dazzling visual styles of many Italian filmmakers: Antonioni, Pasolini, Visconti, Leone, Fellini, Bertolucci, and others can be attributed to the peculiarities of Italian Film Production. For instance, Italian film scripts are split down the middle of the page to allow one side for images and the other side for dialogue. This split page technique puts an equal emphasis upon the pictorial aspect of cinema as opposed to solely the dramatic or theatrical aspects of a typical American screenplay. (Cf. ONCE UPON A TIME: Sergio Leone, documentary on the DVD, ONCE UPON A TIME IN AMERICA, Warner Bros. 2003)

FURTHER READINGS\VIEWINGS

"A Dialectic Approach To Film Form," in FILM FORM: Essays in Film Theory
by Sergei Eisenstein

FILMS

BATTLESHIP POTEMKIN (1925), by Sergei Eisenstein

PSYCHO (1960) by Alfred Hitchcock

THE TRIAL (1962) by Orson Welles

PICKPOCKET (1959) by Robert Bresson

BALANCING THE STORY:
After the First Draft

A fter writing a treatment or a screenplay the technique of balancing the story is a key procedure to undertake when looking over a completed first draft. The concept behind balancing a story has to do with being able to discern whether or not various characters, circumstances and situations are succinctly germane to the story and have been utilized to their greatest dramatic potential throughout the screenplay or treatment. Another important aspect of balancing the story is to make sure that you have utilized your auxiliary and/or donor characters on both sides of the hero or heroine's process of inner-transformation so that there is someone within the story who recognizes the change in the character; oftentimes even before the character recognizes the change in themselves.[1]

Every story has to show the inner transformation of its hero\heroine from darkness to light or from ignorance to true self-knowledge. This transformation is usually revealed via a self-less act that has the hero or heroine sacrificing their egocentricity for something beyond themselves; a goal that could not otherwise have been recognized, pursued, or attained had they not sacrificed their egocentricity.[2] Perhaps the best way to grasp this concept is for us to look at a current film whose story is unbalanced to see both why the concept is so important and what key points one should look for in one's own screenplay to balance the story in a subsequent draft.

WAIST DEEP (2006), written and directed by Vondie Curtis Hall, is the story of a two time felon named O2 (Tyrese Gibson) whose son is kidnapped by vicious crime lord, Big Meat (Rap artist, The Game), and held hostage under threat of dismemberment unless O2 can raise a $100,000 ransom within 24 hours. O2 embarks on a rapid crime spree with the help of a young woman named Coco (Meagan Good). He first attempts to turn a rival gangster named P-Money against Big Meat and then later decides to pay up the ransom from his stolen loot and regain his son.

Right off the bat, during the opening scenes we can discern that the story of WAIST DEEP is severely unbalanced as two-time felon O2, just recently released from prison, has a security job that requires him to be armed. This is a circumstance that in 'real life' would be highly unlikely and thus would not be germane to the realism that such a story demands. Even if we accept the laconic explanation for this imbalance (O2 was participating in a state sponsored program for ex-cons) writer/director Vondie Curtis Hall has O2 "accidentally" take his firearm with him from his job. The flimsy pretense is that O2 forgot to turn in his weapon because another guard who was to relieve him was 30 minutes late. These are severe imbalances that undermine the realism of the film and ultimately the dramatic urgency of its story.

When you are looking over the first completed draft of your screenplay you must look at the circumstances and situations and see if they are germane; that is, consistent with the level of realism you are trying to achieve.[3] You are really looking to see if what you have written "makes sense". In the case of WAIST DEEP: does it make sense that a two-time felon and ex-con would have a job as an armed security guard? Moreover, does it make sense that this two-time felon and ex-con would be able to "accidentally" remove a weapon from his workplace? If the answer to these simple questions is yes, then the level of realism is diminished considerably and it has a deleterious effect on the overall story within the film. I believe that the answer was yes to those questions because the screenwriter was rationalizing his imbalances instead of redressing and/or fixing these imbalances to balance the story. I will discuss the rationalization of story imbalances in detail momentarily.

The next imbalance in the story of WAIST DEEP has to do with the incomplete use of an important auxiliary character. In the film, Coco details her relationship with the notorious gangster, P-Money, who is shown briefly in a couple of non-speaking flashback shots. P-Money and Big Meat are rival gangsters engaged in a growing street war. O2 has the cunning idea to begin his crime spree against Big Meat's illegal businesses to raise the ransom money disguised as one of P-Money's henchmen. O2's idea is to get the two gangsters to go into a full scale war with each other and distract Big Meat from his plot against him.

Yet inexplicably, P-Money is never given a speaking role, he has no dramatic screen time and there is no retaliation from Big Meat for the crimes O2 did when he was disguised as one of P-Money's henchmen. If the opening imbalances in the story were somehow forgivable, this glaring imbalance—the non-use of an auxiliary character that would have been integral to the plot of the film—is a crushing flaw. It is as if WAIST DEEP aborted one plot line in favor of another in mid-script.

Indeed, the use of an auxiliary or donor character to recognize the inner-transformation of the hero or heroine is a fundamental dramatic necessity that aids in giving the story a sense of balance in its overall construction. Just as it makes no sense to introduce a slew of characters who are not somehow intrinsically germane to the story and have some dramatic importance, it equally makes no sense to introduce a single character who would be germane to the story but never use him or her in dramatically important scenes. In some instances the dark auxiliary character (someone who was against the hero) transforms into a donor (a helper) to the hero because this character has recognized the inner change in the hero.

Clearly, this would have been the role of P-Money in WAIST DEEP. Obviously, he would have been upset that someone disguised as one of his own henchmen was causing the street war to escalate, but if the old saying is true,' the enemy of my enemy is my friend,' then it would have been simple to transform P-Money into a donor character; especially if he was in a position to recognize how much O2 had changed from years before and how deeply he cared for his son. The real dramatic utility of auxiliary and donor characters is to be able to recognize the inner-transformation of the hero or heroine and this recognition is a significant key to balancing a story.

There are many other plot-holes and problems within the entire film, WAIST DEEP, but the majority of these problems are directly connected to these two major imbalances in the story. Why was the story of WAIST DEEP so unbalanced? Vondie Curtis Hall gives us a clear hint when he was asked what inspired him to write the film. He answered," It was an existing script developed for Tupac Shakur. When 'Pac died, it sat on a shelf for a while. Then the company that did GRIDLOCK'D (1996) called me and said,' We've got this urban Bonnie & Clyde type of thing.' I said,' Yeah, but I will have to change everything to make it my own.' I did change everything, but I kept the Bonnie & Clyde aspect of it."[4]

I believe from this answer that the reason why the story of WAIST DEEP was unbalanced was because it was essentially a first draft screenplay that was cobbled together from Curtis-Hall's existing unused script for Tupac and the production company's urban Bonnie & Clyde concept. Moreover, I intimate from Curtis-Hall's answer that there was pressure on him to rapidly complete the screenplay and shoot the film while the production company had the funding and the actors were attached to the project. Thus, I speculate with a reasonable amount of intuitive certainty given the resulting film, that Curtis-Hall did not have a chance to balance his story and that the film was made from a first draft screenplay. If it was not a first draft screenplay, then it is clear to me that Curtis-Hall rationalized the imbalances in the story because of his blinding need to show," . . . something you don't often see in urban movies. [He] created a brother (Tyrese Gibson) who cares about his son."[5]

This is a key point in understanding why so many of the stories in our first drafts remain unbalanced: we as screenwriters have an agenda; usually a noble social, political or racial cause that is so important in our own minds that we rationalize stories that are unbalanced. We believe our subject matter to be so important that it doesn't matter what shape the story is in so long as the agenda is transmitted. This is ultimately a debilitating form of artistic hubris that causes otherwise gifted artists to create "agenda" films whose unbalanced story flaws become more and more noticeable as said agenda fades into the background of history. A good rule of thumb is to never mistake an agenda for a theme. A theme is an exploration of a human truth that can be posed as a question that your story asks, answers, or explores. Alternately, an agenda could be seen as a one-sided perspective on a situation, circumstance or character that is really more a half-truth than the whole truth.

Perhaps it is prudent to point out now that the first step in beginning the procedure of balancing the story after the first draft of a screenplay is to resist the urge to rationalize imbalances such as implausible situations and circumstances or the misuse of auxiliary and/or donor characters that are not germane to the story. This, unfortunately, requires the kind of mature, objective skill that is accumulated with practice and patience over time—natural genius notwithstanding. Balancing a story is as much a question of the author's inner-maturity as it is a willingness to accept the fact that no draft of a screenplay is complete until its story has been balanced.

EXAMPLES OF BALANCED STORIES

Let us merrily turn our attention to some examples of balanced stories in film. Our first example gives us a skillful use of an auxiliary character that functions to help the 'hero' recognize his true nature after his dark inner-transformation is nearly complete. Oliver Stone and Brian DePalma's SCARFACE is essentially a tragic story of a Cuban immigrant's rise to power in the 1980's drug world of cocaine in the United States. Although this film is analyzed in greater detail in a later chapter, it is the use of an auxiliary character, near the last act of the film that gives us an illuminating example of the true function of an auxiliary character in a story.

When a sting operation brings Tony "Scarface" Montana up on drug conspiracy and money laundering charges he hires a high priced and powerful criminal lawyer named Sheffield (Michael Aldredge) who in a single scene delivers a damning recognition of Tony's dark inner-transformation. After Tony offers his lawyer $800,000 to keep him from going to jail, the lawyer looks at him with a hardened seriousness and says," Tony the law has to prove beyond a reasonable doubt, I'm an expert at raising that doubt. But when you've got a million three undeclared dollars staring into a videotape camera . . . Honey, baby it's hard to convince a jury that you found it in a taxicab."

This lawyer is trying to convince Tony to accept his fate and his true identity as a drug peddling, money laundering kingpin caught up in a system of laws that no one is above, but Tony will not accept the truth. Stone and DePalma created a single use auxiliary character that was important to the story and who functioned to reveal the main character's inability to recognize his own dark inner-transformation. The key here was that the auxiliary character was not pulled out of thin air; the lawyer, Sheffield, was a logical consequence of Tony's actions and circumstances. Although he was only in one scene, Sheffield was germane to the story and was necessary to balance the story.[6]

Although typically an auxiliary character or donor character is introduced before or during a hero's inner-transformation, the important fact to remember is that as long as that auxiliary character is germane to the story then the true function of that auxiliary character is to recognize the hero or heroine's inner transformation in or near the final act that is a dramatic necessity that must be realized for a story to have a true sense of balance.

Paul Thomas Anderson's BOOGIE NIGHTS (1997) provides us with an excellent example of a succinct use of various characters that are all germane to the story. BOOGIE NIGHTS is essentially a Rags to Riches story archetype centered on the rise of 'Dirk Diggler' (Mark Wahlberg, no pun intended) in the 1970's pornographic film industry. Besides its emotionally frank yet sexually discreet presentation of the participants within this fictionalized portrayal of the porn industry, the film contains many notable performances from its ensemble cast; particularly a superlative performance from 1970's film icon, Burt Reynolds as Jack Horner pornography director/dark father figure. But our concern here is not with the principal characters, but instead with a peripheral character whose situation and circumstance might first appear to be negligible to the story but in fact are crucial to it.

Throughout the first half of the film the wife of Jack Horner's Assistant Director, Little Bill (William H. Macy) is indulging in sexual infidelities and throwing it in his face in ever increasing explicit, careless, and emasculating ways. He is powerless (impotent would be a better word) to stop her from engaging in such sexually flagrant behaviors in social settings or even in the privacy of their own home. One has to wonder whether or not seeing sexual acts performed all day at his job as an assistant 'porn' director has inured him from engaging in sexual pleasures within his own marriage. Moreover, each one of his wife's indiscretions only seem to underscore his own degenerating sense of male inadequacy hinted at through his nickname, 'Little Bill'.

The climax of this peripheral character's story comes during the New Year's Eve celebration at Jack Horner's house just minutes before 1980. Little Bill finds his wife having sex with yet another man in a back room just as everyone is counting down in anticipation of the arrival of the new year. Little Bill calmly goes out to his car, gets a handgun, returns to the back room and kills his wife and the man. While the party guests are still in shock from hearing the gunfire he walks out into the living room and in full view of everyone, sticks the gun in his mouth and blows his brains out. Paul Thomas Anderson immediately cuts to an inter-title that simply reads," 80's", as if this terrible event were an ominous harbinger of things to come in the new decade.

Now it should be understood that the character of Little Bill is germane to the story because he works as the assistant director during the production of Dirk Diggler's porno films, yet his situation and the circumstances of the murder of his wife and his own suicide are germane to the theme Paul Thomas Anderson was exploring within the overall story. It is through the shocking death of a peripheral character that Anderson presents sexual freedom without emotional attachment not as rejuvenating, life giving, or hedonistic, but instead as a destructive, debilitating and recklessly ego inflating force that can be ruinous to the lives of those who profit from its uninhibited practice.

The death of Little Bill is significant because it acts as a 'death knell' signaling the end of Dirk Diggler's dreamlike rise to fame and fortune and his swift and dark decline into an egocentric nightmare. More than this, the murder of Little Bill's wife and his suicide can be taken as a direct consequence of the sexual freedom without emotional attachment indulged in and exploited by the pornographic film industry. Perhaps due to the livid subject matter and to reduce the predictability of the Rags to Riches plot, Paul Thomas Anderson used a peripheral auxiliary character to reveal the true purpose and theme of his story. The idealized illusion of sex for sex's sake has far reaching real life ramifications in that it amplifies the egocentricity of each member of the emotionally crippled ensemble cast; this is a human truth explored as a theme within the story.

SUMMARY

For every first draft of a screenplay or even a treatment a writer must go through a procedure of balancing the story before a subsequent draft can begin in earnest. Balancing the story consists of reviewing the screenplay with as much objectivity as possible to discern whether or not various characters, circumstances and situations are succinctly germane to the story and have been utilized to their greatest dramatic potential. To determine whether or not a situation, circumstance, or character is germane to the story one has to ask oneself," Does each of the elements as utilized make sense?" "Are they consistent with the level of realism I am trying to convey?" But most importantly," How do said elements contribute to the exploration of a human truth or theme rather than the pursuit of an agenda?"

To determine whether or not you are utilizing your auxiliary character or characters to their greatest dramatic potential you should simply make sure that an auxiliary character that is germane to the story recognizes the hero or heroine's inner transformation. If this sounds too formulaic to you, then you must remember that the recognition of this change can be presented in a wide variety of creative possibilities. The example from SCARFACE revealed an auxiliary character used in only one scene whose sole purpose was to reveal (to the audience) the main character's inability to recognize his own dark inner transformation.

The example from BOOGIE NIGHTS revealed a peripheral auxiliary character whose situation and circumstance were used to illuminate a major theme within the story. And finally the examples from WAIST DEEP hopefully revealed the necessity of balancing the story so that various circumstantial and situational incongruities do not distract from the realism within the story—as well as insuring a full dramatic use of auxiliary characters. By far the greatest danger from not balancing a story is that we can easily rationalize a story's imbalances because we have an agenda and we want our stories to communicate that agenda even though the characters, circumstances and situations aren't strong enough or fully realized to support that agenda. So hopefully we understand that balancing the story is a matter of making sure that we have a balanced use of donor and/or auxiliary characters that are used before and after a hero or heroine's inner-transformation, and making sure that you have utilized all the circumstances, situations, and characters that are germane to the story to their fullest dramatic potential within the screenplay.

NOTES

(1) It helps to think of auxiliary characters as simply supporting characters who recognize the inner transformation of the hero or heroine, but donor characters are supporting characters who are in a position to give important help or information to the hero or heroine during the course of the story.

(2) Tragedies and Comedies usually invert this rule in that the character moves from knowledge to ignorance or from selflessness to egocentricity. A comedy will usually provide a last minute change of heart to save the hero or heroine whereas a tragedy will not. See: The Seven Basic Plots by Christopher Booker, pages 150-152.

(3) Obviously, fantasy films, science fiction and comedies can forgo such attention to circumstantial realism; instead screenwriters of these genres are urged to look at their character's behaviors and actions as "real" credible responses that are consistent within their retrospective circumstances and situations. An example would be the fear that is palpable within the faces of actors running from computer generated dinosaurs in Steven Spielberg's JURASSIC PARK. In fantasy and science fiction films the soft realism of emotions supplants the hard circumstantial realism of other genres.

(4) Cf. A Chat With Vondie Curtis-Hall by Kimberly Hayes Taylor, The Detroit News, June 22nd, 2006.

(5) Ibid.

(6) In keeping with the tragic circumstances of SCARFACE and the increasingly cocaine influenced egoism of Tony Montana each of the major supporting characters in turn try to get him to recognize his own terrible inner transformation (his mother when she throws his drug money back in his face, his wife Elvira in the famous Jacuzzi and restaurant scenes, his pragmatist friend Manny Rivera and finally his sister before she is killed).

THE DIFFERENCE BETWEEN
STORY AND NARRATIVE

It is a common misunderstanding to assume that a story and a narrative are one and the same, but the two are quite different. A story is the sum of its events, characters and the consequences of the characters behaviors, decisions, and actions. A story is what happened in the duration between the beginning and the ending. A narrative is how the story is presented to you. "Its order of presentation need not be the same as that of the natural logic of the story."(1) Whether the ending was presented first and the story told in reverse or the story leaps from time period to time period, a narrative is distinguished from a story because it is the *way* the story has been told as opposed to *what* has been told.

The difference between story and narrative corresponds directly to the old Russian Formalist's Fabula/Syuzhet distinction. (2) The fabula is the mental reconstruction of a story in a linear and forward progressing chronological fashion. It is what all cinema spectators do no matter how the story has been presented to them and relates directly to the way we experience and perceive reality, as Andrei Tarkovsky would say," through time." The syuzhet (pronounced like *Suzette*) is the actual presentation of the story within the film. For instance, the films of Alejandro Gonzalez Inarritu (Amores Perros and 21 Grams) are presented in a non-linear structure or syuzhet, but the fabula (the actual story) is mentally reconstructed by the spectator during or after the film has concluded. In the following chapters we will be examining the four general types of cinematic narratives: Linear (events presented in a contiguous chronological order), Non-linear (events presented in a non-contiguous and/or anti-chronological order), Discovery narratives and Conceptual narratives.

Since the original version of this book was presented in 1997 I have encountered a marked increase in a hybrid version of the Discovery narrative that I call the Seduction narrative. The seduction narrative has been brought back to the commercial forefront in the films of M. Night Shyamalan (1999's THE SIXTH SENSE and 2004's THE VILLAGE) as well as Ron Howard's A BEAUTIFUL MIND (2001). Since this is a hybrid narrative style we will pause here to examine it before moving on to the general types.

THE SEDUCTION NARRATIVE

The seduction narrative is a narrative that *seduces* the spectator into looking at a character, set of characters or circumstance in a particular way only to reveal the true nature of the character(s) or circumstance in the final act or finale. M. Night Shyamalan's THE SIXTH SENSE was one of the most commercially successful seduction narratives. In this film, the finale reveals that child psychologist Dr. Malcolm Crowe (Bruce Willis) was actually dead during the course of the story. His death was the result of a gunshot inflicted by a disgruntled former patient who had broken into his home in the prologue of the film.

A seduction narrative takes great pains to seduce the spectator into seeing its character(s) and the events they encounter in a particular and ultimately tentative way. In THE SIXTH SENSE, scenes that first appear as typical marital distress and dysfunction are (after the revelation) understood to be scenes of inconsolable grief. Specifically, the restaurant/anniversary scene between the wife and Dr. Crowe which is shown to us twice in the film: once in its entirety and then again in a shortened version after the revelation. This is often a typical feature of seduction narratives; events require a double presentation and a double interpretation: The first interpretation, before the revelation of the final act or finale and the second or final interpretation after the revelation.

The first interpretation, which we might call the 'prima facie' is made during the spectator's immediate experience of the story during the actual course of the narrative and is the most elusive interpretation. After the revelation, the prima facie is irreparably damaged if not permanently destroyed and the events can only be understood as they relate to the final interpretation. It is often terribly important for spectators, reviewers and critics not to give away the ending (the final act or finale) while the film is in theatrical release. This is to give new spectators the pleasure of the prima facie and the post-revelation interpretations that are central to conceptualization of the seduction narrative. There is also a discreet commercial conceit for many seduction narratives in that the double interpretation can often translate into repeat screenings and doubled box office receipts and DVD/Pay-per-view sales. Titillated and intrigued spectators often return again and again to experience the second interpretation in its entirety and to check to see if all the sequential details and events match this second interpretation.

The seduction narrative is a form which intentionally misleads the audience with its own prejudices or jaded views and then turns those prejudices and jaded views back upon the audience as a revelation (often but not always) about a new or alternative mental, spiritual or physical state. In THE SIXTH SENSE the idea of a character's unrecognized afterlife was a revelation of an alternate spiritual state. In A BEAUTIFUL MIND it was the revelation about the subjective perception of Schizophrenia—an alternate mental state.

Most of us are inclined to recognize Shyamalan's THE SIXTH SENSE as the first successful version of a seduction narrative, but actually it was Alfred Hitchcock's PSYCHO (1960) that was the first successful seduction narrative.(3) In this film the audience is seduced into believing that Norman Bates' mother was alive. Only in the finale is it revealed (in emphatic Hitchcockian fashion) that the mother has been dead for years and Norman was only imitating his mother's voice and wearing her clothing. We can tell with certainty that PSYCHO was the first deliberately successful seduction narrative because author Robert E. Kapsis tells us that Paramount adopted the unusual admission policy of allowing no spectators in after the start of each screening and that," Hitchcock decided not to hold advance screenings for critics and other opinion makers. (Pg. 59, Hitchcock: The Making of a Reputation)" This is evidence of the master filmmaker's attempt to keep the prima facie and the final interpretations of the story distinct and insure the success of the seduction.

To reiterate, a seduction narrative always plays upon the prejudices and jaded views of its audience. The timid and supplicating demeanor of Norman Bates (Anthony Perkins) supported the illusion in the spectator's mind that the domineering voice and emasculating content of Mrs. Bates' speech was from a real living character. Other seductions were purely visual and are a testament to Saul Bass and Alfred Hitchcock's pictorial genius in having a figure in the window of the house that is thought by the supporting characters to be the living Mrs. Bates. Also, Norman carries the corpse of his mother down the staircase as he speaks in her voice. It is the revelation that makes us go back and review the film to see how we were seduced into believing the prima facie interpretation.

For instance, in THE SIXTH SENSE, the fact that Dr. Crowe was a child psychologist and began a therapeutic relationship with the young boy who could see 'dead people', seduced the audience into thinking that he had not been killed by the intruder's bullet. In A BEAUTIFUL MIND, the very fact that the government had actually contacted John Nash (Russell Crowe) to decipher a Russian code helped to seduce the audience into believing that, later in the film, his schizophrenic fantasy of working for the government to find hidden Soviet codes in magazines and newsprint was real.

Seduction narratives are usually impressive to an audience because 'the reveal' (as it is called in the business) forces the spectator to mentally re-trace the way the narrative was presented and reconstruct the story to align it with the revelatory information. The seduction narrative throws light upon the syuzhet which is often discarded after an audience has seen a film. The late Seventies horror film, PHANTASM (Don Coscarelli—1979) is another interesting seduction narrative as the death of a teenager's older brother is revealed only after the brother had been seen throughout the film as if he were alive. PHANTASM attempts to reveal an altered physical state of existence through an alien conspiracy to use reanimated human remains as extraterrestrial slave labor.

The Seduction narrative is a hybrid form of the discovery narrative, but the essential difference is that the revelatory information presented in the finale of a seduction narrative forces the spectator to re-dress his opinion of the characters, events, and actions as presented in the film. A discovery narrative, as we shall examine later, does not usually force a spectator to reinterpret the entire story and its characters. The seduction narrative tells two stories as one, whereas a discovery narrative demonstrates two themes in a singular story context. There are usually two specific strategies of seduction: 1) through carefully controlled characterizations that deceive the spectator (as in the voice over characterization of Mrs. Bates that proves unreliable in Hitchcock's PSYCHO) or 2) an ellipsis that forms a pivotal lacuna in the story and forces the spectator to make an assumption about the character or circumstances that proves to be false after the revelation. (i.e., THE SIXTH SENSE there is a quick fade to black after Dr. Crowe had been shot and another quick fade in to him as if he survived the shooting.)

Essential Features of a Seduction Narrative

1) Must have a revelation in the final act or finale that gives a second and ultimately final new interpretation of the character(s) and events that contradicts and supplants what was previously understood by the audience.
2) Gives a doubled presentation of key events or characters: once during the course of the film and again in a shortened version after the revelation.
3) Requires a certain amount of secrecy from previous spectators, reviewers, and critics to protect the prima facie or first interpretation and the revelation.
4) Uses the audience's own prejudices and jaded views against them to capitulate the revelation.
5) And finally, but most important, a seduction narrative usually reveals a new or alternative mental, physical, or spiritual state that is otherwise hidden by the audience's prejudices.

You can understand why it is very important to grasp one's story (or stories) first when writing a seduction narrative since the revelation is going to alter the first interpretation of the events and characters. Another reason is that the sequential order of the details and events must ultimately match both the first interpretation and the final interpretation. A seduction narrative requires that a filmmaker choose events, actions and characters that have a duality or a potentially doubled nature. In THE SIXTH SENSE Malcolm Crowe was a husband and a psychologist. The question of perception or how events are perceived is one of the most striking features of seduction narratives. Whether one tells a story as a linear, non-linear, conceptual, discovery, or seduction narrative it is critical that the writer/filmmaker grasp the story first so that one does not confuse the narrative (syuzhet) with the story (fabula).

If we recall the seven basic story archetypes discovered by author Christopher Booker from the first chapter (1: Overcoming The Monster, 2: Rags to Riches, 3: The Quest, 4: Voyage & Return, 5: Comedy, 6: Tragedy, 7: Rebirth) these seven basic story archetypes, as I call them, are fabulations: they are the mental reconstruction of characters, events and circumstances thought through and re-arranged into a chronological linearity after we have witnessed and understood the hero or heroine's transmutation from moral darkness to light or from ignorance to knowledge. Modern cinematic narration allows for a dynamic presentation of these all-too-familiar heroes, villains, events and circumstances in such a way that the syuzhet or structure of the film itself is not chained to a linear chronological presentation. Theoretically, as long as the story contains the fundamental elements that reveal a character's transmutation (from moral darkness to light or from ignorance to knowledge), the story itself can be presented in any order the author finds most cinematically stimulating to his purpose and theme. We will now turn our attention to the presentation of a story via the four general types of cinematic narration.

Other Seduction Narratives of Note:

SPIDER (David Cronenberg 2004)
VANILLA SKY (Cameron Crowe 2002)
MULHOLLAND DR. (David Lynch 2003)
THE USUAL SUSPECTS (Bryan Singer 1999)
FIGHT CLUB (David Fincher 1999)

NOTES

[1]   Pg. 43, Story and Discourse, Seymour Chatman.
[2]   C.f. Page 140, REFLEXIVITY IN FILM AND LITERATURE: From Don Quixote to Jean-Luc Godard by Robert Stam. Please note that Syuzhet may also be spelled, sjuzet. Also see: STORY and DISCOURSE: Narrative Structure in Fiction and Film by Seymour Benjamin Chatman or Narrative Discourse: An Essay in Method by Gerard Genette which calls the same distinction, l'histoire et recit.
[3]   At the risk of contradicting myself there is some evidence that THE WIZARD OF OZ (1939) by Victor Fleming (1883-1949) might actually have been the first successful seduction narrative. It certainly seduces the audience into believing that Dorothy was swept away to a magical world only to reveal that she was in what had to be a coma (alternative mental state) when she awakens. It is difficult to know whether or not Dorothy's miraculous recovery was simply a convenient plot device (the dreaded," it was all a dream" ending) or a deliberate attempt at seducing the audience. I have chosen to keep my original assertion about PSYCHO only because there is a critical consensus of opinion and a researchable fact that Hitchcock was deliberate in his intentions concerning the way the audience should perceive the prima facie of the narrative and the subsequent seduction and revelation.

Four General Types of Narratives
LINEAR, NON-LINEAR, DISCOVERY, and CONCEPTUAL

THE LINEAR NARRATIVE

There are essentially two readily identifiable types of general narrative forms in screenplays and subsequent films: Linear and non-linear. The linear screenplay has the most basic features and simplistic assembly: some characters, a plot, and a number of events that occur one after another in a contiguous chronological A/B/C/D/E/F/G order until the end. Non-linear screenplays or narratives have the same basic features (characters, events and plot) but the events occur in a non-contiguous meta-chronological order (moving forward and backwards in fictional time). For instance: A/C/B/D/C/F and so on; the narrative can repeat scenes, break scenes into two parts or for the truly daring present scenes in a coincidental order as in Paul Thomas Anderson's films, BOOGIE NIGHTS (1997) and MAGNOLIA (2000) or Alejandro Gonzalez Inarritu's AMORES PERROS (2000) and 21 GRAMS (2004).[1]

With this general outline in place, let's give some concrete examples and explanation. The first time screenwriter is usually the first person to tackle a linear screenplay because it seems so simple to set up a plot, a few characters and have a number of events happen to the characters in a compressed and forward progressing time frame. But first drafts of these types of screenplays are the least dramatically satisfying because although the writer creates spectacular events for the characters to encounter, the characters themselves lack feelings or emotional depth and as one event unfolds to another event; eventually the explosions, killings, beheadings, last second escapes, and dare-devil stunts get tiring. In fact, linear narratives are actually the most difficult screenplays to write although on the surface they seem the easiest. There are two successful writer/directors who have employed this linear method of screenwriting to spectacular results: French director, Jean-Luc Godard and American director, Spike Lee.

For Godard, during the early Sixties, his films were a collage of sight gags, cinematic tricks, and quotations from literature, painting, and classic American films; a tongue-in-cheek drama that threatened to destroy all narrative conventions. Godard's work was comical, genuine, unique, and fascinating. For Spike Lee, in his masterpiece,' DO THE RIGHT THING,' a day in the life of one Brooklyn neighborhood provided an excellent linear narrative where one thing led to another to exacerbate a tinderbox of racial tensions that at the beginning of the film seemed benign. The most crucial point that determines a linear narrative is that the characters must be established quickly and with a great economy of dialogue; this is what usually trips up the first-time screenwriter. Although the characters are established quickly and with little dialogue, such screenplays run the risk of containing uncompelling characters and maintaining dialogue that is most often quite unoriginal.

Much of the success of Spike Lee's,' DO THE RIGHT THING,' must be attributed to how the establishment of his characters in the beginning of the film closely patterns itself on traditional racial/cultural stereotypes while simultaneously keeping those characters original and their dialogue fresh. The genius of this single film is that once Lee had set up his stereotypes he proceeded, one event after another, to break each stereotype down and the characters are actually developed *through* the events they encounter. How can anyone ever forget 'Radio Raheem' (Bill Nunn), a character molded from the age old racial stereotype of the, 'Boom box carrying Negro,' which Spike Lee deliberately usurps by sacrificing this character/stereotype to a brutal death at the hands of White police officers. It is the sacrifice of 'Radio Raheem' (coupled with his speech about Love and Hate) that allows this character to transcend the stereotype and makes his senseless death a symbol of a community's outrage. A linear narrative is the best way to enrich characters first presented as one-dimensional by revealing their inner-transformation through the events and circumstances they encounter.

For Godard, the linear narrative provided him the greatest opportunity to take classic American genres and give audiences what they least expected: the creation of events throughout the course of the film, which would threaten to destroy the genre itself. ALPHAVILLE (1965) is a prime example of a splicing of a Gumshoe detective thriller (The Big Sleep/Maltese Falcon) with the Science Fiction genre, which Godard ingeniously set in present day Paris. ALPHAVILLE, is Paris controlled by a mega computer called ALPHA-60 which makes robots out of people by tempering their intelligence (censoring illegal words like 'love' or 'poetry') and emotions. "The voice of Alpha-60, which controls this totalitarian world of the future, was not produced mechanically but by someone who had lost their vocal cords and had relearnt how to speak using a mechanical voice box." [2]

Godard's lead character, detective Lemmy Caution (performed by American actor, Eddie Constantine who had immigrated to France) continuously encounters the absurdity of ALPHAVILLE which is really the absurdity of modern day Paris and Post-war French culture. Again, as with all linear narratives, character and dialogue are stereotypical and sparse, considering the wide spread appeal of gumshoe detectives of Film Noir (Mickey Spillane/Sam Spade) Godard was able to swiftly set his narrative in motion through the most original and surprising events that Science fiction could provide him. The cold, calculating, absurd, and emotionally vacuous world presented in ALPHAVILLE is given a dazzling romantic and optimistic conclusion as Lemmy Caution discovers the only word that can destroy the demeaning logic of the mega-computer ALPHA-60 and restore ALPHAVILLE to normal. "Much of ALPHAVILLE is derivative of other dystopian futures (the obvious reference, which Godard never makes, is to George Orwell's 1984). But it is difficult to think of any parallel work which so successfully shows the future in the present, and which can sustain viewings forty years after it was made."[3]

"The cold, calculating, absurd, and emotionally vacuous world presented in ALPHAVILLE is given a dazzling romantic and optimistic conclusion." (Anna Karina & Eddie Constantine, ALPHAVILLE—1965, Courtesy Chaumiane Production-Film Studio)

So this is the key point of linear narratives, if as a screenwriter you must use this form: you must develop your characters *through* the events they encounter within your story. Just because a linear narrative allows you a quick set up and little dialogue in the beginning of the script does not mean that you cannot develop your characters as you throw one explosion on top of another during the course of the script. Many stories that feature a Quest, Overcoming a Monster (human or inhuman) and Rags to Riches story archetype favor a linear narrative presentation because the inner strengths and/or weaknesses of characters (heroes and villains) are developed and revealed through a succession of dramatic events and circumstances that increase in emotional intensity. Each event must have an effect that is either physical, emotional, or psychological upon the characters that deepens and/or enriches an audience's first impressions set up by your stereotypes and sparse dialogue at the beginning. Also characteristic of linear narratives is an absence of flashbacks; fictional time remains chronologically informed by the scenes that precede each other. For example, a lap dissolve may show the same characters later that day or even (with the use of an inter-title) later that year, but the time frame still moves in a contiguous chronological order that is contingent upon events that preceded it whether shown on screen or not; the organization is still linear.[4]

In general, another major hurdle of all linear narratives is the ending. It is within the ending that the point of the film, the meaning of its title, and the dynamics of the drama are resolved. But coming up with an ending is very hard to do if you are writing a linear screenplay because you are usually thinking up the next event as you go along and you haven't considered an ending until you get tired or run out of ideas; sometimes with a linear narrative it seems there is no place to stop. Several Spike Lee films have suffered from not having proper or dramatically satisfying endings and other linear narrative films have endings that are just contrived to bring a halt to the story without demonstrating the theme or fully exploring the demands of its character's goal or their circumstances. The advice here should be clear: have your ending before you start to write or else you cannot help but lose your way and the best way to grasp your ending is to know the goal of your character(s).

Linear Narrative: A Specific Analysis
ALI: FEAR EATS THE SOUL

Another major filmmaker who worked almost exclusively in the linear narrative form was the late German filmmaker, Rainer Werner Fassbinder. This 'enfant terrible' of the 1970's state financed New German Cinema movement was as controversial as he was prolific. He made some 41 feature films, two shorts and a multi-part television film from 1966 before he was found," dead, a cigarette still between his lips," in his editor, Julianne Lorenz's rented flat in 1982.[5] His sudden death was attributed to exhaustion, continued drug and alcohol abuse, and his refusal to simply take care of himself physically. Fassbinder's films, taken separately or collectively, comprise a sharp form of social criticism by exposing the cruelty and oppression hidden beneath veneer of polite German society after World War II.

The linearity of his work contains the best attributes of what distinguishes a linear narrative: 1) Characters are developed through the events and circumstances they encounter; that is, his films often start with discriminating caricatures or at least readily identifiable "types" that by the end of the film have developed into multi-dimensional characters through their reactions and responses to the events and circumstances they encounter. 2) His films contain some of the best, enigmatic, abrupt and provocative endings in the history of cinema. Not all of Fassbinder's films are satisfying (partly attributable to the rapidity of their production or his own lack of total involvement if he got bored with material), but each film has a unique ending that in some cases salvages the entire effort. To put it simply, the endings of many Fassbinder films are arresting in that the terminal point demonstrates the theme that was running through the material and surprises us only because we were distracted by the melodramatic story context. As he has said," I want to give the spectator the emotions along with the possibility of reflecting and analyzing what he is feeling." [6] If we can say the least about Fassbinder's work, we can say that his endings were always "shocking" because they caused us to reflect on all that we had seen no matter how ridiculous or cruel.

In one of his many masterworks, ANGST ESSEN SEELE AUF (1973—Ali: Fear Eats the Soul), Fassbinder loosely 'transcribes' the 1950's melodrama, ALL THAT HEAVEN ALLOWS (1955) by Douglas Sirk, the German director who emigrated to America during the Nazi era. By making a romance between an elderly German widow and an Arab immigrant worker, Fassbinder brought together a neglected aspect of German society (the elderly survivors of Nazism) and a despised aspect of German society (the foreign workers who had immigrated to Germany for jobs). His use of a melodramatic story context is the "sugar cube" that distracts us from the needle's prick—in that he is revealing the cruelty at the heart of corrupt social interaction: the need for a defined line between insiders and outsiders and the extremes to which insiders will go to protect this line.

When the lonely and old Emmi Kurowski (Brigitte Mira), a widowed cleaning woman "accidentally" comes into a pub frequented by foreign workers to get out of the rain, she becomes the victim of a seemingly cruel joke. A scorned barfly dares one of the workers, Ali (El Hedi ben Salem) to dance with the old woman. When he does, Emmi invites him home with her. Both are lonely, (he, as a stranger in a strange land and she, as a widow), and wanting companionship, they marry. "Emmi's children are outraged and Ali's friends ridicule him for marrying 'a grandmother'." [7] The social denigration pushes the two characters together with the pathos of 'us against the world'.

Fassbinder, ever the acute social observer, reveals to us a tacitly understood social custom: mixed company. Mixed Company is a social custom that censors and/or modifies what is said publicly in informal or formal social settings that contain more than one gender, race, sexual orientation, age, class or religion. For instance, what a bachelor might say about women when only in the company of other bachelors would not be uttered if that bachelor were in the company of men and single women; otherwise known as mixed company. The reasons for this self-censorship are simple:

1) Any disparaging remarks about women could lessen his chances of appearing favorable to the single women; it would besmirch his charm.

2) The remarks could lead to the open ridicule of the bachelor by his male competitors, thus increasing their chances of attaining sexual satisfaction or a relationship with any of the single females in the room and decreasing his own.

Returning to ALI, FEAR EATS THE SOUL, after Emmi and Ali go to her apartment together, the neighbors begin gossiping with explicit disdain for the dark-skinned Arab by demonstrating what is said in unmixed company. Moreover, after Ali and Emmi are married, the outrage of her children and the continued disdain expressed by the neighborhood grocer reveals the deception of a polite society that pretends to be tolerant publicly, but privately harbors prejudices and resentments that betray a deep seated xenophobia. "Fassbinder goes beyond Sirk in that he exposes a social mechanism. As long as Emmi and ben Salem are faced with direct animosity, they assure themselves of their mutual solidarity and stick together. But when their people try to come to terms with the situation and they are both taken back into their respective circles (and then always betray each other), the real, previously hidden conflicts come to the surface."[8] So we see how characters that are first presented to us as discernable "types" or caricatures are developed through the events and circumstances they encounter (in this case racism) into fully fleshed out characters born from the conflicts that block the fulfillment of their goals.

Yet it is the sudden event of Ali's painful ulcer that seems to snatch away a precious reconciliation between the two and leads directly to Fassbinder's most touching and simple ending—patterned after Sirk's ending for ALL THAT HEAVEN ALLOWS, but decidedly different in tone and feeling. To care for someone deeply can mean sitting by their sickbed waiting for things to get better in the world. Fassbinder's early childhood experiences are what contributed to his direct insight into these social mechanisms of oppression. "In Cologne, [Fassbinder] was given the job of collecting rent from his father's [immigrant] tenants. The experience was crucial: he was suddenly in touch with a group of outsiders, a persecuted minority, and he felt a strong affinity with them."[9]

Fassbinder reveals through the simplicity of a linear narrative the complexities of two different social realities by comparing and contrasting their respective cruelty, joy and their need to have outsiders to ostracize and define and maintain their boundaries. He continued to make these observations throughout his career in films about the internal cruelty and oppression within the gay community in FAUSTRECHT DER FREIHEIT (1974—Fox and His Friends), business, DIE EHE DER MARIA BRAUN (1978—The Marriage of Maria Braun), and among women, DIE BITTEREN TRANEN DER PETRA VON KANT (1972—The Bitter Tears of Petra Von Kant) to name a few. No one was beyond the target range of his acute social biopsies, alas not even himself.

NOTES

(1) We might note that the films of Paul Thomas Anderson and Alejandro Gonzalez Inarritu are uni-linear, which is a fancy way of saying that they are parallel linear narratives of several characters whose lives are connected around a central narrative event. Quentin Tarantino did much to bring this narrative style into vogue with PULP FICTION (1994), but it has since been perfected, and some might say overused, by other filmmakers like Paul Haggis in CRASH (2004) and Rodrigo Garcia in NINE LIVES (2005). Older master filmmakers had flirted with the parallel linear narratives which no doubt opened the door to these new attempts today. Steven Spielberg's CLOSE IN ENCOUNTERS OF THE THIRD KIND (1977) and Stanley Kubrick's THE KILLING (1956) were also very interesting journeys into this narrative style.

(2) Pg. 167, GODARD: A Portrait of the Artist at Seventy by Colin MacCabe. 2003. Farrar, Straus, and Giroux. New York.

(3) Pg. 168, Ibid.

(4) I assume that the reader is very familiar with the technique and function of a FLASHBACK in narrative form, but a FLASHFORWARD is a much more complex narrative technique whose underused function in a majority of movies is to speed up the telling of an epic story. A brief example is the 'Sollozzo meeting' sequence of 'THE GODFATHER'. As Tom Hagen (Robert Duvall) describes the reputation of Sollozzo the would be narcotics trafficker to Don Corleone (Marlon Brando) the day before the actual meeting, Director Coppola, cuts to the actual meeting so that by the time Hagen is finished describing Sollozzo, Don Corleone is already greeting him. A much more detailed FLASHFORWARD can be found in Brian DePalma's,' MISSION: IMPOSSIBLE (1996)', just before the 'Langley' episode. Ethan Hunt (Tom Cruise) begins describing the security system of the 'Black Vault Lockdown' located inside the CIA headquarters at Langley, via shots and voiceover which gives all information the spectator and the characters need to prepare for the suspense and complexity of the following episode which takes place with the characters assuming their roles at the actual headquarters.

(5) Pg. 135, FASSBINDER\FILMMAKER by Ronald Hayman. 1984. New York. Simon & Schuster.

(6) Pg. 182, THE CINEASTE INTERVIEWS ed. by Georgakas & Rubenstein. 1984. London. Pluto Press.

(7) Pg. 54, RAINER WERNER FASSBINDER, ed. Kardish & Lorenz, 1997. New York. Museum of Modern Art.

(8) From Michael Toteberg's presentation of Fassbinder's screenplays, FASSBINDER'S FILMS Vol.3, 1990. Frankfurt. Reprinted in The Criterion Edition DVD liner notes of ALI: FEAR EATS THE SOUL, 2003.

(9) Pg.13, FASSBINDER\FILMMAKER, Ibid.

THE NON-LINEAR NARRATIVE

For the first time screenwriter, contemplating the task of *not* writing a script with one event logically following another event in fictional time is daunting. Non-linear narratives have events or circumstances that occur in a non-contiguous meta-chronological order (e.g. A/C/D/C/E/A).[1] Flashbacks, which are verbally cued by the dialogue or music have become the standard and cliched method chosen to escape a linear narrative, but if we really look at,' THE GODFATHER II,' we would not see any verbal flashback cues throughout the entire film; transitions to the past from the present are arbitrary to fictional time, but thematically justified. Francis Coppola's,' THE GODFATHER II,' has a non-linear narrative that enhances a certain thematic depth within the film that would not otherwise have existed had the film been edited into a linear progression. The non-linear narrative can be based on something more than simple temporal or fictional time logic; such films can often have the logic of a dream or recurring memory. A non-linear script is actually easier to write and yields much more complex results because:

1) Characters are already fully developed and involved in the emotional or physical vacillations of their circumstances.
2) Thematic depth is achieved via the inter-connections between non-contiguous meta-chronological scenes. For instance a scene *relates* to another scene that follows or precedes it for reasons beyond chronology.

The key here is that the writer is totally immersed into the emotional world of the characters. Dialogue becomes easier to write because the writer knows exactly how his characters are feeling and these feelings, attitudes, and actions can be expressed without the slightest hesitation—or indecision. Moreover, the writer and filmmaker can connect scenes in a variety of intriguing ways. For instance, in Bernardo Bertolucci's Academy Award winning, 'THE LAST EMPEROR,' the story of Pu Yi was presented through a non-linear narrative: scenes were connected via highly charged emotional moments that were similar in Pu Yi's childhood and his adult life.[2] A brief summary of the story is necessary before clarifying this example. Pu Yi was Imperial China's 'last emperor'. Crowned as the emperor at the tender age of 3, he was uprooted from his parent's home in Northeast China and literally imprisoned in 'The Forbidden City': the palace designed for all Emperors. As various republics, warlords, and political upheavals ravaged the people of China, Pu Yi was completely sheltered and without any external political power while inside the walls of the Forbidden City. When the Japanese invaded Manchuria (Northeast China) Pu Yi was installed as this occupied region's puppet emperor. After Japan's surrender at the end of WW II, China became communist; Pu Yi was completely dethroned and imprisoned again as a traitor and counter-revolutionary. He died in 1967 at the age of 53 as a gardener and an unfavorably remembered citizen of China's imperial age.

The thematic depth fore grounded in a non-linear presentation of the life of Pu Yi can be felt immediately in two of the film's early scenes. In the opening sequence a 45 year old dethroned Pu Yi (John Lone) is unceremoniously brought to a communist prison camp to be re-educated after being convicted as a traitor. Upon his entry into this prison he promptly locks himself in a lavatory and slits his wrists in a sink full of hot water. As Prison guards knock and order him to 'Open the door,' Pu Yi looks at his reflection in a mirror and Bertolucci cuts to a scene 42 years earlier when Imperial troops ordered Pu Yi's parents to,' Open the door,' to their villa so that Pu Yi (aged 3) could be taken away and crowned as China's new emperor. The effect of this single cut is startlingly dramatic and swiftly reveals much about Pu Yi's emotional state. In a reflection, during the present suicide attempt, Pu Yi remembers another time when his life was taken away from him. It is also significant to note that this non-linear sequence is not random, by virtue of the matched dialogue (for both the prison guards and the imperial troops),' Open The Door,' and the use of the color red (Pu Yi's blood mixing in the hot water and the red door of the villa) to make the 42 year transition between the two scenes accessible on both an emotional and visual level.

A major point in almost all non-linear narratives is that the theme of the film is fore grounded as its content and the subject matter are broadened as a result to encompass both the main character(s) and their times. For instance, a major thematic point of 'THE LAST EMPEROR,' is Pu Yi's actual imprisonment as an emperor forbidden to leave,' The Forbidden City,' as a puppet emperor forbidden to leave his occupied country and as a communist prisoner, forbidden to leave the prison. At every turn throughout Pu Yi's life he is a trapped individual struggling to free himself from the traditions and politics of his culture and his people. "Pu Yi is insistently portrayed not as the Agent but as the Patient of historical processes: the film stresses his hermetic removal from history, in the conventional sense."[3] Only a non-linear narrative could communicate this over-arching theme so lucidly by shifting between historical time frames based on the mental state and the emotional world of its main character throughout a variety of circumstances.

To return to an earlier example, Coppola's,' THE GODFATHER,' is primarily a linear narrative, following the exploits of the Corleone crime family in one time period within a chronologically contiguous narrative. But,' THE GODFATHER II,' is a non-linear narrative, and a broader film as a result. The sequel encompasses the immigration of Vito Corleone to America in the 1920's and Michael Corleone's trials and tribulations as a mafia Don in the 1950's. The dramatic effect of presenting both stories in a non-linear narrative is found in the violence both father and son must commit to achieve and maintain power. Moreover, the non-linear narrative allowed Coppola to evoke different time periods through dual characters and foreground not simply the content (the mafia), but the themes of crime and power. For the screenwriter, an intensely acute awareness of the over-arching themes of his story, as well as, a total immersion into the emotional world of his characters gives a non-linear narrative much of its dramatic and cinematic impact. Although, my examination may lead one to believe that non-linear narratives work best on period films, there are many recent examples of non-linear films that are not historical dramas.[4]

The key to non-linear narrative can also be found within the over-arching theme that may be dormant within the story which can be elevated and brought to the foreground through a crosscutting of different time periods, from different characters, and actions whose similarity and variations support the theme. Many stories that feature a Voyage and Return or a Rebirth favor a non-linear presentation in that the character who is now changed can narrate the events and circumstances that precipitated their inner change and can allow us to easily discern the transitions between time periods. For Bertolucci and his writers, the themes of imprisonment and rebirth in,' THE LAST EMPEROR,' is found in a multitude of repetitions and variations through similar dialogue, locations, and emotional states that the main character, Pu Yi, experienced throughout his life. Indeed, the entire film has a deja vu-like quality of an absurd dream, whose ending—the suggested transformation of an elderly Pu Yi into a cricket recalls the same insect that was given to him as a child many years ago. Non-linear narratives can be rich with meanings, poetry, and all the while retain the elusive qualities of a dream.

REPETITION, VARIATION and CONTRAST
in the Assembly of a Non-Linear Narrative

As a rule, many non-linear films are not written to be non-linear, that is, they are written to be linear, but the filmmaker and/or the editor(s) create a non-linear narrative during the process of editing.[5] A non-linear narrative is usually an authorial process of discovery found during the assembly of the separate shots and scenes of the film. As Bertolucci has said himself," editing is going into an underground mine where you find incredible precious metals you didn't know were there while shooting . . ." [6] The first discovery is *repetition*; the repetition of similar events, actions, or circumstances in various contexts throughout the scope of the story. These repetitions are usually exploited to convey the non-linearity of the film's arrangement. The "open the door" moment in THE LAST EMPEROR connects two distinct periods in Pu Yi's life where guards were demanding that someone," open the door."

The second discovery also found during the process of editing a non-linear film is *variation*. Although events, actions or circumstances are repeated there are variations that change the perspective upon what is being repeated. Returning to our previous example, when the young Pu Yi heard the palace guards shouting, "open the door," he didn't know they were coming to steal him from his life. Conversely, when the older Pu Yi heard the communist guards shouting," open the door", they don't know that he is attempting to take his own life. A variation is evident within the two similar moments. So there is repetition, there is variation and there is a *contrast* between the scenes or shots that have been intercut that dynamically moves the narrative forward thematically as opposed to chronologically.

A non-linear narrative is a narrative whose dramatic structure is supported more so by contrasts rather than conflict. It would seem that once contiguous chronology is destroyed the filmmakers are free to juxtapose events, circumstances, and actions according to the way these elements contrast and contradict each other. A stunning example of how a non-linear narrative's drama is supported by contrasts rather than conflict is found in Michel Gondry's film of Charlie Kaufman's screenplay, THE ETERNAL SUNSHINE OF THE SPOTLESS MIND (2004).

The foibles, fickleness and obsessions of human nature are revealed in the romance, breakup, longing and recriminations of a love affair. The contrast between the way Joel Barish (Jim Carrey) feels about Clementine Kruczyuski (Kate Winslet) during their courtship and romance is continually interpolated with the way he feels during the decline and destruction of their relationship. It is a drama constructed by the non-chronologically motivated repetition and variation of scenes, events, actions and characters. Although we can safely say that this particular non-linear narrative was written for the expressed purpose of being non-linear, a fact highlighted by the fictional conceit of memory cleansing (Lacuna Inc.), it is worth repeating that a non-linear narrative is usually created during the post-production editing of the filmed elements.

It is there, in the editing room, alone and intimately familiar with the material that the filmmaker/editor "discovers", as an author, a theme that can be conveyed more readily by destroying the contiguous chronological framework of events and reassembling these events to better convey that theme via similarity, variation and contrast. This is an authorial process of discovery that we can now contrast with the fictional process of discovery called, a discovery narrative.

NOTES

(1)   I call non-linear narratives, Meta-chronological, because although this narrative structure destroys the temporal contiguity of the presentation of events, it actually intensifies and highlights the perception and experience of time. Whether the perception and experience is conveyed through the use of title cards (e.g. Bertolucci's use of the title card," Many years before . . ." in 1900) or through the careful forensic matching of child and adult actors faces and the modification of costuming in Sergio Leone's ONCE UPON A TIME IN AMERICA (1984), non-linear narratives appear to highlight and foreground temporal relationships among scenes while simultaneously destroying their chronological contiguity. Time takes an active as opposed to a passive role in the telling of the tale.

(2)   All of my comments concerning Bernardo Bertolucci's THE LAST EMPEROR are in reference to the original theatrical release version of the film and not the re-released director's version which deviates from many of the actual scene arrangements as discussed. This is one of the instances that reveal the danger of DVD in that a film is not allowed to retain its original arrangement and develop the patina that will distinguish it as a classic because it can always be 'changed' after its theatrical release.

(3) Pg. 109, BERTOLUCCI'S 1900: A Historical and Narrative Analysis, by Robert Burgoyne. Wayne State University Press. 1991.

(4) One classic non-period film that utilizes a non-linear narrative, if the reader is pursuing this challenge, is recommended: **LAST YEAR AT MARIENBAD** (Alain Resnais—1961). The structure of this film mixes past and present together through precise editing on the similar gestures of characters in different time frames and during repeated, but slightly changed, dialogues. Ostensibly, the story concerns an obsessed man, a woman, and her husband who are all vacationing at a luxurious Chateau. The obsessed man attempts throughout the movie to convince the woman that they are lovers who had met at the chateau last year and had planned to meet here again and runaway together, this year. The woman denies this story, although it is unclear whether she is doing this to fend off her husband's suspicions or to cover her own change of heart. But the obsessed man continues trying to convince her, even though he begins to doubt his own story, mix up the details and dates. When both the past story and the present story converge, the truth of the matter wins out in this highly stylized and obsessive drama.

(5) Whether this non-linearity is a consequence of boredom with the filmed elements or not, we should be more optimistic and say that it is an objective process of discovery wrought from a deep and intimate familiarity with material as was the case with Coppola and THE GODFATHER Part II. As most films are shot out of linear sequence it is inevitable that during the editing process the opportunity for an alternate non-linear way of putting the film together could be discovered.

(6) DVD Liner notes, THE LAST EMPEROR, Director's Cut, Artisan Films 1998.

The two previous examples of narrative structure (linear and non-linear) were intimately related to the syuzhet or the physical ordering of the presentation of the events, but our next two examples of narrative structure (discovery and conceptual) are intimately related to the fabula in that these are narrative structures conceived and dependant upon the fictional representation of events as oppose the their physical order. In short, what is suggested by a particular ordering of the events, beyond the temporal.

THE DISCOVERY NARRATIVE

'A Discovery is, as the very word implies, a change from ignorance to knowledge, and thus to either love or hate, in personages marked for good or evil fortune'

-Aristotle, The Poetics, 11

A discovery narrative is a narrative of deception that presents a series of mysterious events, actions or circumstances that are inevitably revealed to be a plot against a naïve, innocent or trusting character. As we will discuss in greater detail later, a discovery narrative is distinguished by having two themes: a fictional theme that unifies the actual story and the characters and a reality theme that is projected outward towards the audience watching the film. Weak discovery narratives usually have weak reality themes: a theme that is false, implausible or that does not relate to the audience in a palpable or profound way.

Another essential feature of a discovery narrative is a peculiar dramatic division of characters: there is always a naïve or innocent character being deceived by a worldly or wicked character or set of characters. This is a very important feature of all discovery narratives, because to create a sense of discovery in both the audience and the fiction, there must be at least one character who doesn't know what is really going on in the story. There must be at least one guileless individual caught up in the mysterious circumstances for a discovery narrative to function properly. Just as there must also be one knowledgeable and discerning character that is leading the innocent by the nose, until that innocent character "discovers" that the plot is against them.

Discovery narratives are the oldest and most ubiquitous narrative forms whose origins of structure can be discerned in the story of Adam and Eve in the Bible, the epic of Gilgamesh, Joan of Arc, Faust, and even Bram Stoker's Dracula and world creation myths and stories of indigenous people. Simply put, all discovery narratives are narratives that tell stories of a loss of innocence; a loss of naivete that must be replaced by guile, cunning and duplicity if the character is to survive. Perhaps one reason discovery narratives are such an enduring narrative form is that the form itself can be placed into a wide variety of contexts: mythical, historical, contemporary, futurist, and spiritual. These are narratives best suited to reveal corruption, mendacity, hate, and inhumanity.

When faced with corruption in the world, a discovery narrative renders the process of that corruption visible to audiences who are unwittingly the participants and victims of that very same corruption. Depending upon the artist's subjective worldview, the context and progression of the discovery narrative can go from corruption and wickedness toward redemption and forgiveness. But this is a much rarer occurrence since the essential elements of the narrative require that a character be naïve or innocent for there to be a discovery revealed. Anything less and the naïve character is made to look too foolish, too much of a victim for the audience to understand and accept.

There is often a Sleuth-like quality to these narratives that should not be over-simplified; the process is more than just playing 'Sherlock Holmes'. At the core of the best Discovery narratives is a powerful dramatic tension between the sudden irrational presentation of mysterious fictional events as they are encountered throughout the course of the film being viewed and the rational deduction of what these events mean by the characters within the fiction. For Sherlock Holmes, murders are solved by piecing together clues which are flaccid until the entire puzzle is fit together: the murderer caught, and the crime explained. For Discovery narratives, the clues are actually symbolic events or actions that intensify a mystery, impinge dramatically upon the behaviors and actions of the character(s), and retain an irrationality—even after explanation—that can be quite disturbing to an audience. A good example would be the hideous murder victims of David Fincher's, 'SEVEN.' The horrible murders encountered one after another in this film are offset by the rational—yet deeply disturbed—murderer discovered by the end of the film. The difference is sublime: Mr. Holmes knows at the outset that someone has been murdered and his business is to find out who did it and why? A discovery narrative may reveal who has been murdered and maybe who did it, but the most troubling part is why? The often irreconcilable tensions in a discovery narrative are generally what places this kind of narrative at the moral fringes of acceptable entertainment.

Another important quality of discovery narratives is the accumulation of partial answers that obscure more than reveal the whole truth. For instance, midway through Ridley Scott's,' ALIEN,' the creature is found to have a kind of molecular acid for blood. We first encounter this acid blood exactly the same way as the characters: by watching it mysteriously flow from one of the creature's wounded tentacles as it melts through floor after floor of the ship. Note here, how the graphic presentation of this mysterious liquid is presented before any character's dialogue defines it and gives it meaning within the narrative. Once the liquid ceases to melt a character ascribes a fictional meaning to the mysterious event, by suggesting that," I haven't seen anything like that since . . . molecular acid. It must be using it for blood." The tentative delivery of this meaning and others like it accumulates from one graphic event to the next graphic event. As we 'discover' more about the creature the more terrifying and mysterious the irrationality of such a creature's existence affects the audience and the behaviors and actions of the main characters. [1]

If we concern ourselves simply with the mysterious fictional events of discovery narratives, the films themselves become excessive exercises in fantasy, that one would pay little attention to, but what is key to such narratives is how these events are explained, or given meaning—if any—within the film. Moreover, how the behaviors and actions of the characters change dramatically as these fictional meanings and partial answers accumulate. For the writer, the major points he or she should concern themselves with before approaching the task of writing a discovery narrative are:

1) The mysterious events and the accumulation of fictional meanings that are partial answers to the whole truth.
2) The emotional reactions and physical actions of the characters to these events appear as realistic as possible.
3) The immediate need to get the audience to identify with the naïve or innocent character.

Discovery narratives are much harder to write and require certain refinements in dialogue or cinematic technique to succeed. Such films also yield dynamic dramatic results in visualizing the most extreme emotional states. I'd like to turn our attention to a seminal Discovery narrative film of the late Sixties which spawned a profitable genre: Roman Polanski's adaptation of Ira Levin's novel, ROSEMARY'S BABY (Paramount—1968).

Audience Identification with the Protagonist

In this narrative we discover, just as the protagonist discovers, that her newly wedded husband has promised a satanic cult their first born child in exchange for success and stardom. The film starts off as a routine enterprise concerning a young, modern and aspiring bourgeois couple renting and moving into a New York apartment that is slightly above their means. Slowly and with maniacal attention to detail the story becomes a twisted parable about ambition, greed, Catholicism abandoned and satanic practice. Polanski weaved this incredibly layered web by making sure that the first act of his script and the visual aspects of his film encourage the audience to safely and securely identify with Rosemary Woodhouse (Mia Farrow). I must digress here slightly to reveal how Polanski achieves the audience's identification with the main character that is so necessary for the success of a Discovery narrative. Looking at 'ROSEMARY'S BABY' now, audiences are jaded by other films with satanic themes and they may dismiss Rosemary's character as too naive, but Polanski achieved the ultimate in character identification because by the film's conclusion the audience could read the 'inner speech' of Rosemary Woodhouse: in other words we know exactly what she is thinking and feeling. Polanski does this in two ways: through inflective dialogue and subjective camera techniques. I will give two examples of his technique to examine the whole.

1) Early in the film Rosemary meets a young woman named, 'Terri Gionoffrio,' in the laundry room of the apartment building. The young woman is staying with an elderly couple across the hall from Rosemary's own apartment. Later, when this woman mysteriously commits suicide by jumping out of a window, the police question Rosemary and her husband about the woman's full name. Rosemary has trouble remembering the woman's last name and the audience struggles with her because when *we* were introduced, the woman announced her

full name quickly and in a causal, but realistic manner. A moment later, when a police officer provides the full name, both audience and character affirm the remembrance. It seems like such a tiny detail, but it's just such a detail—and others like it—that encourages an audience to identify with a naive character they would otherwise dismiss. We might call this type of dialogue, inflective, because it encourages the audience to mirror the 'inner speech' of the character, as opposed to dialogue that describes, explains, or objectifies a situation.

2) The visual example comes from the very same scene in the laundry room where Terri and Rosemary are introduced. It seems Terri has been given a splendid silver charm to hang around her neck by the elderly couple. The charm contains a mysterious substance called 'Tannis Root,' that smells something awful. When Terri invites Rosemary to smell the charm the camera moves ever-so-slightly into a tight medium two shot. As Rosemary jumps back in disgust from the smell, the camera reacts suddenly by shifting back to a wider two shot of the women; as if the camera itself had smelled the pungent odor and 'agreed' with Rosemary about the smell. The shift in camera movement and framing to simulate a character's psychological perspective is something Mr. Polanski talks about in-depth in his autobiography,' Roman by Polanski':

"Much of the film is seen through Rosemary's eyes. In trying to convey this subjective immediacy, I often staged long, complicated scenes using short focal lenses that called for extreme precision in the placing of both camera and actors. A common expedient is to use longer focals, which enable the camera to shoot a scene from farther away. This is far less time-consuming but also far less visually effective and convincing. Ideally the lens should be at the same distance from the subject as the eye of the notional observer [The Character looking.]" (ROMAN BY POLANSKI, pg 254, Ballantine Books, 1984)

Again, this is a precise detail, but it is just such a visual detail that encourages an audience to identify with the usually naive and/or deceived character that is essential to a discovery narrative.

So it must be clear for the writer attempting to approach a discovery narrative that he or she must carefully construct their script to encourage audience identification with the main character(s). This task is very difficult because the character's innocence and lack of worldliness can put off an audience, particularly if you put that character in a highly charged dramatic scene where an audience will take sides with the character whose guile and cunning immediately defeats the naïve and weak lead character of a discovery narrative. You must find typical or ordinary ritualistic situations **in the first 10 minutes of the first act** that will provide an opportunity to get the audience to identify with the way that innocent character views the world.

Ritual is an inherent part of our day to day lifestyles, so if the writer/filmmaker can find a ritual that is typical to a large demographic, specific to the character and their

113

environment that is supported by the story context (e.g. Rosemary's new apartment and it was the first day doing her laundry in the building) then that ritual may provide an excellent opportunity to get the audience to identify with the character and begin the process of discovery. This is why the laundry scene of ROSEMARY'S BABY is so significant. It was a modern ritualistic situation that allowed the audience to identify with Rosemary through a skillful alternation of the dialogue, the situation and the shot. Although, our primary analysis concerns ROSEMARY'S BABY the reader is encouraged to watch and carefully study the first acts of all such films identified as Discovery narratives to see how both the writer and the filmmakers attempt to handle this important task.

What Has Been Discovered?

The real discovery in the discovery narrative of 'ROSEMARY'S BABY,' is not the fictional existence of the Devil's Son (The Anti-Christ) but the true existence and nature of Satanic Cults. We cannot afford to be jaded on this point, for there had been no serious major motion pictures to dramatize a satanic cult before, ROSEMARY'S BABY. And there is the horrible and tragic coincidence that writer/director Roman Polanski's beautiful wife, Sharon Tate, was murdered by the Manson Family cult whose horrific actions in 1969 revealed the existence of murderous anti-social cults in America for all the world to see. Many writers and critics agree that the American counter-culture movement lost its innocence with these murders and never fully recovered.

For the writer there are actually two films or rather two thematic levels within all discovery narratives: 1) the fictional theme which is encountered, explained, and dealt with in the fictional world of the characters. 2) The reality theme which is the dramatic foundation for the entire film. For 'ROSEMARY'S BABY,' the fictional theme is the birth of the anti-Christ and the reality theme is the existence of satanic cults. It is also significant to note that it was Rosemary's husband, Guy Woodhouse (John Cassavetes) who was the primary deceiver of Rosemary. His need for worldly success, money and fame fueled his hand in the deception against his wife.

As previously mentioned, the powerful dramatic tension that discovery narratives provoke in the spectator is created by the interaction of the two themes within the single film; that is an interaction between the real and the fictional. A majority of flawed discovery narratives are failures because the filmmakers either reject a reality theme in the hopes of playing up the fictional theme or discourage audience identification with a naive character through miscasting. One tragic example is a film by John Frankenheimer: "DEAD BANG" (1989) which starred Don Johnson as a police officer who discovers the existence and murderous conspiracy of a White Supremacist Cult. Although, I will always maintain that the film has great merit, and actually includes a real performance from its former Miami Vice television star, apparently audiences were just unwillingly to accept Don Johnson in this role and the commercial appeal of the film suffered as a result. Clearly, there is a delicate balance that must be struck and maintained between the fictional theme as revealed through the audience's identification with the main character(s) and the reality theme for discovery narratives to work.

114

THE COMPLICITY POINT

An important and specific dramatic point that is also peculiar to all Discovery Narratives is whether or not the naïve character will decide to become an accomplice in the corruption that they have discovered. The complicity point is as old as Eve being offered the apple; wickedness always offers gifts to fetch its accomplices. It is the complicity point that reveals the true internal strength or weakness of the once naïve character by testing their ideals and most importantly their/our morals. The complicity point is a major dramatic moment that is always explicit in discovery narratives.

Where the complicity point occurs within the narrative usually determines whether or not the naïve character will accept or reject complicity. It usually occurs in one of two places: between the second and third acts of the story as a turning point for the naïve character (who denies becoming an accomplice) or at the end of the film for the naïve character who agrees to be an accomplice. The ending of ROSEMARY'S BABY reveals a reluctant, some would even say ambivalent, acceptance of what Rosemary had discovered. There is a complicity point mid-way through ALIEN when Ripley is encouraged to go along with the way the mysterious creature has been interpreted. In SEVEN, the point of complicity is found when Det. Mills (Brad Pitt) must struggle with delivering vengeance/revenge and becoming the murdering executioner of someone else who executed others in judgment.

"The ending of ROSEMARY'S BABY reveals a reluctant, some would even say ambivalent, acceptance of what Rosemary had discovered." (Mia Farrow, ROSEMARY'S BABY 1968, Copyright Paramount Pictures and William Castle Enterprises, Inc.)

In films like,' ROSEMARY'S BABY,' or 'ALIEN', we are introduced to characters in banal or routine settings where the dramatic eruption of mysterious events leads to a consistent layering of meaning about the events until the actual plot is discovered. [2] Again, the technique of Discovery rests on the accumulation of fictional meanings given to mysterious events that erupt throughout the course of the narrative. There is a continuous process at work that presents an event and then gives that event a partial answer and meaning: Event + meaning, Event + meaning, until both the chain of events and the build up of meanings and answers reveal the discovery of the plot. But I would argue that although my description of the process seems a bit mechanical, the best discovery narratives also have at their core a moral theme which is what is usually the key to their disturbing quality. In, 'SEVEN,' once the killer is caught his speech about who should die and who should live strikes a cord in all of us about the way we judge people. Moreover, in Coppola's, 'APOCALYPSE NOW,' the graphic realization that Kurtz has gone mad and should be killed is a moral judgment that upsets the viewer's values. These moral themes require that the character(s) make a difficult choice: to become complicit with what they have discovered or reject the discovery with the same moral perforce that led them to it.

DISCOVERY NARRATIVE: A SPECIFIC ANALYSIS
TRAINING DAY
Written by David Ayer
Directed by Antoine Fuqua

We must add to our discussion of discovery narratives the powerful police drama, TRAINING DAY (2001). Adding this film to our discussion should not be so difficult once we fully accept the superbly modulated and layered performance of its lead actor, Denzel Washington. His well deserved Best Actor Oscar for this film only seemed to highlight the fact that he was not awarded one for his stand out performance as MALCOLM X in the Spike Lee film several years earlier. Some have opined about the fact that he was awarded a Best Actor Oscar for so dark and disturbing a role as that of a corrupt Los Angeles police officer. But when a great actor is typecast or holds him or herself back from playing roles opposite our expectations, they are only coasting on the limitations of small minds that constricts their talent rather than broadening it. The same holds true for great actors who only play "heavy" roles and not the contrary.

Yet when the great actor does decide, by fate or inspiration, to broaden their performance and they do so with such incredible results, then their accomplishment should be recognized. After all, the Motion Picture Academy snubs of Cary Grant's dark role in Alfred Hitchcock's SUSPICION (1941) and Henry Fonda's formidable dark turn in Sergio Leone's ONCE UPON A TIME IN THE WEST (1969) live on in infamy among critics. In accepting Denzel Washington's superlative performance we cannot discount what his performance added to the script and the overall film. It's just that since such performances are rare, we must concern ourselves with the method and the content of the story and the narrative, which are the subject and scope of this discourse.

A FINE DISTINCTION

It would most likely seem that TRAINING DAY is a seduction narrative in that the story seduces us into believing that seasoned LAPD officer, Alonzo Harris (Denzel Washington) is training his new rookie partner, Jake Hoyt (Ethan Hawke) for the vagaries of the law and dangers of the streets that face an undercover narcotics officer. As the film progresses we realize during an intense revelatory scene that Alonzo Harris has been planning "all week" to use his rookie partner in a precarious scheme to pay back a huge gambling debt and save his own life before the actual day the two are working together. The narrative does feature two of the defining characteristics of a seduction narrative:

1) It gives us a doubled presentation of characters and locations
2) It does reveal, through the character of Jake Hoyt, an altered mental perspective that was not present before the revelation.

The doubled presentation of the drug dealer Roger and "the Jungle" the ghetto where Alonzo's woman and child live have distinctly different tones in connection with Alonzo's actions each time we see them. After the life threatening events of the day, Jake Hoyt has clearly been changed from a naïve rookie to a seasoned officer of the law by the end of the film.

But I believe that what keeps TRAINING DAY from being a seduction narrative is that the seduction is carried out upon a character within the story and not upon the audience watching the film. This is a subtle distinction, but it is supported by the fact that the revelation of the film (that Harris was using Hoyt for his own ulterior motives) is not the finale of the film. Most seduction narratives conclude once the revelation has been revealed to the audience and/or the characters, yet TRAINING DAY continues beyond the revelation into the realm of discovery.

Moreover, the prima facie of the film is not destroyed once the revelation has been revealed. It is still possible to enjoy the first interpretation of the film because much of what Harris is telling Hoyt is plausible and relevant information that a seasoned officer would tell a rookie officer. Here again, the seduction is not for the spectator, but for the character and TRAINING DAY is a richer film as a result. And in the final analysis, TRAINING DAY is not about seduction at all, it is about *deception* and therein lay the essential distinction that makes the film a discovery narrative as opposed to a seduction narrative. We can discern a motif of deception being played out against all of the lead characters of these films, from Rosemary Woodhouse being deceived by her husband in ROSEMARY'S BABY, Ripley being deceived by the corporate robot in ALIEN, and finally the deception between Harris and Hoyt in TRAINING DAY.

There can be no question also that the narrative follows the familiar dramatic structure of presenting mysterious events and then giving those events fictional or (temporary) meanings until the actual plot is discovered. The only difference is that rather than events it is the actions of Alonzo Harris and Jake Hoyt that are enigmatic and must be temporarily explained. For instance, when Hoyt jumps out of the car to stop an assault in progress upon a woman, Harris is completely bemused and quickly resolves the situation. His 'temporary' motives for this resolution were because they had more important things to do, but his real motives were because he was trying to keep on schedule for his own plot against Hoyt.

WHAT IS BEING DISCOVERED IN TRAINING DAY?

Ultimately, there are multiple deceptions within this film, but an important discovery is that the appearance of law and order is at times more important than upholding the law and keeping the order in a modern society. "For in their everyday work the police, although they intrinsically possess great dramaturgical potential, must dramatize the appearance of control."[3] If the first half of the film is a training session for both Jake Hoyt and the audience, then both learn that to keep law and order, laws must be broken and the peace must be disturbed—particularly as it concerns undercover officers. We are deceived about the true intentions of Alonzo Harris because much of what he says in the first half of the film is palpably true.

> *"To be truly effective, a good narcotics agent must know and love narcotics.*
> *In fact, a good narcotics agent should have narcotics in his blood."*

Alonzo Harris makes this statement before he tells Jake Hoyt to smoke some of the "laced" marijuana they have just confiscated from some scared suburban kids after witnessing their drug purchase. When Jake refuses to smoke the narcotics, Alonzo stops his car in the middle of the street, points his gun at Jake's head and says," If I was a dealer you'd be dead by now, mutherfucka. You turn shit down on the street and the Chief brings your wife a crispy folded flag. What the fuck is wrong with you?" And this statement, given the nature of undercover police work (the lengthy investigations, drug buys, and acting) is certainly true; to continue a ruse a narcotics agent would not be able to deny certain things in his interaction with criminals if he wanted to stay alive.

Alonzo Harris is able to deceive Jake Hoyt with a unique strategy of planting the truth in his head with provocative macho rhetoric—"You want to be a wolf or a sheep?"—while simultaneously using Jake's own masculine pride against him. For instance, Jake does smoke the laced marijuana after Alonzo orders him to get out of his car, saying that he doesn't want to work with a "rookie". Denzel Washington puts such a derogatory emphasis on the term "rookie" in the rhythm of his speech that it cuts incisively into the pride of Jake Hoyt—who does not want to be treated as a rookie on this his first day as an undercover officer. Thus, the deception played out against Jake Hoyt by Alonzo Harris is rooted in truth, but it is propelled by the pride of the character that is being deceived.

What is ultimately discovered in TRAINING DAY is the deception that Alonzo Harris was playing against himself. When he extemporaneously speaks Jake's epitaph in the revelatory scene, he is in essence really speaking his own: "A Los Angeles police department narcotics officer was killed today serving a high risk warrant . . ." The reality theme, so characteristic of all Discovery narratives, in TRAINING DAY is that the police, control, modify and manipulate how crime is perceived in a civil society and they do so with the willful intent to cover up their mistakes and sometimes to embellish their successes. This is, of course, not the first police drama—nor will it be the last—to dramatically render such a theme, but in the pantheon of police\crime films TRAINING DAY ranks high in the substance and force of its drama and narrative style.[4]

The re-staging of the character Roger's murder scene by Alonzo Harris and his co-conspirators demonstrates that the information about crime can be "freely" manipulated by the police for the embellishment of success or the obscuring of mistakes, defeat or corruption. When Alonzo shoots one of his conspirators, to add to the veracity of their cover story, the bullet slips past the officer's protective vest and wounds him. Harris immediately calms the situation by saying," Alright, alright you'll get a medal, don't worry about it . . . Hey, you want to go to jail or do you want to go home?" Harris is turning what was essentially a mistake of his own aiming ability into an accolade for his wounded comrade.

It is clear that since the police are usually the first responders to a crime scene all information about the crime is filtered through their investigative and cultural prejudices; all of which are manipulated to put the officers in the best light. Wasn't this really the suspicion behind the social demonstrations that marked the tragedies of Amadillo Diallo case or even the Rodney King verdict? "That is, [the police] must segment their audiences so that certain presentations are available only to some segments of the society; they must control the information available on their actions in order to be effective (both in crime control and in the maintenance of public credibility) . . . they must decrease the amount of information available to their public that indicates the dirty, the boring, the ineffectual, the illegal or potentially immoral; and they must, through the management of appearances create the sense of commitment to and enforcement of rules and tenets on which there is only an "as if" public agreement." [5]

The dramatic complicity point for officer Hoyt comes right during the creation of the cover story for Roger's murder. He is first asked to agree to his part in the cover story, but he refuses and takes a shotgun that was pointed at him and turns it on Alonzo. He is then offered a portion of the money dug out from Roger's kitchen, but he refuses again. Since this complicity point comes two-third's of the way through the narrative it becomes a turning point that eventually leads Hoyt to create a deception against Alonzo. As with most Discovery narratives Hoyt has to act as if he has become an accomplice to deceive and ultimately defeat the villain. This is again another key aspect of discovery narratives, once the naïve character has refused to become an accomplice, he or she must perform a deception against the deceiver(s) to escape or destroy the plot against them.

It is the fate of Alonzo Harris—riddled with bullets in the middle of the street near L.A.X. airport—that reveals that Harris was trying to thwart a plot against himself by deceiving Jake Hoyt. If Hoyt had not been saved by a twist of fate induced by his selfless act of heroism (the saving of a girl from a potential rape) Hoyt would have been discarded by Harris and avoided his own appointment with death. Yet, beyond the self interest and egoism of Alonzo Harris the lesson behind the reality theme of TRAINING DAY is that," In this business you got to have a little dirt on you for anybody to trust you," and this is a how the cynicism that obscures the black and white truth is perpetuated in police work and ultimately in modern society.

The characteristic features of all great discovery narratives can be summarized below as:

1) A naïve or innocent character deceived by the guile, cynicism, or wickedness of another.

2) These films usually contain a fictional theme and a reality theme; the former theme relates directly to the characters and the latter theme to the audience watching the film.

3) A narrative construction that presents ambiguous or mysterious events that are intentionally misinterpreted by the deceitful character for his or her ulterior motives until the deception is discovered and the truth is revealed.

4) The Complicity Point, the point in the story where the innocent or naïve character is offered a chance to join in the deception or corruption by actively participating, accepting a bribe, or simply not acting at all on what they know.

5) The deceived naïve character must usually perform a deception against the deceiver to destroy or escape the plot against them.

Discovery Narratives favor the use of a Rebirth story archetype in that the naïve main character is placed into a position of "living death or imprisonment" by their deceivers before they are "reborn" through their discovery and the eventual defeat of or escape from their deceivers. We should remember the pain and imprisonment of Rosemary Woodhouse during her pregnancy as she drank "Tannis Root" and felt like there was," a wire tightening," inside of her; also the death of Jake Hoyt's heroic idealism in TRAINING DAY as he was held captive by Alonzo Harris during their 24 hour journey.

So let us be clear that though there are several differences between discovery narratives and seduction narratives a major methodological difference can be simplified as: Seduction narratives seduce the spectators into interpreting mysterious events, actions and characters one way and then reveal an alternate interpretation in the final act. Discovery narratives require that the characters be deceived by the initial interpretation of mysterious events until that deception is made clear by their own actions and/or destroyed by their discovery of the truth.

Seduction narratives ultimately deceive the audience and erode the tacit bond of trust between an audience and the filmmaker. Underneath the most successful seduction narratives (beginning with the initial negative critical reception of PSYCHO) there is the insipid suspicion that the filmmakers are making fools of their audience.[6] Over time, if too many seduction narratives are released consecutively audiences can become jaded and dismissive, even of films that are not seduction narratives but contain similar events or the same actors. On the contrary, Discovery narratives, enrich both the audiences who are watching and the characters upon the screen with the doubled themes that under-gird the structure and the content.

NOTES

[1] The tentative words and delivery of the meaning is crucial. By having characters act as if they are making their best guesses about the mysterious events, there is a heightening of the discovery aspect of the narrative, giving the planned events within the film a sense of having been created as the film is being viewed, rather than a hackneyed style of simply placing the mysterious event and immediately giving it a secure meaning moments later. This is a question of talent rather than technique.

[2] Although, Outer Space can hardly be called a routine setting, the inter-personal relationships within 'ALIEN' creates a routine setting because of the work ethic imbued within the opening scenes: a crew of laborers waking up from a 'routine' mining expedition, who immediately begin arguing over work assignments, union contracts, and bonus pay. This is exactly what offsets the spectacular setting and the mysterious events to follow: the idea that if man conquers space travel the benefits would simply feed back into the industrial corporate structure and man would still treat himself like he always has: A day's pay for a day's work.

[3] Pg.30, POLICE WORK: The Social Organization of Policing 2nd Edition, by Peter K. Manning, Waveland Press, 1997.

[4] That pantheon includes SERPICO (1973, Written by Waldo Salt and Norman Wexler, directed by Sidney Lumet), THE FRENCH CONNECTION (1974, William Friedkin), TO LIVE AND DIE IN L.A. (1985, William Friedkin), INTERNAL AFFAIRS (1990, Written by Henry Bean, Directed by Mike Figgis) and many others.

[5] Pg. 30, ibid.

[6] Indeed, this might be the real explanation for the mixed and dour critical reactions to Alfred Hitchcock's PSYCHO during its initial release and a contributing factor to the commercial decline of his career—with PSYCHO Hitchcock had irreparably broke a tacit trust between himself and his audience that no matter how creative his subsequent films were (THE BIRDS, MARNIE) or commercial (TORN CURTAIN, TOPAZ) he could never recover. He literally destroyed the 'prima facie' of his own career. Also note the vehement and dismissive criticism leveled at M. Night Shamaylan's THE VILLIAGE (2004)

CONCEPTUAL NARRATIVES

The final narrative in General Types is the most difficult to describe and to approach as a prospective screenwriter: The Conceptual Narrative. A conceptual narrative is a film whose overall vision is based upon a utopian or dystopian theory about life that most often recapitulates itself into a startlingly different stylistic approach. If this sounds general, then you are quite right because I am trying to be delicate at the expense of being obtuse.

Everyone adheres to what they might be inclined to call a 'theory about life', but in our day to day social reality it is better to call these theories: Belief Systems. For our society to operate as a civilized society large segments of the population must share similar beliefs. These shared beliefs form a system where in which we function as individuals and as groups. Sociologists have long attempted to explain what these shared beliefs are and how these shared beliefs are created and maintained.

Author James Q. Wilson, has identified this shared belief system as,'The Moral Sense,' which is patterned after four general sentiments (Sympathy, Fairness, Self-Control, Duty) springing forth from three general sources (the Sociability of Man, the Family, and Gender) that are consistent throughout the history and culture of man. But any artist who holds a 'theory about life' is usually stepping into boundaries far outside of our traditional belief systems to reveal the abundance or absence of the previously mentioned sentiments and sources. To express his or her theory, the artist must devise a concept to communicate it.

It is the conceptualization of the theory that causes an artist to redress or reinterpret the form of film (structure or visual style) to suit his or her needs and express the theory succinctly. There can be no doubt that Russian filmmaker, Sergei Eisenstein (1898-1948) was a conceptual filmmaker whose theories about film supported his own theories about Socialist/Marxist life. Conceptual narratives are audacious, difficult, and controversial all the more so because while being decidedly theoretical, these narratives require often radically different approaches, in terms of spectatorship, to be appreciated. One cannot sit through James Cameron's,' TERMINATOR II,' the same way one would sit through Stanley Kubrick's,' 2001,' and expect the same appreciation; although I would argue both films are conceptual narratives.[1] These types of films either require great thought to create and/or provoke great thought and debate.

Before attempting to articulate how a writer/filmmaker should approach creating a conceptual narrative it is best that I describe through example a few conceptual narratives. Two films will serve as challenging examples: Jared and Jerusha Hess' NAPOLEON DYNAMITE (2004) and Pier Paolo Pasolini's,' TEOREMA' (1968).

NAPOLEON DYNAMITE

True comedy classics are rare and often dependent upon a singular dynamic performer (Buster Keaton, Charlie Chaplin, Richard Pryor), but the film NAPOLEON DYNAMITE is spotlighted here not solely because of its humor (and it is hysterically funny) but also for its striking conceptualization. NAPOLEON DYNAMITE is a conceptual narrative that uses costuming, art direction and music to construct a deliberately anachronistic fictional world that defies a specific time period to tell a timeless tale of heroism and individuality. Such grandiloquent words are rarely used to describe a comedy, but comedy is an important dramatic form and I see no reason why we shouldn't take our comedies as seriously as we take our dramas.

The Issue of Time: TEMPORAL DIASPORA

It can be argued that all films present a theory about life and that we only notice the films that deviate from our own belief systems and rituals or present themes that we rarely acknowledge or contemplate. Yet, in spite of rendering the previous definition of conceptual narratives moot, such an observation should serve to intensify our scrutiny of these films. The importance of many conceptual narratives is found in that presentation of theories about life that deviate from our long cherished beliefs and rituals or highlight themes that are obscured by the conformity and/or routine of our day to day lives. Wasn't this fact the real underpinning of the success of the first MATRIX film?

Much of the charm and incandescence of NAPOLEON DYNAMITE is found within the film's uncanny ability to frustrate the spectator's intuition about what time period the film is recreating. This is done primarily through an inventive and contradictory use of costuming, music and art direction. For instance, Napoleon's (Jon Heder) well-worn Moon Boots are a costuming detail that signifies the mid-to-late 1980's, when such boots were in vogue. But the film's reference to "the Internet" is a verbal reference to the mid-1990's, further complicated by the old model desktop computer that was used by Napoleon's brother Kip (Aaron Ruell).

Throughout the film there is a calculated effort to obfuscate a time period, whether we look at Uncle Rico's (Jon Gries) Early Eighties customized van to Napoleon's three piece suit that he purchased for the high school dance, a specific time period is lost in the details. The long, long coiled phone cord used in Napoleon's house is indicative of a pre-cellular and pre-cordless phone time period. Even the music played in the film particularly Cyndi Lauper's eighties hit "Time after Time" during the school dance and the retro seventies sound of late nineties pop star Jamiroquai used during the election speech dance further heightens our awareness of the film's temporal Diaspora. The obfuscation of time is finally rendered literal by Uncle Rico's Internet purchase of 'The Time Machine' and his yearning to return to 1982 and have the coach put him in during a championship football game and change his present situation.

We refer to the fictional world presented in NAPOLEON DYNAMITE as a temporal Diaspora because the rural town inhabited by the characters retains all the shattered bits and pieces of several different time periods and manages to present them all seamlessly in a narrative that is mostly chronologically contiguous. The contradiction in time periods can be seen in Deb's (Tina Majorino) mid-eighties side angle pony-tail to Perdo's cousin's early nineties hydraulic low rider which plays the early eighties hit,' So Ruff, So Tuff," by Roger Troutman. We know that this temporal Diaspora was intentionally created because of the fact that one of the co-writers, Jerusha Hess, was also the costume designer. This atypical screen credit-writer and costuming designer—reveals the attention to detail and the significant role that costuming and art direction would play in the total conceptualization of the film.

We might speculate that the theory about life presented in NAPOLEON DYNAMITE is that we are defined by our past, but we can only transcend the past by committing ourselves totally to the present. The frustrated efforts of Uncle Rico and later Napoleon to go back in time forces both characters to turn their attention to the present. We are victorious over the past that shapes us only by committing ourselves to the present. The only character who delivers his past to us verbally is Pedro (Effren Ramirez) in his flashback about why he shaved his head. A wig immediately replaces Pedro's real hair; this change of costuming forces his character to deal with the present and the impending school presidential election. The concern for the present while being trapped in the details of the past is finally transcended in Kip's sudden elopement with LaFawnduh (Shondrella Avery); the very act is a total divestment from his past as a nerdish character without a woman and a leap into an uncertain future.

If by utopian we mean the satisfaction of all wants and needs then NAPOLEON DYNAMITE presents us with a decidedly dystopian world. The fragments of different time periods within the film (through costuming, art direction, music and dance) represent a comically dystopian world where no one was getting what they really wanted and their dissatisfaction was a steady diet. The effort to go back in time and satisfy what one thinks one needs now, the need to have a friend and wanting to have a girlfriend, the effort to be class president are all frustrated desires that make the world of NAPOLEON DYNAMITE comically dystopian.

So we see that conceptual films need not always be thought of as science fiction as in THE MATRIX Trilogy. In NAPOLEON DYNAMITE the concept can be created in comedy that uses the left over bits and pieces of multiple time periods. The husband and wife team of Jared and Jerusha Hess, far from creating a new cinematic language to communicate their conceptual film, put intense scrutiny upon an aspect of film form that is usually contiguous and taken for granted (costuming, music and art direction to represent a single time period) and forced it to be poly-temporal or rather comically anachronistic.

TEOREMA

"After a series of disillusionments you wind up by seeing reality as a horrendous, intolerable thing—as a perfidious game played by some devilish god . . . or else as a game"

—Pier Paolo Pasolini[2]

Another example of conceptual filmmaking is a strict example of the rules that define such films. TEOREMA (Translation: Theorem-or-Theory), made and released in Italy in 1968 was yet another scandalous film for its scandal plagued creator: Pier Paolo Pasolini (1922-1975). The resultant controversy surrounding the film and its author necessitates that we begin this analysis with a severely constricted overview of the filmmaker before approaching the film.

Pier Paolo Pasolini: known homosexual, Marxist, writer, film theorist and filmmaker was one of the most formidable intellectual and artistic talents to ever engage in the art. His career began as a celebrated poet and Marxist intellectual after World War II (Le Ceneri di Gramsci-Ashes of Gramsci); later as a novelist whose books were about the post-war slums of Italy and its adolescent inhabitants (Ragazzi di Vita). In 1960, after a fast and furious rise as a talented screenwriter for the likes of Frederico Fellini, Franco Rossi, and others, Pasolini announced his entrance into filmmaking as a director and writer. His first film,' ACCATTONE,' (Literally translated as, beggar/thief) was a magnificent, if somewhat late-coming, work in the tradition of Italian Neo-Realism. (For an in-depth discussion of ACCATTONE see the last part of chapter: BUILDING THE CHARACTER)

The film follows the life and times of a pitiful pimp (Franco Citti as the 'Accattone' of the title) who would rather put his woman out on the street with a bandaged leg than work for a living himself. The film is noted for its bold language and the simple, yet fascinating, construction of its shots and editing. What was scandalous was the fact that here is a story about a pimp (the pure embodiment of Pasolini's *idée fixee* on socially worthless characters) set to sacred music of Johann Sebastian Bach.

It is particularly through the work of Pasolini that we can discern that the true mission of Italian Neo-realism was an unassuming humanism that cast light upon the underbelly of the Post-war economic miracle that swept Europe aided in no small part by America. This humanism revealed the crisis of those who were being left out and the intrinsically Italian ways of life that were being destroyed in the process. From Visconti's LA TERRA TREMA (1948—The Earth Trembles), DeSica's THE BICYCLE THEIF (1948), Antonioni's IL GRIDO (1957-The Cry) and Fellini's I VITTELONI (1953) and LA STRADA (1954) more than any other Italian Neo-Realist, Pasolini's work was the epitome of the passion, the poetry and the social criticism of the Neo-Realist movement.

Pasolini's theories on film, most importantly his essay,' A Cinema of Poetry,' completely turned the work of film semiotians and theorists who claimed to be studying 'the language of the cinema' on their heads, by proclaiming,' cinema expresses reality with reality,' as opposed to operating with a system of signs and signifiers as the written language operates. His incredible and serious work in film theory has connections with the cinematic visions of several other directors, including: Orson Welles, Bernardo Bertolucci (whose first film,' The Grim Reaper,' was from a short story by Pasolini), Michelangelo Antonioni, and the late Russian filmmaker, Andrei Tarkovsky, and the influence of Pasolini's work is constantly being rediscovered today. Though despite Pasolini's fascinating filmography (most notably his 'trilogy of life': THE DECAMERON (1971), THE CANTERBURY TALES (1972), and ARABIAN NIGHTS (1974)—his entire output of highly challenging and diverse works and writings will, perhaps, be overshadowed by his last film, SALO (1975) and his brutal death allegedly at the hands of a male prostitute in that same year.[3]

SALO, a notorious film, still banned in many countries and shrouded in controversy is one of the most infamous films of commercial cinema's history. "No film, if the director is famous and the subject one that gives rise to gossip, can escape rumors—they are the business of the publicity department. It is a way of keeping alive that sense of the marvelous on which the film industry feeds. The subject of SALO had more than its share of reasons for the most unbridled gossip."[4] Loosely, based on the Marquis de Sade's novel '120 Days of Sodom,' this final film features graphic violence and clinical sexual sadism/masochism so disturbing its scandal will long be remembered as a dark foreshadowing of Pasolini's own horrible death just a few weeks before its release. Hence, there is no need to go into specifics about the work; I'm sure any interested reader can find out about it on their own.

We will conclude this overview with a description of Pasolini by Director Orson Welles (who acted in the short film, LA RICOTTA, by Pasolini in 1963) when he was asked to describe him by interviewer Peter Bogdanovich, he said he was," Terribly bright and gifted. Crazy mixed up kid, maybe—but on a very superior level. I mean Pasolini the poet, spoiled Christian, and Marxist ideologue. There's nothing mixed up about him on a movie set. Real authority and a wonderfully free way with the machinery."[5]

TEOREMA, Pasolini's fifth feature length film, occupies an important place in our analysis of conceptual filmmaking because so bold is its approach, subject matter, and presentation that it will intrigue the would-be screenwriter who imagines himself as a conceptual writer and it will reveal the great labor of the soul and provocation of accepted sensibilities that such films require to make and appreciate.

The story of TEOREMA is fantastic: The lavish household of a modern bourgeois family is suddenly visited by a mysterious stranger who possesses either divine powers of love or demonic sexual charms. The stranger engages in seemingly sexual experiences with the mother, the son, the daughter, the father, and their maid. "The allegorical, religious nature of this "scandalous" love is, perhaps, clearest in the scenes between the father and the visitor—scenes where the overtones of homosexuality and incest bathing the film are also strongest."[6] Later, just as suddenly as his entrance, he must leave. Before leaving, each household member confesses the profound effect his presence has had upon them.

When the stranger finally does leave, everyone reacts severely over the loss. "Each finds the knowledge of the authenticity they have lost and of the impossibility of refinding it and hence refinding their lost souls."[7] The Mother (Silvana Mangano), unable to continue her empty life of being a chaste lady begins picking up men from the street for various sexual encounters in ill-fated attempts to relive the sexual liberation she experienced with the visitor. The Son (Andres Jose Crux) becomes a disturbed artist unable to communicate his vision of a totally new world," never before seen or painted by any man," in his own work. The Daughter (Ann Wiazemsky) falls into a closed fisted catatonic state and is sent to a mental hospital. The Father (Massimo Girotti) gives away his prosperous factory to its workers and abandons his previous life. Finally, the most sublime effect befalls the maid (Laura Betti), who quits her job, returns to her village, and is given the miraculous 'Saintly' powers of healing and levitation. When she asks to be buried to her eyelids in the earth, her tears create a fountain of hope.

The theorem of the film is 'What if' a divine creature entered the pristine and loveless confines of a bourgeois household, spreading his love and healing powers like a mania? How would this family change? But Pasolini's divine creature, at once sacred (he heals some of those he touches) and profane (his sexual fecundity spares no one in the household), forces us to see him as destructive. "TEOREMA was disconcerting because of its content. A combination of eros and religiosity—it was the first time that a completely nude male body, that of the protagonist Terence Stamp, had appeared on the screen in a film that disavowed pornography."[8] The conceptualization of Pasolini's film and his attentive camera rests on what Michel Foucault described as the intersection of mankind's most controversial ideologies: Politics (Marxism), Sexuality, and Religion in the nude male body of its star.

By recreating a very subjective and pointed view of a bourgeois household for the divine creature to inhabit, Pasolini expresses the classical Marxist division between the noble and oppressed proletariat versus the modern bourgeois typified by the loveless and alienated household with its dutiful maid and the father who owns a factory. Prior to the stranger's entrance, the family rarely speaks to each other, shows little affection, nor invades the privacy of each others personal worlds. Pasolini explains his overall view of the bourgeoisie in a BBC television interview in 1968:

> **"But my hatred for the bourgeoisie is really a kind of physical repugnance towards petit bourgeois vulgarity, the vulgarity of hypocritical 'good manners', and so on. And perhaps it is above all because I find their cultural meanness insufferable."**[9]

It is this disparaging view of the bourgeoisie that the entire theorem of Pasolini's film interrogates by simply exploring the idea of 'what if' a divinity from a lost or past age interrupted this family and its stifling values. By creating a divine creature in the personage of the handsome British actor Terence Stamp, Pasolini mixes the sacred and the profane, giving this creature a mysterious quality that cannot simply be exploited for its sexual openness or its divine connotations.

> **"I had adapted my character to the physical and psychological person of the actor. Originally, I intended this visitor to be a fertility god, the typical god of pre-industrial religion, the sun-god, the Biblical god, God the Father. Naturally, when confronted with things as they were, I had to abandon my original idea and so I made Terence Stamp into a generically ultra-terrestrial and metaphysical apparition: he could be the Devil, or a mixture of God and the Devil. The important thing is that he is something authentic and unstoppable."**[10]

And finally, notwithstanding the swarm of controversy surrounding the release of this film, the left wing faction of Italy's Catholic Film Office awarded the film a prize while the right wing faction denounced the film as perverse. Moreover, Italian officials quickly confiscated the film in Rome on September 3rd, 1968 for obscenity. At the trial in November of '68 Pasolini," explained the irruption of the divine into the everyday world, and the philosophical role of eros in existential crises. The trial ended with acquittal—the film was judged to be a work of poetry."[11] Despite this controversy,' TEOREMA', was simply an ideological pit stop for its creator as his penetrating criticism of the bourgeoisie changed and his later views and subsequent films broadened into a caustic critique of the 'Neo-capitalist' consumer society rising in Italy and the Third World:

> **"The bourgeoisie is at present undergoing a revolutionary change: it is assimilating everybody to the petit bourgeoisie: the whole of mankind is becoming petit bourgeois. So there are new problems, and these will have to be solved by the members of the bourgeoisie themselves, not the workers or the opposition. We dissident bourgeois cannot solve these problems, and neither can the "natural" bourgeois. That is why the film remains "suspended' . . . ."**[12]

It is the disquieting formal aspects of the film, coupled with Pasolini's public/private persona that creates the most profound effect upon the overall film and its fascinating events. TEOREMA communicates mostly in its silence: image conveys the theory more so than dialogue. After a brief documentary-like prologue (actually an epilogue, hinting at a reverse linear narrative structure) where the workers are questioned about their opinions concerning their sudden acquisition of the factory, Pasolini continues with virtually silent black and white images of each of the family members and their daily routines. With the arrival of the visitor, the images change to color and dialogue returns; but the film is still filled with long passages of silence, particularly during the scenes involving the sexual/mystical powers of the visitor.

Because the spectator must interpret the 'silent passages' and the actions of the visitor much of the controversy surrounding this film is also based on those contemporary spectators who were looking for Pasolini's homosexual vision in the perceived sexual encounters. Clearly, Pasolini's early legal entanglements concerning the buying of sex from young male prostitutes and his public homosexual lifestyle contributes to the discreet sexual symbolism seen in all of the 'silent passages' of this highly stylized film. Indeed, there are no sexually explicit scenes in the entire work, but the camera does linger in silence upon the crotch of Terence Stamp as the divine creature, subjectively seen through the point of view of the desiring family member. "A camera that lingers on male bodies is, perhaps, only the most obvious and specific sign of Pasolini's attraction to men. His very taste for ambiguity expressed through smiles we cannot interpret, gaps between narrative and image—may well be still another indication of a homosexual sensibility."[13] But even this lingering is equivocal, because the camera lingers upon his silent face as seen in front of the glare of the sun, giving him a halo in another sequence.

It is the alternating point of view of the visitor as divine and sexual, coupled with Pasolini's controversial public persona that caused the controversy for the film's contemporary viewers: when trying to see the visitor as divine the silent passages seem sexual, when trying to see the visitor as (homo) sexual the silent passages seem to express a deep religiosity. Modern viewers of the film, given the extensive knowledge of Homo-erotic codes through deep-seated homophobia will no longer see the ambivalence in these scenes and, no doubt, discount any pretensions of divinity. Whether these 'snap' judgments are the cause of the promeninance of the openly "Gay" in modern society or a lack of religiousity in modern society, we can only be certain that there has been a 'social' loss of innocence concerning sexuality that is a contributing factor.

Now there can be no doubt that the visitor's encounters with the Mother and the Son are concretely sexual, but even in these sequences the sexual contact is initiated by the family members. More succinctly, it is as if the very presence of the visitor is drawing out repressed desires from within these characters. The silent presentation of the other encounters can be viewed in a religious context either as salvific (the visitor saves the maid from a suicide attempt brought on by her own fits of passion while gazing upon him) or healing (the visitor cures the father's physical ailment). It is this second view of the 'silent passages' as being imbued with a divine religiosity that allowed the film to win an award from the Catholic Film Office and gives credence to Marc Gervais, a Canadian Priest's comments," that despite its "suspect" erotic sensibility, TEOREMA's mystical character cannot be questioned. It is an interrogation into the human condition. It is a work on the need to [reach] the absolute and reject the bourgeois condition that alienates man."[14]

Pasolini holds a view that man's pursuit of the absolute is "suspended" and this view is given to us via the Father's severe reaction to the loss of the divine stranger and the structure of the film itself. Throughout the film (even during the opening credits) mysterious shots of an eerie prehistoric landscape (Mt.Etna) are interspersed. At times, the shots 'erupt' in-between scenes, other times the shots are inserted into the film over a biblical quote or after a character's episode is complete. The shots are disconcerting, but not obtrusive to the flow of the story. It is only at the very end of the movie—the completion of the Father's reaction—that these mysterious shots are integrated fully into the narrative and we realize that these shots of a prehistoric landscape were actually flashforwards.[15]

The Father, after giving his factory away to the workers, wanders aimlessly into a busy train station. There, he caresses a young child and is 'chosen' by a male prostitute's unflinching gaze. As if in a trance, he turns away from the prostitute and begins removing all of his clothes until he is completely naked. Pasolini brings the camera down to the Father's feet and cuts to the prehistoric landscape of Mt. Etna, which we can now understand as having been the same landscape intercut throughout the film. The Father walks across this landscape into a close up in front of the camera and in desperation releases a blood curdling scream which ends the film. Clearly, out of options after the divine stranger's abrupt departure, the Father can find no solace in his ownership, in the countenance and caress of a small child, or in the leering eyes of a sexual predator. He is like the solitary figure in Pasolini's poem, LINES FROM THE TESTEMENT, who can find," no lunch or dinner or satisfaction in the world equal to an endless walk through the streets of the poor where you must be wretched and strong, brothers to the dogs."[16]

Pasolini seems to suggest at the conclusion of his 'theorem' that the bourgeois, no matter how great the effort, cannot hold on to the absolute neither in today's world of neo-capitalism (where bourgeois rationalism and consumer ethics control the minds and behaviors of even the poorest of workers) or by trying to return to a pre-industrial or prehistoric past. This severe social critique puts Pasolini and this film in league with radical French sociologist, Jean Baudrillard and his pessimistic critique of consumer society, THE SYSTEM OF OBJECTS (1968); although I can find no evidence that the former was familiar with the work of the latter. It is the structure of the work with its documentary-like beginning (the actual end result of father's reaction to the loss of the divine), silent black and white images, the divine and profane visitor, silent passages, and flash cuts to the prehistoric landscape that provides this, "abandon all hope, ye who enter here," interpretation of TEOREMA. The radical form of this film conceptualizes a radical theory about life.

> **"I too, like Moravia and Bertolucci, am a bourgeois, in fact, a petit-bourgeois, a turd, convinced that my stench is not only scented perfume, but is in fact the only perfume in the world. I too am thus endowed with the characteristics of aestheticism and humor, the typical characteristics of a petit-bourgeois intellectual. This is not a run-of-the-mill confession, but purely and simply a statement of fact."[17]**

Some may suspect that Pasolini was pushing an agenda instead of pursuing a theme given his polemical comments about the bourgeoisie, but with Teorema Pasolini attempts to construct a neo-myth as an intellectual means for resolving what he understood as a conceptual contradiction or duality in post-war Italian society: the loss of the rich and diverse cultural identity of Northern and Southern Italy (exemplified in part by the plurality of regional dialects in the Italian language) through the social conformity brought about by the post-WWII economic miracle and vertically mobile class expectations. Thus, it can be said that Pasolini had an agenda that he transformed into a theme by making the film less an attack on the bourgeoisie and more of an exploration of the tragic changes in modern society.

An American film with a similar mythic conception as Pasolini's TEOREMA is Charles Burnett's TO SLEEP WITH ANGER (1990). In this film, the arrival of a distant friend "from back home" into the restrained family relationships brings not the devastating sexual havoc as Pasolini's divine stranger, but instead baits the tensions that were already repressed within the family relationships. The religiosity of the distant friend's arrival in Burnett's film is one of a pagan sort; ancient Southern superstitions coupled with a biting and bitter irony. Burnett's 'distant friend' is named Harry (Danny Glover) and his sudden unannounced arrival and pagan rituals give him a classic trickster persona.

Harry is a trickster archetype that is evocative of the African Yorba religion's Eshu, the trickster who was," understood to have gotten one of the creator gods drunk at the beginning of time, and that is why there are cripples, albinos, and all others sorts of anomaly in the world."[18] Harry gets everyone he comes into contact with intoxicated by his destructive influence. Soon after his arrival, Gideon (Paul Butler), the patriarch of the family becomes incapacitated with an unexplained illness, the marriage of the younger brother begins to fall apart, the mother, Suzie (Mary Alice), is besieged by an obsessive suitor from her past, and finally the two brothers, Junior (Carl Lumbly) and Sam/Baby Brother (Richard Brooks) are at each other's throats with murderous intent.

Like most trickster archetypes Harry's existence begins and ends in the doorway, at the crossroads, or the transitional spaces that mark the indecision and resistance to change that inflict mere mortals. The powerful emotional tension that Burnett creates and sustains in this film highlights his original presentation of ordinary characters in extraordinary circumstances that grow darker and increasingly malevolent with each subsequent event. Where Pasolini led a pointed attack upon the bourgeoisie in TEOREMA, Burnett's attack is *'intra-racial'* in the sense that Harry is a wicked primordial force from the painful past of African-Americans that exposes the underlying hypocrisies of African-American life in the contemporary post-Civil Rights era. Both Pasolini and Burnett use their 'thaumaturgic' characters to critique the relationships, contingencies and shortcomings of their contemporary society. Burnett reveals the new social chains that enslave contemporary African-American society through the destructive influence of the trickster Harry character. Whether it is the selfish pursuit of money (Baby Brother), control over the female, or the expected rules of behavior that are socially enforced with exacting emotional brutality in familial relationships; Harry exacerbates these and other tensions if not by his actions then also by his mere presence in the household. Burnett, like Pasolini, reveals a "false" utopia (one wonders if those are the only kind) in a familial circumstance that pretends to be satisfactory. But with the arrival of a destructive force from the past, the façade of harmony is threatened with destruction and no one is revealed to be satisfied as circumstances continue to get worse.

Approaching the Conceptual Narrative

Perhaps the first thing to do in preparation for the construction of a conceptual narrative is to determine whether your vision or theory of life is a utopian or dystopian view. By making this determination at the outset it is a rather simple undertaking to see that the story will move in either of two directions:

1) A utopian view presents a self-satisfied world that is disturbed and/or threatened with annihilation by the knowledge of a revealed truth that contradicts its basic assumptions and results in a move towards the acceptance of an alternate/ compromised world view. (e.g. Adam and Eve's banishment from the Garden of Eden and their acceptance of Man's labor and Woman's pain of childbirth.)

2) A dystopian view presents a compromised world of dissatisfaction that is disturbed and/or threatened with a violent overthrow or mass exodus by the

knowledge of a revealed truth and results in a move towards a new beginning or a utopia with a new harmony of relations among its subjects. (e.g. The flood and Noah's Ark)

If a utopian view leads to a compromised pessimism wrought from the indulgence of satisfactions now lost, then a dystopian view leads to a guarded optimism; a kind of recalcitrant hope or wisdom wrought from the pain of dissatisfaction now relieved. In a utopian world view everyone is satiated—or seems to be—until the revelation of the knowledge of a truth that disturbs or threatens this satisfaction.

A perfect example is Steven Spielberg's MINORITY REPORT (2002) where the perfect deterrent to murder is compromised and threatened by the revelation of the knowledge of a truth that directly contradicts its perfection. Another example is the utopian society in Michael Anderson's LOGAN'S RUN (1976), a place where," computerized servo-mechanisms provide all needs and everyone can pursue endless hedonism. Endless, that is, until Lastday."[19] That's when anyone who is age 30 must submit to a ritual that promises rebirth but is actually a forced euthanasia. LOGAN'S RUN and MINORITY REPORT are utopian visions that exaggerate a particular social or political ethos inherent in the present (respectively, the hedonism of the 1970's and the post 9/11 reactionary political agendas) and become subversive protests of contemporary society disguised as science fiction. This was a prophylactic tradition that was perhaps started with Sir Thomas More's book, Utopia, which stands as a subversive critique of contemporary 16th century religious and political vacuousness.

In a dystopian world view the revelation of the knowledge of a truth inspires the dissatisfied to fight or flee the prevailing situation and establish a world that rectifies the injustice. We see this pattern in conceptual films as disparate as Cecil B. De Mille's THE TEN COMMANDMENTS (1956) to Franklin Schaffner's THE PLANET OF THE APES (1968). In THE TEN COMMANDMENTS the revelation that the Pharaoh's son, Moses was born a Hebrew slave threatened both the sovereignty and the absolute hegemony of the Egyptian utopia while simultaneously providing a new hope, a prophet and monotheism to the Hebrew slaves. In THE PLANET OF THE APES the revelation that the dystopian world of apes ruling over humans was the result of a 20th century nuclear holocaust is confirming evidence that the knowledge of a revealed truth is a powerful and motivating catalyst for conceptual narratives. By contrast, dystopian world views seem to function as cautionary tales that warn of the dangers that may develop if contemporary injustices are left unchecked. This is an eschatological tradition that was perhaps wrought from the apocalyptic vision of the Judeo-Christian religion and the recurrent millennial prophecies that," instigate an armed revolution or keep its permanent possibility always alive."[20]

One can easily surmise that utopian and dystopian views are simply two polemical perspectives of the same coin (heads or tails?), but what should interest the screenwriter is how the belief systems of either world view are sustained. What are the lies, omissions, recriminations, inequities and false reasoning that keep the participants believing in the world view that is being threatened with a revealed truth? It is a matter of presenting a worldview as a place where a number of different types of characters need to believe a certain 'hypothesis' that is threatened when a particular character, event or action reveals a truth that contradicts and/or undermines that 'hypothesis'. As a rule most Conceptual Narratives favor a quest story archetype with the goal being the confirmation of the revealed truth through the escape and/or search for a new equitable world, kingdom or circumstance.

So a crucial starting point for the construction of a conceptual narrative is to determine whether or not your story will be utopian or dystopian in context and to establish the nature and subject of the truth that will be revealed to threaten that worldview. It is the revealed truth that will create the conflict which will motivate the characters and set the drama of the narrative in motion.

The conceptual writer/director must have two ingredients for a successful approach to this form:

1) A theory about life that is usually utopian or dystopian
2) Detailed knowledge of the formal aspects of film: narrative and/or technique and a willingness to break these forms to communicate that utopian or dystopian theory.

Although the writer/director can learn the formal aspects of film through academic or technical schools, developing a theory about life whether through copious erudition or personal predilections is quite unique to the individual artist. The films we have previously examined: NAPOLEON DYNAMITE and TEOREMA all begin with the artist's subjective view of life which *necessitated* a different approach to film to conceptualize that theory. The advice here is clear: the writer cannot force the conceptualization of the work without having something to say about life that is revealed through the new approach and vice versa. It is only by finding the right approach formally and finding a certain *personal conviction* about life that the conceptual writer can ever hope complete his work successfully.

NOTES

(1) While it might be prudent to point out that writer/director James Cameron's TERMINATOR II skirts the perplexing issue of time travel/time reversal/and relativity to play upon its new Computer Generated Imaging, Kubrick's 2001 effectively integrates time into its narrative by condensing millions of years of human development into a singular vision.

[2] Pg. 182, PIER PAOLO PASOLINI: CINEMA AS HERESY by Naomi Greene. New Jersey, Princeton University Press. 1990.

[3] There is much controversy surrounding the arrest, trial and conviction of Pino the frog, the male prostitute accused of Pasolini's murder. In the 1981 film WHOEVER SAYS THE TRUTH SHALL DIE by Dutch filmmaker Philo Bergstein an interesting counter-theory concerning Pasolini's murder by Right Wing extremists was postulated. Pressure to reopen the case was increased after the release of Marco Tullio Giordana's 1995 film, PASOLINI: Un Delitto Italiano and these counter-theories have gained such ground that the case was finally reopened in 2005. As of this writing there has been no conclusive evidence that disproves Pino the frog's guilt. I am inclined to side with this political conspiracy theory given the large number of enemies Pasolini created and encountered relating to his outspokenness, success, and his openly homosexual lifestyle in the last years of his life. It stands to reason that the investigation of his murder was not conducted with the same juridical zealousness of other celebrity murders because of his lifestyle and his politics. Moreover, the idea of a conspiracy is supported by writer and friend of Pasolini, Enzo Siciliano in his descriptions of the horrific wounds Pasolini suffered the night of his murder and the," spurts" of blood that left large deeply soaked stains on Pasolini's shirt in his biography of the filmmaker.

[4] Pg. 385, PASOLINI-A BIOGRAPHY by Enzo Siciliano. New York. Random House. 1982

[5] 'This Is Orson Welles,' Orson Welles and Peter Bogdanovich, pg.270.

[6] Pg. 132, Green, Ibid.

[7] Pg. 159, The Passion of Pier Paolo Pasolini, by Sam Rohdie, BFI, 1995

[8] Pg. 317, Siciliano, Ibid.

[9] Pg. 155, PASOLINI by Oswald Stack. Extract from a BBC interview. Bloomington and London. Indiana University Press. 1969

[10] Pg. 155-156, Stack, Ibid.

[11] Pg. 318, Siciliano, Ibid.

[12] Pg. 524, PASOLINI:REQUIEM by Barth David Schwartz. New York. Pantheon Books, 1992.

[13] Pg. 50, Greene, Ibid.

[14] Pgs. 135-136, Greene, Ibid.

[15] For a definition of a flashforward see Linear Narrative footnote #2.

[16] Pg. 213, POEMS by Pier Paolo Pasolini. Trans. MacAffee, Norman and Martinengo, Luciano. New York. Noonday Press. 1996.

[17] Pg. 283, ITALIAN CINEMA: NEO-REALISM TO THE PRESENT by Peter Bondanella. New York. Frederick Unger Publishing Company. 1983.

[18] Pg. 121, TRICKSTER MAKES THIS WORLD by Lewis Hyde. New York. North Point Press. 1998.

[19] Cf. LOGAN'S RUN DVD Linear Notes, Warner Bros. Films, 2002.

[20] Pg. 158, THE HISTORICAL JESUS by John Dominic Crossan, New York. HarperCollins, 1992.

VOIR-DIRE: *IRREVERSIBLE*
Analysis & Interpretation of The Film

The controversy and vehemently dismissive criticism that has been leveled at this film and its creator cannot be ameliorated by the stroke of anyone's pen. The film, itself, is simply meant to elicit opinions and *that* it surely does—and then some. But I will offer an alternative commentary and interpretation. It is my sincere hope that if we can accept this interpretation of Gaspar Noe's IRREVERSIBLE that I will present, we will be able to see that IRREVERSIBLE is in actuality a very spiritual film and not just an empty subversive exercise. But before going any further, a synopsis of the actual story of the film must be recounted.

IRREVERSIBLE: The Story

A woman, who just found out that she is pregnant earlier in the day, goes to a party later that night with her boyfriend and her ex-boyfriend who still loves her. Annoyed with her boyfriend's drug-induced antics and immaturity, she leaves the party to go home alone. She attempts to avoid the danger of crossing a busy boulevard by using an underground tunnel. In the tunnel, she is brutally raped and savagely beaten by a homosexual pimp named, Le Tenia.[1]

As her boyfriend and ex-boyfriend leave the party they discover what has happened to her. The boyfriend becomes enraged and seeks revenge. The ex-boyfriend tries, in vain, to talk him out of it. With sketchy information from two street hoodlums, they track the man named Le Tenia to a sado-masochistic Gay nightclub called Le Rectum. Once inside the club, the boyfriend searches for anyone who knows Le Tenia while the ex-boyfriend follows him in protest.

When the boyfriend confronts two men, he unwittingly picks a fight with the man standing next to 'Le Tenia' and is beaten into submission after getting his arm broken. Just before he can suffer the greatest humiliation, the ex-boyfriend comes to his aid and uses a fire extinguisher to literally beat the brains out of the attacker and kill him. The police and an ambulance come and remove the two. Le Tenia is never questioned or caught.

What Kind of Narrative is This?

Of course, what intrigues us about this now legendary film is the fact that the story in the film is told in reverse; that is, the events are presented in a reverse chronologically contiguous order. So the film is still a linear narrative, but its linearity is not disturbed by the reverse presentation of events; it is still chronologically contiguous. Yet, the reverse chronological presentation of events does have an extraordinary effect upon the reception of the story. The story as its writer/director, Gaspar Noe, has acknowledged in numerous interviews, is just a simple story of revenge. But when one is first watching the film it is difficult to discern the revenge aspect of the tale until the woman is recognized by her boyfriend.

Indeed, by reversing the chronological order of these contiguous events, Gaspar Noe is presenting the audience with a series of mysterious events that are given fictional meanings as the film progresses until the actual story is finally 'discovered'. This is our exact definition of a discovery narrative, as you recall. In reversing the chronological order of events, yet keeping them contiguous, Noe has created a challenging discovery narrative that mystifies otherwise intelligible events, for the first half of the film. Mystifies is not the exact word; what Noe has really done is, he has stripped away our moral veil: the rational and reasonable veil through which we can watch and consume fictional violence without immediate repugnance.

Further evidence that supports the idea the IRREVESIBLE is a discovery narrative is 1) Marcus (Vincent Cassel) is a naïve character confronted by extraordinary wickedness and deceit (the savage rape and beating of his girlfriend by Le Tenia) and 2) the film has a complicity point that separates the 2nd and 3rd acts. On the first note, Marcus naively believed he could exact revenge on his girlfriend's rapist and his machismo was elevated when he discovered that the assailant was Gay. To his chagrin it was he, himself, who was severely injured and almost sexually humiliated in the revenge attempt. On the second note, after the discovery of his girlfriend's condition and some routine police questioning, two shady street characters approach Marcus and Pierre (Albert Dupontel). The street characters offer the opportunity of revenge which Marcus, despite the warnings of Pierre, agrees and becomes a willing accomplice.

If we had known that the events presented to us were part of a plot of revenge beforehand, we would better rationalize the violence and tolerate it. If a man's woman has been brutally raped and savagely beaten, the motive of revenge is not only justified it is expected. Yet Noe, rips this rationalization away from us by deliberately presenting the events in reverse chronological order and destroying that moral veil. The reverse presentation makes the events seem, at first glance, to be the simple recording of unmitigated immoral and savage behavior. It is an understatement to say that the first half of the film is so difficult to swallow that many spectators leave the theatre or television screen in disgust.

An Ignis Fatuus?

Yet, why reverse the chronological order of events? Is it just a stylistically empty exercise in how to present violence out of context? Is this simply a subversive way to present Gay hate crimes and horrific misogyny? Was this peculiar structure just an Ignis fatuus, the so-called deceptive goal or hope drawing attention to a morally repugnant and socially reprehensible film? Gaspar Noe has said that IRREVERSIBLE is not a "brainac" film, but we have to attribute his anti-intellectual/anti-theoretical comments to his own personal hubris.[2] Whether or not he conceived of IRREVERSIBLE as a high concept film with spiritual, moral and artistic intentions is beside the point. The events as presented in the film literally coerce the viewer, critic or theorist to deal with the events as artistic, moral and spiritual phenomena.

Indeed, given the final editorial structure of the film, (e.g. reverse chronology, episodic construction, digital re-framing, free-floating camera work, and DVD chapters arranged according to a counter-clockwise time frame) we are forced to downplay the director's public claims of near total happenstance and naked intuition in the construction of the work. Although Gaspar Noe claims to have prepared the film on the whims of his own intuition and with improvised dialogue—We can assume with certainty that his intuition was informed and guided by some thoughts or observations of human nature and some kind of narrative preparation; narrative preparation in the form of his previous films and the thoughts and observations about human nature that preoccupy all artists, whether they write it down or not. After all, no one can successfully tell a story in reverse without some type of intellectual and artistic preparation or thematic purpose.

A Spiritual Interpretation

There are actually two stories that get told within IRREVERSIBLE and this assertion refers us back to our formal dichotomy stated earlier: the fabula and the syuzhet. The fabula is the mental reconstruction of the events after they have been presented. Once we realize that this is a story of revenge that is being told in reverse through what physicist Hans Reichenbach called," the emotive significance of time," and those specific thermodynamic processes that we witness as irreversible (e.g. Marcus' broken arm, the bludgeoning, and the rape) we can easily reassemble the story in our minds by following the causal chain of those irreversible events.[3] But the syuzhet, which is the physical act of reversing the presentation of events, tells us an alternate story. The 'detached' camera work and the reverse chronology actually suggest an alternate narrator and point of view. To discern this alternate point of view we must look at the difference between: How the story begins and how the film ends. The final shot of IRREVERSIBLE *the film* is really the opening moment of IRREVERSIBLE *the story*.

The film ends with a shot of the stars after the camera has detached itself from all the principal characters and passed through the earth's atmosphere. The moment is the prologue of the story and the epilogue of the film. This suggests to me that the story begins as this 'alternate' narrator has descended from the heavens. After the camera settles upon the character of Alex, it then moves into the apartment and reveals to us a view of the poster of the star-child returning to earth from Stanley Kubrick's film 2001. The detached and rotating camera, coupled with the 2001 'Star child' poster and the final shot of the stars suggest that the alternate narrator and point of view of the film is that of Alex's unborn child.

This is an extremely profound suggestion because the soul of an unborn child might not have any moral framework (and certainly no rational framework) with which to decipher the horrifying events it is witnessing "for the first time". There is no moral connection between the violence and the motive of revenge for this unborn child. This "tabula rasa" justifies presenting the material in reverse and makes literal the notion of philosopher Henri Bergson, who said that," the irreversibility of time must be an appearance relative to our ignorance."[4] We, as spectators, are put into the same position of ignorance as the newly conceived embryo. The hate, violence and revenge are first presented to us without a rational veil which we have been conditioned through experience to accept.

If this interpretation is germane, the syuzhet or narrative suggests something more about this unborn child. The opening shot of the film, a gloomy hallway detached from all principal characters and events, is actually the final moment of the story. The suggestion here is that after Alex's savage rape and brutal beating she physically 'lost' the child. Thus, the soul of this child followed the other parent for the second half of the film: the father, Marcus. It is Marcus who supplied the other half of the genetic material for the child's conception. The detached soul of the unborn (miscarried) child follows Marcus on his journey of misspent revenge. (Again Le Tenia is not captured and the wrong man is murdered)

After Marcus' beating and humiliation, the soul as the camera "floats" away and into an apartment where a man is confessing to have engaged in incest with his daughter. Finally, the "soul" or alternate narrator floats away down the dark hallway. This moment is the epilogue of the story and the prologue of the film. The hallway, itself, becomes a metaphor for transition from this world to another. It is also strangely reminiscent of the underground tunnel where Alex was raped and beaten and the dream she had of a tunnel; all of these places being places of transition.

So to sum up, I believe, IRREVERSIBLE tells us two stories:

1) The fabula of revenge that tells the direct story of a boyfriend desperately searching for the man who has brutally raped and beaten his girlfriend.
2) The syuzhet which passively tells the story of the soul of an unborn child descending from the heavens, attaching itself to the spirit of the mother who is carrying it, the rape and beating that causes the miscarriage and finally the departure of the soul which is suggested by the transitional space of the hallway.

This is the "what" that has been discovered at the end of the film: this suggestion of a 'detached' narrator whose alternate point of view is what thematically justifies the reverse chronology and the uncompromising presentation of the events. The free floating camera work and digital re-framing is obviously not motivated by the characters on screen. This alternate point of view is being suggested by the filmmaker and my 'spiritual' interpretation is rooted in my understanding of the final shot of the film as the opening moment of the story: the heavens. There can be no doubt that the fictional theme of IRREVERSIBLE is revenge, but the reality theme is an exception to the previously expressed rule in that the film substitutes a metaphysical theme (that of the subjective consciousness of an unborn child) for the usual reality theme that is peculiar to most discover narratives.

In many ways there is room for argument that IRREVERSIBLE is a conceptual film as well, since it clearly presents a dystopian view of life and breaks conventional film (narrative) form to tell it. But this is pretty much obvious so I will leave that discussion to the pens of others. What is most important to understand about IRREVERSIBLE is the fact that it is a linear discovery narrative whose mysterious fictional events are given meaning as the film progresses. This was achieved by using an ordinary story of revenge and reversing the chronology of contiguous events. More than any contemporary film IRREVERSIBLE reveals the heightened narrative possibilities that are still being discovered within the medium that so many of us had thought was exhausted.

NOTES

[1]   Le Tenia is French for Tapeworm. See: The Breakthrough Scene chapter for a detailed discussion of the infamous rape scene of this film.

[2]   Various interviews with Writer/Director Gaspar Noe are available on the internet. At iofilm he says," His starting point was," a rape and revenge movie, told backwards." Also see,' Tunnel Visionary: Gaspar Noe's Brutal IRREVERSIBLE,' on Indiewire.com.

[3]   Cf. Hans Reichenbach,THE DIRECTION OF TIME. 1956. University of California. Berkeley.

[4]   Pg. 7, CREATIVE EVOLUTION by Henri Bergson. 1911. Dover Publications. New York.

ALTERNATE REALITIES

"Reality is that which, when you stop believing in it, doesn't go away."

-Philip K. Dick

Truly compelling dialogue always implies something else other than the immediate subject within it. There is a great saying among screenwriters, it goes: *People sometimes don't say what they really mean.* We often have to infer what someone is really trying to say to us even though the person speaking feels that they are speaking directly. Some people attempt to infer alternate meanings from the most direct statements or honest actions. In life, we might call this build up of inferred meaning: ulterior motives. In film, we should call this build up of inferred meaning: An Alternate Reality. It is crucial that we absorb the meaning of the phrase, ulterior motive, into this phrase, alternate reality, because life, for some people, is a continuous process of decipherment through inference, whereas, a single film is a discontinuous process of decipherment through image and sound of a fictional reality. In short, a film requires an average of two hours worth of decipherment and life just goes on. The deciphering of an ulterior motive is the lens through which an alternate reality can be viewed. By alternate reality, I mean an alternate goal for a character or group of characters that is hidden by the feigning of allegiance to others or the emotionless practice of rituals that gain and control the confidence of others.[1]

For the spectator viewing a narrative film, assumptions, judgments, prejudices, and inferences are drawn from the interaction of dialogue, action, sound and image. If a character gets out of the driver's seat of a car, we assume the character owns this car until we are told or shown otherwise. When characters speak to each other the spectator is immediately engaged in an attempt to decipher the real meaning of the words exchanged to infer or discover the plot of the film. It is the plot—and the process of uncovering the plot—that creates an alternate reality in film.

To be specific, an alternate reality is the completed build up of inferences and assumptions that gives relevance to the entire construction of a film's narrative. Hitchcock once said that,' drama is life with the dull bits cut out.' Well, the alternate reality produced by narrative film is the audience's inferences about what has been cut out. For instance, a majority of Alfred Hitchcock films (particularly those films of his magnificent decade: 1954-1964) are pure exercises in the establishment and maintenance of an alternate reality, that is usually confirmed for an audience by an explanatory scene within the final act.

This establishment and confirmation is quite pronounced in,' NORTH BY NORTHWEST,' which has Roger Thornhill (Cary Grant) as an advertising executive mistaken as a government secret agent. The inference throughout the first two acts of the film reveals the intricacies of a secret society of criminals and government agents, that is finally confirmed for us by a meeting of high level government officials who discuss what to do about,' Thornhill.' The plot of the film is the spectator's process of deciphering this alternate reality which dovetails into the confirmation. Although much of the dramatic power of Hitchcock's films are hinged upon the fact that his confirmation scenes do more than confirm the audience's assumptions and inferences, these important scenes often reveal a deeper level within the alternate reality that has been established.

For example, it is revealed that the man Roger Thornhill has been mistaken for,' George Kaplan,' does not even exist; he is a fictional character within the fiction that these high level government officials have created to entrap a foreign spy. Much of the pleasure of this film involves the decipherment of its plot through the engaging performances within performances of glamorous Hollywood stars (Cary Grant, Eva Marie Saint, and James Mason) and the effective use of double entendre in its dialogue to temporarily cloak its themes of homosexuality, sexual licentiousness, and covert government operations. To return to the opening statement, the alternate reality is that 'something else' underneath the immediate subject of the dialogue that undermines our first impressions of a character or their inter-relationships to other characters.

Many people feel that they speak directly and there is no need to infer what they have actually said, but it is this direct speaking person who has the most rumors, slander, and misconceptions surrounding his or her persona. In our times, the truth is circumspect, heroes have feet of clay, and everybody seems to want something from everybody else. And while this conception of an alternate reality has cynical underpinnings it is just such underpinnings that intensify drama.

THE DECIPHERMENT

'Politicians, ugly buildings and whores all get respectable if they last long enough.'

-John Huston (Chinatown, Dir. Roman Polanski/Wri. Robert Towne-1975)

Sociological evidence supports the idea that as we become socialized we learn to conceal our true feelings and we simultaneously begin to disguise our immediate wants in the present to secure our distant goals in the future.[2] It is a second birth from childhood to adolescence which manifests itself in white lies, flattery, and manipulation. For a growing teenager it becomes extremely important that they learn to decipher the intense behaviors and actions of others so that they know how to protect their feelings and themselves. It is the time when the school bully is revealed as a lonely coward and the girl and boy who loath each other are revealed to actually like each other.

This process of decipherment through inference becomes continuous for most of us, creating an alternate reality that can only be understood when one looks behind immediate words and actions to uncover the unspoken motivations and circumstances of an individual or group's behaviors. Indeed, isn't this process of decipherment exactly what Vito Corleone (Marlon Brando) was trying to teach Michael Corleone (Al Pacino) during the last days of his life in Francis Ford Coppola's,' THE GODFATHER'?

> *"Now listen, whoever comes to you with this Barzini meeting—He's the traitor. Don't forget that."*

If this line from the script does not betray the memory, Vito Corleone was wise to the fact that Barzini was behind the troubles that befell the Corleone family, including the assassination attempt on his life and the death of his son Santino (James Caan). He learned (deciphered) this from a formal meeting with all of the mafia 'families' where a glance conveyed to him this important fact.

In effect, nothing is genuine: no feeling, expression, sentiment, or gesture carries with it an absolute certainty that one could understand as purely altruistic. Life becomes an enormous scheme to achieve goals by indirect, indecent, and indefatigable means. If this sounds like a paranoid socio-political theory more so than everyday life, it might be true, but so pervasive and innocuous is this process that it need not be a theory of simple cynicism than it is a dispassionate observation of human behavior. As noted science fiction author Philip K. Dick pondered," Maybe each human being lives in a unique world, a private world, a world different from those inhabited and experienced by all other humans. And that led me to wonder, If reality differs from person to person, can we speak of reality singular, or shouldn't we really be talking about plural realities? And if there are plural realities, are some more true (more real) than others?"[3] Film is not only the perfect medium to record this process, narrative film actually solicits the audience's attention to decipher alternate realities.

Each time we enter the theatre we want to know,' What is this film really about?' Even after numerous television advertisements, celebrity appearances, newspaper ads and reviews—we just have to know what the film is really about. What is the plot of this film? No one wants to feel gullible if there is a surprise ending. The spectator is primed

142

into inferring from his need to decipher, literally why something has been filmed. The success of a particular film depends on how well the prospective audience has been primed as much as it does on the quality of the actual work.

The Alternate Reality: A Specific Analysis
GOODFELLAS
Written by Nicholas Pileggi and Martin Scorsese

It seems that the emerging screenwriter has no way of penning words that do not evoke an alternate reality. Every portion of dialogue can reveal another level of meaning. Many writers have attempted to remove the veil and decode this odd plastic world of words and actions that mean something else other that its direct intentions: a specific example of this decoding is actually practiced by the characters throughout Martin Scorsese and Nicholas Pileggi's film,' GOODFELLAS (1990). Billed as 30 years of life in the mafia, Goodfellas was a swift moving documentary-like drama whose violence was not nearly as chilling as the levels of inferences within the dialogue which forced its audiences to judge and re-judge, assume and confirm the 'uncloaked' motivations and intentions of its cast of mafia characters.

One scene, in particular, gives us a dynamic example of how this script weaved an intricate web of decipherment and the use of this decipherment to both remove the cloak of unspoken intentions and increase the dramatic tension. The scene comes late in the film after lead character, Henry Hill (Ray Liotta) had been busted for narcotics trafficking and is out on bail. He meets with one of his best friends and partner in crime, Jimmy Conway (Robert DeNiro) in a local diner to discuss his case:

INT. SHERWOOD DINER. LATE MORNING

HENRY walks in and finds Jimmy at the window booth. Although there is food on the table, nothing seems to have been touched.

HENRY: (Voice-over) If you're part of a crew, nobody ever tells you that they're going to kill you. It doesn't happen that way. There aren't any arguments or curses like in the movies. So your murderers come with smiles. They come as your friends, the people who have cared for you all your life, and they always seem to come at a time when you're at your weakest and most in need of their help. So I met Jimmy in a crowded place we both knew. I got there fifteen minutes early and I saw that Jimmy was already there.

JIMMY: Hey. Hi. How you doing?

HENRY: (Voice-over) He took the booth near the window so he could see everyone who drove up to the restaurant. He wanted to make sure I wasn't tailed. He was jumpy. He hadn't touched a thing.

HENRY: I'm just a little fucked up, but I'm, you know, I'll be okay.

JIMMY: You want something to eat?

HENRY: Naw, my stom-

JIMMY:	Eat something.
HENRY:	Naw, the aggravation's got my stomach going. I'm just gonna get a cup of coffee. That's it.
JIMMY:	(To Waitress) Could we have a cup of coffee, please?
HENRY:	(Voice-over) On the surface, of course, everything was supposed to be fine. We were supposed to be discussing my case. But I had the feeling Jimmy was trying to sense whether I was going to rat him out to save my neck.
JIMMY:	You made sure nobody tailed you, didn't you?
HENRY:	Oh, yeah. Yeah, you know, drove around for about half an hour before I got here. In and out. So it's all right.
JIMMY:	I been telling you all your whole life, don't talk on the fucking phone, right? Now you understand, huh? But it's gonna be okay. I think you got a good chance of beating the case. Yeah, well . . . You know that kid, you know, from the city we're talking about? You know I 'm talking-
HENRY:	Ye-ah . . .
JIMMY:	Well, the kid turned out to be a rat. As soon as he got pinched, he ratted everybody out, he ratted youse all out. But I know where he is. He's hiding now. He's, you know, he's—Know what I'm saying? Would you have a problem going with Anthony on vacation? You know, take care of that?
HENRY:	Uh-huh. No, not at all.
JIMMY:	That way they got nothing. Huh?

(JIMMY slips a matchbook across the table to HENRY. Freeze frames on JIMMY and then HENRY.)

HENRY:	(Voice-over) Jimmy had never asked me to whack somebody before. But now he's asking me to go down to Florida and do a hit with Anthony. That's when I knew I would never have come back from Florida alive.
JIMMY:	Thank you.
HENRY:	You know, um, I think I'll have another coffee.
WAITRESS:	Yes, sure.

[GOODFELLAS, Martin Scorsese and Nicholas Pileggi, pgs. 125-127, Faber and Faber, 1990]

Immediately, the viewer is aware of four elements evolving throughout this brief scene:

1.) The suspicion Henry Hill harbors against his friend, Jimmy Conway.
2.) The discussion of Henry Hill's impending trial.
3.) The murder Jimmy Conway wants Henry Hill to commit.
4.) And most importantly, Henry Hill's decipherment of an alternate reality.

It is Henry Hill who tips the audience off into deciphering the alternate intentions of Jimmy Conway. Had the scene have been written without Hill's voice-overs it would have taken an incredible amount of inference to decipher that Jimmy wanted to kill Henry: more than an average audience would have been willing to infer. But beyond prompting the audience, Henry Hill's voice-over actually increases the tension between the fictional reality and the alternate reality, by giving a banal meeting in a diner a life threatening connotation.

The location of the scene is almost pure Hitchcock: a crowded diner, during the day, with a polite waitress is the meeting place of the Mafioso to plan murder and treachery. Safety in a public commercial establishment is challenged and usurped. The tension of this scene is based on the audience's identification with Henry Hill as a guilty, but truthful, character in his voice-overs. He had been guiding us through his experiences for a majority of the film, deciphering the real meanings behind otherwise cloaked mafia actions and meetings.

The threat of death hangs both within the dialogue (Conway wants Hill to murder someone out of town) and beyond the dialogue, if we understand Hill's voice-over it is clear that Conway is also trying to infer what are Henry Hill's true intentions. If we were to apply Jean Cocteau's comment that the cinema captures," death at work," then the freeze-frame itself is evocative of a sudden death; a temps mort or caesura of the 'imprint of recorded time' that stuns the spectator like the sudden death of an acquaintance we would have adored to become our friend. [4] Finally, in the concluding voice-over Henry Hill confirms for us the alternate reality of Conway's conversation:

HENRY: (Voice-over) Jimmy had never asked me to whack somebody before. But now he's asking me to go down to Florida and do a hit with Anthony. That's when I knew I would never have come back from Florida alive.

Although, this decipherment of an alternate reality has been important for the length of this entire movie, it is most crucial here in this scene because of the friendship between Conway and Hill. How could we ever suspect a breach in this thirty year criminal partnership unless Henry Hill told us how to decipher the banal fictional reality? GOODFELLAS is a very sophisticated example of a film whose entire plot is about the decipherment through inference of a nefarious alternate reality. Scorsese tells us, himself, that, "GOODFELLAS is an indictment. I had to do it in such a way as to make people angry about the state of things, about organized crime and how and why it works. Why does it work? What is it in our society that makes it work so well and operate on such a grand scale?"[5]

It might be fruitful to point out that a film from Martin Scorsese's adolescence, which he has presented in re-release on DVD, utilizes an almost total dependence on the decipherment of an alternate reality; that film is Abraham Polonsky's,' FORCE OF EVIL (1949).' This fascinating drama uses the criminal numbers racket as a reality theme that must be deciphered via a coded language identified and defined by its lead character in voice-over. Clearly, the similarity between Polonsky's,' Force of Evil,' and Scorsese's,' GOODFELLAS,' rests on this need to document, or rather, decode a criminal underworld.

But now it is best to apply this examination of an alternate reality and its mechanics to the construction of a writer's original material.

THE MEANING OF A SCENE

"Hide the ideas, but so that people find them. The most important will be the most hidden."

Robert Bresson, NOTES ON THE CINEMATOGRAPHER pg.34

Because in real life we try, often desperately, to infer what someone really means, even if the person speaking is sincere and truthful, to construct a scene to effectively solicit a viewer's penchant for decipherment through inference of an alternate reality, the writer must: 1) identify how the scene anticipates or is a variation of the demonstration of his theme; 2) isolate which actions, dialogue, setting or circumstance will first attract the audience and distract them from your ulterior purpose for using the scene. (Remember the banal setting and routine meeting between Henry Hill and Jimmy Conway) This sounds more complicated than it really is, but a useful tool in understanding how this all works is to sit back in a theatre or living room while others are watching a movie (preferably one that you have already seen) and listen to the comments of an audience. If you listen close enough you will hear how the audience is deciphering the events on the screen, even though you know that the meaning of the scene is unclear or won't be fully apparent until the end of the film. What you will be witnessing is the 'process of decipherment through inference' that I have been trying to describe.

In some theatres and in front of many television sets the comments about the events on screen are loud and distracting . . . and quite often more entertaining than the movie itself. Therefore, knowing that the audience is trying to decipher your movie starting at the opening credits, you can bait, elude, or reverse this process by the way you construct your scenes. You can either reduce the amount of words spoken on the screen by your characters and utilize their actions as counterpoint (this technique is the very key to understanding films by Michelangelo Antonioni) or you can fill up the screen with tons of dialogue to force the audience to aggressively attempt to decipher what is really going on on-screen (as the script from a film like THE USUAL SUSPECTS (1995) makes abundantly clear).

For instance, two characters are in love with each other, it would be undramatic to just have the male say,' I love you,' and the female say,' I love you too.' The audience would balk at the crystal clear sentimentality of such a display. But if the writer sets aside the immediate meaning of the scene (the two characters are in love) and baits the audience by constructing the scene to *reveal* that the two characters are in love with each other, then that scene will have a greater dramatic potential.

The writer/director must remember that he is not in the position of 'preaching a story' or hammering the meaning of a scene into the audience's heads—he is in the position of showing, or rather, revealing a story; if done sincerely and with enough originality, the writer may not even have to use the word,' Love.' The dramatic potential is unlimited here, even with this our most dramatized human emotion, because by eliminating the word love the writer now has a variety of alternative options that are either specifically cinematic or heightened by the language of cinema to reveal that one of the characters is in love, while the other is insincere-or-one is loved, but the other doesn't know what real love is. By eliminating the word 'love' the question for the writer\filmmaker is how can love be demonstrated without being cliché?

The variations and possibilities are as endless as the creativity inside the writer. The immediate meaning of a scene, for the writer, is simply a guidepost. The words he chooses or chooses not to use must ignite the audience's hunger for an alternate reality. But the writer must always stay within sight of his guidepost or else he may lose his way during the scene. This is why he must identify the major theme and figure out how best to demonstrate it. But most importantly, the writer must remember that there is going to be an audience for his work and this audience is heavily involved in the production of meaning during his scene. Hitchcock was a master at this ability to play upon the way audience is trying to decipher his films through inference.

If we remember the murder of Marion Crane in 'PSYCHO', contemporary audiences were quite concerned with the $40,000 dollars Norman Bates was forgetting about after the murder, but in actuality the money was the least of Norman's concerns and his murders were murders of passion not profit as the audience may have incorrectly assumed. To conclude, even though the audience was incorrect, they 'entertained' themselves with the money and the idea that Norman seemed to be forgetting about it as he cleaned up the murder scene. It was Hitchcock, as author of the film, who knowingly baited the audience with the money as a detail within his shots. The key here is that the drama of the film reveals the plot or alternate reality; many writers start with a plot and have no real drama that allows the audience to entertain themselves while they attempt to decipher the plot.

NOTES

[1]   For an in-depth discussion of goal see the chapter, Conflict and Goal: The Substructure of Dramaturgy.

[2]   'The family can moderate or magnify any natural predispositions. The interaction between parent and child may make the latter more or less impulsive, more or less willing to take the feelings of others into account.' Crime and Human Nature, James Q. Wilson and Richard J, Herrnstein, pg. 217.

[3]   Pg. 261, How to Build a Universe That Doesn't Fall Apart Two Days Later, in THE SHIFTING REALITIES OF PHILIP K. DICK, ed. by Lawrence Sutin. New York. Vintage Books. 1995

[4]   Pg. 100, PASOLINI: CINEMA AS HERESY by Naomi Greene.

[5]   Pgs. 275-276, MARTIN SCORSESE: A JOURNEY by Mary Pat Kelly. New York. Thunder's Mouth Press. 1991.

APPROACHING THE BACKSTORY

For the writer approaching any story, he or she must realize that they are writing several stories at once: 1) the story as planned with its dramatic events, actions and circumstances and 2) the back-story that supports almost all of the dialogue, actions and behaviors they are writing about now. One great way to make building back-stories easier is the use of character biographies: a full detailed outlining of each lead and supporting character and their relationships to each other before your story began. Much of this material makes up the foundation of a back-story that can be understood as your script advances to its conclusion. This may seem like a cumbersome and unnecessary task (especially since a back-story is usually only given in short fragments) but character biographies however detailed or brief helps to establish a distinctive perspective for a character as well as defining the interrelationships among characters. A character biography can also help a writer define the ultimate goal of a character for a writer as well as enrich the conflict and the story.

I have already demonstrated how an alternate reality can be discerned in particular contemporary films, but a back-story can be pieced together from selected lines of dialogue, repeated actions, costuming, physique, and art direction within the film that reflects into the past and adds substance to your characters while they are on-screen. What makes up a back-story are the bits and pieces of a group or an individual's past that are carried forward into the present. Much like the French philosopher Henri Bergson's description of duration or memory as," the continuous progress of the past which gnaws into the future and which swells as it advances."[1] The back-story may be simply defined as all the preceding events, circumstances and situations that inform all that which is presently being seen on screen. The back-story is all that has occurred prior to the camera's arrival to record your characters.

For instance, in Ridley Scott's ALIEN the first act of the film tells us a number of important details that reveal a back-story that had existed prior to the actual story we are now watching. When we first encounter the space mining ship, Nostromo, we learn that this is a routine mission to mine ore from a distant planet and bring it back to earth that the character of Brett (Harry Dean Stanton) refers to as,' the old freezerinos.' The original mission and this character's line of dialogue points to the conclusion that the earth has become a frigid wasteland that has to use extra-terrestrial fuel from distant planets to sustain life. This is a back-story, sketched ever-so-delicately by screenwriter Dan O'Bannon.

When we first see the Alien spaceship and the fossilized creature inside of the ship, we can clearly see the ruptured chest with ribs bent outwards as if the creature exploded from inside. After Ripley (Sigourney Weaver) deciphers part of the rescue beacon's message as a warning, we realize that the fossilized creature was another victim of the alien predator. Moreover, that this initial victim attempted to warn any approaching ships about the horror that lay beneath its own ship's deck. Again, the back-story, the history of past actions, events, and thoughts swells into the action, events and dialogue of the story [proper] we are watching as present tense.

A lot of writers fail in writing competent screenplays for two reasons:

1) they attempt to force both the back-story and the actual story together as one without a thematic concept to limit what should stay in and what should stay out of the script. This circumstance can more often than not result in too many situations, characters, and diverse actions going on in their scripts. Specifically, a back-story should be suggested with great economy and precise attention to the details that will give the maximum impact so that the," past gnaws into the future," but does not overwhelm the present circumstances we are watching.

2) The writer attempts to concentrate solely on the actual story without giving their characters a past or future to discuss, react against, or struggle to express. Moreover, characters written this way have a 'cardboard' perfunctory quality reminiscent of the unintentional comedy of early American porno films. This circumstance causes the writer to create caricatures instead of characters and weakens the overall effectiveness of their story. A well thought out back-story gives depth to characters and adds richness to a story.

If we force the back-story and the actual story together as one without a thematic limitation or justification we find we'll end up with a bloated script that is too dialogue laden to support the actual story on the screen. The simplest explanation of this flaw is that the writer is trying to explain the actions of a particular character or set of characters instead of trying to reveal these characters to us. In trying to give all of the back-story in flashbacks or poorly realized scenes with other characters we lose both the actual story and the characters because the flashbacks can become too cumbersome and disruptive or we are introducing too many small supporting characters whom we may never see again. One should not confuse exposition for back-story. In other words, don't confuse explaining how a character or their circumstances came to be with why the character acts that way in those circumstances.

The writer must use the back-story to color the mind set of the characters on screen during the actual story. This coloring can be achieved carefully through precise dialogue exchanges, costuming, actions or inactions of major characters rather than through clumsy flashbacks or long winded conversations. We can find a simple example of this coloring in ALIEN between Parker (Yapet Koto) and Brett in the scene after the Nostromo has left the orbit of the desolate planet and the alien creature has allegedly been taken off of a crew member's face:

PARKER

What I think we should do is just freeze him. I mean, if he's got a disease why don't we just stop it where it is. We can always get to a doctor when we get back home.

BRETT

Right.

RIPLEY

Whenever he say's anything you say right, Brett, you know that?

BRETT

Right.

RIPLEY

(Sighs) Parker what do you think you're staff just follows you around and says right . . . It's like a regular parrot.

PARKER

(Laughing slightly to Brett)

Yeah, shape up, what are you some kind of parrot?

BRETT

Right.

DALLAS

Oh, come on! Knock it off! Cain's gonna have to go into quarantine and that's it!

We note here how this scene, as well as several other smaller scenes between Parker and Brett, establishes both a friendship and the depth of that friendship forged through many space missions together—all without flashbacks or dwelling on the specific nature of those previous missions. **Skillful writing is writing that establishes the personality of a character or the relationships of a set of characters as if they existed prior to our camera filming these characters at this particular moment in time.** In the previous scene the 'in-joking' between Parker and Brett is the sort of camaraderie that can only be forged by two people knowing each other very well in the past or having enough similar and shared experiences to agree to find such nonsense as humorous.

On the other hand, if a writer dismisses or fails to provide or explore a back-story, their characters can easily become flat or simple tools of the plot which makes for excruciating viewing. No matter how wonderful the plot of a story may be the back-story which informs the way your characters interact with each other in dialogue or action is how you give your film depth. It is the back-story that provides the dramatic material for the actual story, because it gives the viewer clues about the personalities, relationships, or emotional worlds of each character they are watching.

The selection of back-story is deeply tied to the theme of your screenplay. At the risk of becoming overly psychological, a writer must observe and explore why people behave the way they do in real life; in learning what makes people tick—which is a lifelong task—you can apply this knowledge to the characters you create. The more complex your observations in real life, the more complex your characters can become in your fiction. For instance, it is not enough to give a lead character a background of childhood sexual abuse, but one must also presume or theorize how such a background would manifest itself in the character's adult life which would be the point upon which this character is now being 'filmed'.

Alfred Hitchcock's much disparaged film, MARNIE (1964) is just such a film which takes an early childhood trauma and dramatizes its adult manifestation. For the eponymous character, Marnie (Tippi Hedren), an early childhood trauma has manifested itself in her adult life as kleptomania and a deep sexual aversion to men. Where contemporary critics were outraged at Hitchcock's 'naive' psychological presumptions, newly uncovered psychoanalytic evidence, initially suppressed by Sigmund Freud, proves that Hitchcock and his screenwriter Jay Presson Allen were right on target in revealing how early childhood trauma can manifest itself as an adult neurosis and severely affect a character's emotional world.[2]

Where back-story can color and shade a character or set of characters, a thorough character biography can also allow the writer to understand how each character in his ensemble might respond in specific conversations and circumstances. So the key here is, even after a story has been written, to invest your story with characters you must understand what makes your characters 'tick' and a hint of advice is not to always concentrate on the character you feel you know the best, but rather, give careful thought to the characters you feel you don't know that well.

For example, I knew a writer who had his flawed character down pat: he knew exactly what made his scarred lead character 'tick', but his weakness as a writer was revealed in not knowing what made his normal co-lead character, so normal. In just assuming that this normal character was normal—this particular character was boring and lacked insightful dialogue and purpose within the story, which in turn, made the entire script seem flat; no dramatics could ensue from an over developed scarred character and an under developed normal character. The question this writer would have to explore, develop, and perhaps answer is what makes his normal character so level-headed? Indeed, what makes us consider someone normal?

Returning to our earlier example, ALIEN reveals itself as a powerful script that was skillfully written because we can discern a back-story underneath what we are witnessing, without losing our way as we watch the story [proper] unfold. We may only discern the particulars of this back-story, after repeated viewings, but any film that warrants repeated viewing, just for the beauty of its back-story, is damn near as close to a classic as we can get now-a-days.

The use of a thematically limited back-story in dialogue forces a writer to use dialogue with as much economy as possible. The writer must find lines that say more while using less. For instance, Jake Gittes (Jack Nicholson) past as a corrupt street officer who threw his career away over a pretty girl in CHINATOWN (1974) is never told directly in Robert Towne's script as directed by Roman Polanski, but the context and the comments from several supporting characters allude to this tragic past. The famous ending line," Forget it Jake, it's Chinatown," intimates the apathetic state of mind that Robert Towne was attempting to explain to an obtuse producer Robert Evans who admits that he," didn't know what the fuck he was talking about," even though he went on to produce the classic film.

In CHINATOWN the back stories of several characters are given with great economy as the part reveals the whole. The skillful use of a back-story is an economical and well selected use of dialogue, costume, behavior—even hairstyle that reveals to us how much of a character's past has been carried forward into the present that we are watching on screen. Towne's concept of 'a state of mind' is a particularly interesting way of describing how back-story influences the characters on screen; it creates a continuous relationship between the past and the present in the mind of the character(s) involved in the story.

IS THE PAST GONE? Film Analysis: BROKEN FLOWERS by Jim Jarmusch

American independent filmmaker, Jim Jarmusch has stated in various articles his disdain for 'back-story', but his film BROKEN FLOWERS (2005) decisively betrays that disdain since it is, itself, a penetrating inquiry into the back stories of an aging Don Juan and his past loves and losses. Bill Murray plays Don Johnston, a gray haired playboy caught in transition when a current girlfriend announces her departure from their relationship. At that moment, he receives an anonymous pink letter, presumably, from a past love who reveals that he had fathered a son and that son may or may not be looking for him. Stunned, but emotionally disinterested by the news, he is encouraged by his neighbor and best friend, Winston (Jeffery Wright) to embark on a quest to discover from a list of five of his former loves (one of whom is deceased) who could be the mother of the son he has never known.

I suspect that what causes such disdain for Jarmusch concerning back-story is the lack of innovation, imagination and the often formulaic approach and rationale that many amateur and studio writers use to tell an audience the back-story of their characters. With BROKEN FLOWERS, Jarmusch finds rich, inventive, and brilliant ways to reveal the back-story of his characters. Unimaginative writers usually have a character tell some personal trauma, defining moment or dream that is used to distinguish that character and give the audience an easy way to understand that character's perspective. The dreaded flashback has become a woeful cliché to present the back-story of a character who exhibits the simplistic "once bitten, twice shy," characteristics.

Yet, Jarmusch demonstrates in BROKEN FLOWERS that back-story can be presented and suggested in a variety of clear and concise strategies. Back-story itself does not always immediately appear as a logical antecedent to the way people are in the present; often the back-story can affect people in ways that are counter-intuitive. The present life and circumstance of each of the four females reveals to us the past relationship Don had with them with a lucidity and economy unique in American cinema to date. BROKEN FLOWERS is in many ways a film about looking back on what cannot be retrieved.

Five Women, One Deceased

The four living women, Laura (Sharon Stone), Dora (Francis Conroy), Carmen (Jessica Lange) and Penny (Tilda Swinton) become a richly textured, but enigmatic quartet revealing a past life that Don accepts that he can never regain. The back-story between Don and the recently widowed Laura who lives with her daughter is presented by analogy through her teenage daughter's precocious and unselfconscious behaviors. One can surmise through a variety of behaviors performed by the daughter (her flirtatiousness, exhibitionism), how a younger Don found himself in a relationship with the mother years ago.

The daughter, Lolita (Alexis Dziena), is a mirror image in behavior, temperament, and body type of her mother. When Don does finally see Laura, she arrives driving a fast muscle car and later we learn (at the very tail end of a "catch up" story) that she was married to a race car driver who died," in a ball of flames," after a racing accident. The muscle car is an obvious object from the past carried forward into the present.

Another significant delivery of back-story comes in a post-coital morning after gesture made by Laura on the porch of her house as Don prepares to leave. She kisses his hand. This is a powerful gesture of appreciation, affection and adoration made all the more conspicuous because it is the woman delivering it to the man. There is a hopeless romanticism in this gesture that tells us so much more about Laura than words could ever explain. Just as Don was told by his friend Winston to," look for clues," concerning which of these women could be the mother of his unknown son, we, the audience, look for clues about the past relationships and current circumstances of all those involved in Don's strange quest.

When Don arrives at the pristine pre-fabricated home of another ex-lover, Dora, he is dumbstruck by the awesome difference between the woman sitting in front of him and the woman he met so long ago. Jarmusch builds up the cloistered, controlled and well kept existence of Dora and her husband, Ron (Christopher McDonald), until with a single stroke the back-story of the past relationship between Don and Dora is revealed with a single photograph. It is a small framed black and white photo of a younger Dora as a free-spirited "hippy-chick" that Dora's husband brings out to show Don. When he leaves the room to return the photo, Don quietly asks," Didn't I take that picture of you?" "Yes," Dora answers him.

It is with this single item and the brief question and answer that a "clue" to their back-story is revealed. The photo and the question give a clear suggestion that these two met during the late sixties or early seventies and that their affair was in many ways tied to the idealism and youth of that era. This photograph also gives a clue about the depth of Dora's current self-imprisonment inside of the pre-fabricated home with her pre-fabricated food and lifestyle of empty perfection. It would seem that the once free-spirited Dora has become a prisoner of her own fears after the hippy era ended.

"It's such a valuable part of life, randomness . . . chance," Jarmusch has said and he uses BROKEN FLOWERS to demonstrate his theme in how back-story is not always a logical progression or immediately recognizable cause of a person's present circumstance. Back-story informs the present rather than explains the present. A specific example of this highly strategic and counter-intuitive use of back-story is on display when Don meets another ex-lover, Carmen. She has become a doctor and presently runs an animal psychiatry clinic. While waiting to see her at her office, Don notices that she has written several books on the subject of animal psychiatry and that she is assisted by a young, temperamental secretary.

In this sequence, Carmen rather straightforwardly details how the loss of her dog, Winston, caused her to notice that she had a gift to communicate with animals. Yet the more back-story she gives about herself the more she ignores the details of the past relationship she had with Don. In fact it is subtly implied that she is now enjoying a lesbian relationship with her secretary. Her current circumstances and her self-disclosed back-story give no indication about her past relationship with Don. She seems an altogether different person. But in this instance it is not the content of the back-story but instead the quality of it that provides a clue.

When Don mentions that Carmen wanted to be a lawyer and that she was," so passionate about," becoming a lawyer we are being given a clue to the back-story that informs the circumstances of Carmen's current life. It is her passion, her ability to change the course of her life intuitively that conveys to us that the same passion is what fueled their earlier relationship. The three books, doctoral degree (after acquiring her law degree) and her current lesbian relationship all point to a woman guided and committed to her passions for as long as they inspire her. When Don mentions the passion of her youth he is at once talking about the passion of their previous relationship and the passion of her current life.

The sequence between Carmen and Don demonstrates that back-story should not always be approached as a facile cause and effect formula. We can change the direction of our lives willingly or have the direction changed by chance. Although a back-story can be fully written out beforehand, in the subsequent film it is usually delivered in tantalizing glimpses and short bursts that suggest a larger story. Back-story usually provides two important foundations in a script: 1) It establishes and maintains a consistent state of mind for a character or among characters and 2) it informs the present with the past through the objects, costume, rituals, and dialogue that are held onto by the character(s).

The final living female that Don visits is Penny (Tilda Swinton) who lives on a farm in a backwoods rural area. When he meets her on the front porch she is not especially moved to see him. Don looks for clues and he sees a pink typewriter and a pink motorcycle that could be clues concerning the pink letter he received that started his quest. When Penny meets him at the door he is received rather coldly. "So what the fuck do you want, Donnie?" She goes on to say that," Well, I don't remember any happy ending between us, no reconciliation, nothing." Don reminds her that she left him and asks if she has a son. Penny, suddenly very angry, pushes him, curses him and runs back into her house.

This moment seems to imply that Don has struck a painful memory for Penny (perhaps of her own child's death). In seeking the son he has never known, Don has reminded Penny of the son that she has lost and can never reclaim. Jarmusch is again very economical in suggesting this back-story and as such this is a very powerful moment in the film that demonstrates his theme of a "random" order of life and how events in our lives don't always lead us the way we think they should.

Don's final moment at the grave of his dead ex-lover, Michelle Pepe, displays an ineffable moment of loss, regret, dignity, and adoration simultaneously with only one phrase," hello beautiful," as he lays some pink roses by her headstone and sits down by a tree as it rains. The back-story here—suggested by a comment made earlier in the film—is that this was someone that Don really loved, but could not keep. So by expressing less, in this scene, Jarmusch expresses more about the multi-faceted character of Don Johnston. The startlingly economy, lucidity, and variety that Jarmusch uses to demonstrate his theme of the often baffling and random ways a person's life is informed by their past makes BROKEN FLOWERS one of his most compelling works. Although it should not be surprising, considering that Jim Jarmusch studied under the great American screenwriter and director, Nicholas Ray (1911-1979) whose comments on back-story we shall examine below.

DEFINING THE BACKSTORY AND THE STORY [PROPER]

Nicholas Ray, told a class of filmmakers and actors that," Creating a back-story requires your using the magic IF and asking yourself," If such a thing happens, what would have happened before that?" In answering that question you must draw on the totality of your imagination, associations, what you have read, past experiences."[3] I find Mr. Ray's insight just as applicable to screenwriters as to screen actors, for the simple fact that his 'magic IF' question probes into the screenwriter's act of preparation before he begins writing his screenplay. The writer may have a number of events happening in their story, but if these events are happening in the story, what has happened or hasn't happened to our characters to make them into the individuals they are now?

We can define the story [proper] as all that which is being experienced on screen through sound or image as the present tense. This should give us a manageable context to understand back-story as not only the unseen distant past, but also the unseen immediate past, just before the camera arrived. "Many narratives and dramas start *in medias res*, and later tell the earlier events more or less succinctly."[4] The suggestion here is that the beginning of a film (or scene) is not exclusively determined by the beginning of the fictional event it reproduces and that we, as spectators, are only the privileged witnesses of events captured at a strategic point in a continuum of time.

One film of many that demonstrates this concept is the opening sequence of Robert Bresson's UNE FEMME DOUCE (1969—A Gentle Woman). A maid opens a door and comes into a room just as a woman leaps from the balcony of her apartment to her death. Yet this sentence is a fabula (a mental reconstruction) that betrays how this information was actually presented cinematically. So let us re-start this opening sequence:

Shot #1:   Bresson gives us a very limited medium shot of a woman's waist (dressed in black) as she opens a door, pauses, and then rushes further into the room.

Shot#2:   Is a shot of an agitated rocking chair and a table with a flower pot and ashtray falling onto the balcony floor. (These actions are presumably a reaction from some unknown force.)

Shot #3:   Is an exterior shot of a long scarf floating gracefully to the ground from the balcony of the apartment as cars can be heard screeching to a halt.

Shot#4:   Is a panning shot of the last car stopping with witnesses running across the sidewalk to the carefully posed body of a dead woman with blood around her head.

The astonishing brevity of this sequence highlights the severity of the suicide it presents. More than this, the sequence emphasizes the arrival of the camera which captures the action too late; later than would be expected for the typical display of a suicide. This opening sequence is constructed with the idea that the events and circumstances that had led to such a drastic action occurred before the story [proper], before what we are witnessing. Bresson spends the rest of the film using the Husband's reminiscence of his wife in voice over as he talks to the woman in black, whom we understand is the maid from the opening sequence, as an unreliable narrator to the accompanying visuals. Thus, these opening sequences of four shots which capture the after-effects of a suicide compel us to look deeply into the film for back-story which will inform us about what we almost witnessed, but otherwise understood has happened after the fact. What was the magic "IF" that informed the terrible circumstances before the camera arrived?

Perhaps it is this single question, the 'magic IF' question, which allows us to begin the task of defining a back-story from the story [proper] and adjusting, checking, and correcting the two stories point for point to make sure that the back-story reveals itself as the point of departure for all the events that follow on screen. While doing this rigorous procedure, the writer must remember that the back-story always affects the way your characters are behaving within your actual screenplay. Therefore, a back-story is not necessarily a previous situation which you must introduce into your script as a flashback or spoken memory: a back-story is a past life experience that informs, shapes, and molds the way your characters exist within your entire script. There may never be a need to reveal the entire back-story, because this extra-story exists in your own mind as you write and helps you give depth to your characters. What you are capturing is the mind set, the psychology and emotional world of your characters as if they are real living people. The four repressions: fear, guilt, shame, and anger control most of us in our daily lives and if you listen to people close enough you can hear which of these learned repressions affected them the most and why they behave the way they do, now, in adult life. But as we have seen from Jim Jarmusch's film BROKEN FLOWERS back-story should not always be approached as a formula. The use of chaos, random events, and the temperament and will of an individual in the hands of an imaginative writer/filmmaker can result in compelling approaches to back-story that can enrich a film beyond our most prosaic expectations.

WE SEE THE PAST IN THE PRESENT

To set up any screenplay one must choose when you are going to start telling us about your characters and when you are going to stop. In fact, you can only make this decision, when to start and end a story, by understanding the major themes of your story and what parts of it best demonstrate those themes. Unlike a biography, where we might understand the underlying themes of a real person's life at the point where they die, your screenplay only has a meaning because you have sought out the major themes and after you have exhausted these themes you must decide to disengage us from them by ending the story at the point where the theme is most explicitly demonstrated, but not explained.

Because a screenplay is less than a novel it is impossible to 'show' every nuance of a character's life experiences and circumstances—one can only hint at it through particular events and circumstances that reveal reoccurring themes in that character or set of characters lives. Screenwriting is not about explaining every detail, but rather it is about revealing as many details as you can through the demonstration of specific themes inherent within your story. What contributes to a writer's decision to collapse both the back-story and the story [proper] into one big monolith is his or her need to show and explain why characters are saying and doing the things they are saying and doing in the script.

It is not enough that these characters exist, but the writer mistakenly feels that he must explain why they exist. Some of the strength of any drama is found within the mystery or ambiguity that surrounds other people's behavior or actions. It is as if the writer is speaking to you and saying,' My character feels this way because when he was a little boy he was raped,' and then their screenplay flashes back to the childhood rape to make you believe what they are saying is true. The opportunities for drama are always wasted by this approach because rather than dramatizing the characters so that we can learn about their past through their present circumstances and actions, we have their past explained to us—and an explanation is not a dramatization. When I see screenplays written with this flawed conception I always find:

1) A multitude of brief sketchy scenes that lack narrative unity.
2) A multitude of flashbacks or montages used solely to explain what could have otherwise been revealed by simply cutting to the next scene.
3) A multitude of characters introduced in both the flashbacks and the story [proper].
4) A multitude of potential dramatic actions that become less and less interesting as the screenplay gets bigger and bigger. (For instance, a rape follows a murder which follows an explosion, which follows more rapes . . . etc.)
5) An incomplete screenplay because even the writer got lost in all the exposition necessary to support their explanations of their character's behavior or circumstances.

The central problem here is that the writer is not theorizing about how the actual back stories would affect his characters present lives. Every writer is a philosopher, to paraphrase and perhaps misquote Albert Camus, the writer presents us with his own philosophy about how events, circumstances, and behaviors affect his characters in their present situations.[5] Yes, childhood sexual abuse is an obviously dramatic event, but a dramatization would reveal how this character deals with this event as he continues through life. A skillful writer may not even have to flashback to this incident when the effect on the character's present life (which we will be watching on screen) is so dramatic that the emotional scarring is felt and its origin need not be shown. Another definition of the back-story is that it is a theory of how our characters function within our story [proper]. To be specific: what we will be *seeing* on screen is affected by what we have *not seen* on screen.

COLLAPSING OF THE BACKSTORY INTO THE STORY PROPER IN Andrei Tarkovsky's SOLARIS

All this is not to say that it is impossible to merge a back-story into the story proper by using flashbacks or cross cutting between present and past tenses, but the writer who wishes to do so must realize that in these instances he is not doing these narrative adjustments simply to explain why a character or set of characters feels the way they do. The idea of developing and exploring your back-story and later collapsing it into the final screenplay is an idea that must be linked to the themes you are investigating and demonstrating in your film. Perhaps it is necessary to state that a theme is not the meaning of your story, nor is it a proverb or moral that explains your story: a theme is the underlying idea, concept, or subject that an artist prejudicially finds or jealously seeks to elucidate within any story and demonstrate within the film.

For instance, writer/director Martin Scorsese has often been fascinated by the theme of redemption and we can trace this thematic concern, particularly within his early films: WHO'S THAT KNOCKING AT MY DOOR (1969), MEAN STREETS (1973), and TAXI DRIVER (1976) as well as his latest film, THE AVIATOR (2004). Sometimes it is not necessary for an artist to be conscious of the themes he seeks, such themes are usually manifested in his choices of subject matter, like the themes of threatened or sustained male camaraderie within the work of director Howard Hawks (b. 1896-d. 1977), but the more aware the writer/director is of his preoccupying themes the better he is able to expand, expound, and elucidate his thematic concerns over a broad range of genres and story telling methods.[6] An example of successful collapsing of the back-story into the story [proper] can be witnessed in the late Russian director Andrei Tarkovsky's film, SOLARIS (1972).

A Russian space station is orbiting a distant planet named SOLARIS. The planet itself has no land surface and is covered entirely by an ocean. After the first scientists subjected the ocean to radiation, strange visitors began to appear on the ship; visitors who seemed to be created from the consciousness or memories of the space station's crew. Many on the space station died or killed themselves due to the involuntary resurrection of the "visitors" from one's consciousness that cannot die or be destroyed. Years later the government, dismissing these strange events, proposed a new mission to send astronaut Kris Kelvin (Donatas Banionis) to the space station orbiting Solaris to determine whether the ship should be salvaged or destroyed. Yet when Kris Kelvin arrives on the space station to pursue his mission he finds out that an old friend, who was part of the skeleton crew left on the space station, has killed himself.

Among many other distractions and bizarre behaviors of the remaining crew, Kris is visited by a perfect replica of his beautiful wife, Hari (Natalia Bondarchuk), who had killed herself years before. Much of the resultant film is centered upon the replica Hari discovering that she is not real (ironically through repeated suicide attempts) and Kris unable to resist believing that this replica of his former wife is real. Far from being a tragic love story, we find when we watch SOLARIS, which was based on a science fiction novel by Polish author, Stanislav Lem, and the from the director's own statements, that this science fiction plot is all set dressing for Tarkovsky's own personal artistic thematic concerns of Man's consciousness and moral responsibilities concerning science and the pursuit of knowledge.

Indeed, Tarkovsky stated," As far as Stanislav Lem's Solaris is concerned, my decision to film it does not denote any affection for the science-fiction genre. For me, the important thing is that SOLARIS poses a problem that means a lot to me: the problem of striving and achieving through your convictions; of moral transformation in the struggle in one man's life. The profound thought behind Lem's novel has nothing to do with the science-fiction genre in which it is written . . ." [7] Tarkovsky achieved this great transfiguration of the science-fiction genre by collapsing his back-story within his story [proper]. The collapsing is not done so much to explain a character, but rather to develop the themes within the story that were hidden within the characters and their circumstances.

We might also note here that literary author Stanislew Lem did not admire film author Andrei Tarkovsky's version of his novel. (This goes a long way in explaining the Steven Soderbergh remake in 2002.) Yet, it was Tarkovsky who used the novel as a spring board to finding his own themes within the material. His bold artistic decisions concerning the work reveals to us that the reverence for a literary author's work need not be a hindrance to the filmmaker who seeks within that work, themes that can justify what he wants to emphasize and where he wants the film narrative to end. [For further discussion of the right of a film author vis-à-vis the work of a literary author, please see the chapter: BOOK ADAPTATIONS] There are three excellent examples of how Tarkovsky choose to include the back-story to support the themes he found in the story [proper]: 1) is the story of Berton (Vladislav Dvorzhetsky), the astronaut who first went to Solaris and returned a broken man 2) is the suicide of psychologist Gibarian (Sos Sarkissian) on the space station, and 3) is the story of Hari, Kris's first wife who committed suicide.

SOLARIS: THE PREVIOUS MISSION

SOLARIS opens with Astronaut Kris Kelvin beginning his last day on Earth with a walk around the sweeping, yet simple, landscape of his father's home near a pond. During his walk, Berton, an astronaut who was previously stationed at Solaris many years ago comes anxiously to Kris' home with an urgent message for him. Berton brings with him an old film of a government briefing concerning his experiences at Solaris which, far from just raising questions about his sanity during his expedition, reveal the strange hallucinatory effects of the alien planet's ocean on human consciousness. It seems, as Berton plays the film for Kris, his father and his aunt, that he believed he saw a garden made of plaster and a four meter tall naked child walking within the ocean as he flew over it in a "hydroplane" while searching for a missing crew member.

Within the briefing, there is another film which Berton took while he had these experiences in flight, but his in flight footage reveals only clouds and glinting sunlight. Berton's report is dismissed and interest in the Solaris expedition is closed. However, what is cinematically fascinating in this sequence is how Tarkovsky used a back-story (Berton's report within the government briefing) inside the story proper, which is Kris

Kelvin's impending mission to Solaris to determine whether the space station should be closed down. Tarkovsky seems to have highlighted this back-story as it elucidates the major themes of the work while simultaneously preparing the audience for Kris Kelvin's hallucinatory experiences upon arriving on Solaris.

What we are witnessing here in this film within a film sequence is the collapsing of a back-story into the story [proper] which is all supported by a major thematic concern within the overall film. From the callous dismissal of Berton's report in the film within the film, Berton's present embittered and defeated demeanor is revealed or 'theorized' as having developed from how he was treated in the past, by his government and the people whom he respected in the scientific and cosmonautic community. He even says after he turns off the tape in disgust,' Today it is considered the thing to laugh at Berton's Report.' A statement which reveals the depth of the wound his prior experiences on Solaris have caused him.

Later, when Berton and Kris have a tense private conversation concerning the intent of his mission,' their argument reveals totally opposite world views, with Kris claiming that science has to follow its own course, no matter where it leads, while Berton sees knowledge as valid," only when it is based on morality."[8] The collapsing of this back-story into the story [proper] is an ironic foreshadowing for Kris's subsequent experiences on the space station and the replication of his first wife, Hari, from his consciousness.

SOLARIS: THE PRESENT MISSION

From the moment Kris Kelvin arrives at the space station a number of strange, even grotesque, events happen one after another. The station is supposed to be deserted except for three remaining crew members: The professor of cybernetics known only as Snouth (Yuri Yarvet), Medical doctor Satorious (Anatoly Solonitsyn), and Kris's old friend, psychologist Gibarian. But a nervous encounter with Snouth reveals that Gibarian has killed himself from depression, perhaps induced by the effects of the ocean and homesickness. When Kris enters Gibarian's cluttered chambers, the collapsing of the back-story into the story proper reaches sublime effect. Kris finds out that Gibarian left a film record for him before he died.

When Kris plays this message he tells him that," By now you know about me, if not, Satorious or Snouth will tell you." This very line of dialogue intimates that Gibarian had planned his suicide to coincide with Kris's arrival. Moreover, within that same message, Gibarian tries to warn Kris, but his message is cut short when Kris rushes to close a door that mysteriously swings open. Both this sequence with Gibarian and the previous sequence with Berton provide important back-story information about the space station and the alien ocean on the planet's surface, but what is ingenious about Tarkovsky's collapsing of back-story into the story [proper] is that he accomplishes this feat in a very unconventional manner: the back-story is not presented as a simple flashback established through the dialogue of present tense characters, but rather, the back-story is presented as separate film recordings of undramatized reality (the documentary like government briefing featuring Berton is presented as a bureaucratic government recording of an official event and Gibarian's posthumous film recording is presented as the last will and testament of a man before he committed suicide).

Far from becoming distracting episodes with numerous characters and explanatory material both sequences are fictionalized events recorded as if they had actually occurred in real life. Taken together, the sequences heighten the realism of the fantastic science-fiction story within SOLARIS. Where Berton's sequence reaches twenty or so years back into time, Gibarian's sequence reaches only a few weeks back into time, but most importantly, the two sequences build the thematic foundations of SOLARIS if only because in presenting the sequences as 'recorded reality' Tarkovsky skillfully edits the material to conform to the themes of the story he wanted to highlight that existed beyond the science fiction genre of Stanislav Lem's novel.

Again, he accomplishes this editing in an unconventional manner, it would seem obvious that all any filmmaker would have to do is physically edit what part of the back-story sequences best elucidates his themes and place it within the current story, but Tarkovsky has the older Berton skip certain sections of his government briefing in disgust. In this manner, the present tense character edits his own back-story within the fictional context of the story proper. This unusual fictional editing occurs again in Gibarian's sequence when Kris turns the sound off during the recorded message to rush and close the door that has mysteriously opened. With this sound off, we miss a large segment of Gibarian's warning. Again, the back-story has been edited by a present tense character within the fiction rather than by the external hand of the filmmaker via the arrangement of past and present tense scenes.

So clearly, in these two sequences Tarkovsky employs a fascinating and unconventional method to collapse his back-story into his story [proper] to develop the thematic concerns that impinge on the emotional world of his characters, rather than explain or conventionally answer questions of narrative logic. In short, the two film within a film sequences add rather than disturb the flow of the story and become more than simple flashbacks cued by present tense dialogue. The final back-story element of SOLARIS, the replication of Kris's dead wife, deviates from this presentation, but is no less important or innovative.

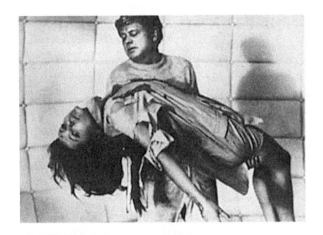

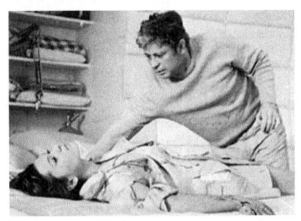

"From the moment Kris Kelvin arrives at the space station a number of strange, even grotesque, events happen one after another." (Donatas Banionis, SOLARIS—1972, courtesy Mosfilm)]

THE ETERNAL RESURRECTION

After learning of Berton's Report which defines the effect of the Alien planet's ocean on human consciousness and witnessing parts of Gibarian's warning when he arrives on Solaris, Kris Kelvin is visited by a replica of his first wife created from his own consciousness while he sleeps in his chambers. The scene itself is given added mystery by the way Tarkovsky cuts from the sleeping face of Kris to an intense close up of the corner of a unknown woman's mouth and cheek with light glinting from her hair. The shot is reminiscent of the fragmented close ups that begin Hitchcock's film VERTIGO, another film concerned with a woman brought forth from the past. The back-story concerning how and why Kris's first wife committed suicide is told in ever increasing dialogues between the two after each time the replica is replaced or attempts to destroy itself.

Slowly, Kris has to tell her that the real Hari killed herself by poison injection after he left her, but he refuses to give her up now and the guilt and frustration on his face during his entire mission reveals to us the effect of his first wife's tragic death on his entire world view. Here in this third example of a back-story collapsed into the story proper, Tarkovsky clearly illustrates the profundity at the heart of Stanislav Lem's novel that intrigued him beyond the science fiction," That man does not want to discover true contact with aliens, he only wants a mirror image of himself."[9] The alien ocean makes flesh the hidden desires within men and Kris Kelvin must finally commit to the hallucinatory effects of this mysterious planet if he wants to redeem himself of his past.

If we look at the construction of Tarkovsky's film we will find that he uses back-story to reveal the forlorn state of mind of his characters which in themselves become the chief thematic nodes within his film. In this sequence, with Hari, one gets the sense that rather than exploring a character's existence within the story [proper] Tarkovsky is giving you a psychological perspective within which one can feel the character's emotional experiences. The importance of feeling the character's emotional world is particularly acute upon the replica of Hari who begins to exude the pain of not being able to love Kris completely as a real woman and yet she says she does love him.

Indeed, in the final sections of the film it is the knowledge of the real Hari's tragic past that is pulling her away from him. If we have understood this collapsing, we should be able to see the 'revolutionary' narrative aspect of Tarkovsky's SOLARIS clearly. Following the three examples discussed we find that: Berton has watched a film of his own past, Gibarian, a deceased character, is brought back to life through a filmed message he left for Kris, and finally the past co-exists with the present when Hari, Kris's dead wife, is re-presented in the flesh as an alien replica from Kris's own memory. I will not ruin the apotheosis of this film as it is presented in its finale, but I will say that the dividing line between memory and the present, the past and reality are merged into one incredible experience for the central character, Kris Kelvin, and the audience.

What does this overview of Tarkovsky's unconventional and idiosyncratic stylistic perspective reveal to us? 1) that it is possible to collapse a back-story into the story [proper] as long as it is thematically justified and supports the emotional world of the characters. 2) That the writer/director must be able to define and isolate his back-story in a way that affords him a style all his own and a style that differentiates him from the herd. "If the filmmaker assimilates himself to his character and, through him, tells a story, or represents the world . . . His operation cannot be linguistic, but stylistic."[10] But we would do well to remember that every writer is limited by the depth of their ability to empathize with their characters and the range of their life experience, so that the creation and maintenance of back-story is ultimately dependent upon these two contributing factors. Perhaps, this is just a fancy way of saying write about what you know or at least what you can competently imagine.

NOTES

[1] Pg. 4, CREATIVE EVOLUTION, Henri Bergson, Dover Publications, New York, 1998.

[2] For more information about the psychoanalytic connection between early childhood trauma and adult neurosis by Sigmund Freud, see: 'THE ASSAULT ON TRUTH; Freud's Suppression of the Seduction Theory', by Jeffery Moussaieff Masson (Harper, 1984, New York).

[3] Pg. 33,—I WAS INTERRUPTED: Nicholas Ray On Making Movies—University of California Press, Berkeley/Los Angeles 1993 Ed. by Susan Ray.

[4] Pg. 22, THE POETICS OF PLOT by Thomas G. Pavel. University of Minnesota Press, Minneapolis, 1985.

[5] The actual quote is more interesting than I have paraphrased,' **A novel is never anything but a philosophy put into images. And, in a good novel, the whole of the philosophy has passed into the images.**' Pg. 18 Modern Novelists: Albert Camus, by Philip Thody, The Macmillan Press, London, 1989.

[6] What is most interesting about Howard Hawks is how he was able to expound, explore, and elucidate his themes of male camaraderie throughout the content of a wide variety of genres: screwball comedies (BRINGING UP BABY—1938), westerns (RED RIVER—1948), film noir (THE BIG SLEEP-1946), action (RED LINE 7000—1965) and melodrama (A STAR IS BORN—1948). "For Hawks, the highest human emotion is the camaraderie of the exclusive, self-sufficient, all-male group." (Cf. Pg.82, SIGNS and MEANING in the CINEMA, by Peter Wollen) Some critics have made the misinterpretation of Howard Hawk's masculine themes as homosexual love, but I am vehemently opposed to this sophistic and revisionist cheating for we find that *then* as *now* men can have a love for each other that is non-erotic and that type of love may be called brotherly love (SEE: Howard Hawk's THE BIG SKY—1952).

[7] Pg. 59, TARKOVSKY, Cinema as Poetry, by Maya Turovskaya, Faber and Faber, London, 1989.

[8] Pg. 273, THE FILMS OF ANDREI TARKOVSKY: A Visual Fugue, by Vida T. Johnson and Graham Petrie, Indiana University Press, 1994.

[9] Excerpt from the Criterion DVD Edition of SOLARIS, 2002.

[10] Pg. 551, The Cinema of Poetry, by Pier Paolo Pasolini, in MOVIES and METHODS, ed. by Bill Nichols, University of California Press, Berkeley, 1976.

THE NARRATIVE ELLIPSIS
Robert Bresson to Quentin Tarantino

An ellipsis is a narrative editorial strategy whereby a specific shot or scene is omitted but clearly implied and chronologically consistent with the rest of the story. An ellipsis is an emphatic demonstration of an artist's ability to guide a spectator toward seeing the thematic underpinnings of a story. Everyone remembers the omission of the actual jewelry store robbery in Quentin Tarantino's RESERVOIR DOGS (1991). This was a shocking and surprising ellipsis in the fact that most of the film was devoted to the preparation of the robbery (selection of accomplices, selection of aliases, meeting place, shares, site of robbery, amount of the take, rules of secrecy, etc.). But the effect, the narrative effect of the omission of the robbery scene is that it forces the spectator to readjust his or her expectations concerning what the story is about. It is not a film about a robbery, but instead, a film about the disintegration of trust among a group of criminals. This is evident in the finale, where Mr. Orange (Tim Roth) reveals that he is an undercover police officer to Mr. White (Harvey Keitel). Trust is the theme of RESERVOIR DOGS and it is mistrust that destroys them all.

Writer Tony Pipolo, in a fruitful essay on Robert Bresson's first feature film, LES ANGES DU PECHE (1943- The Angels of Sin), suggests that at least four conditions must be met for elliptical editing to be effective:

1) "First, one must be able to cut off the segment of the narrative in question and see it as a "unit" of some kind in order to recognize that a key part of it has been omitted.

2) Secondly, that part should be as specific and easily supplied by the viewer as the missing word or term in verse.

3) Thirdly [we recognize] that we are dealing with an elliptic trope rather than a carelessly constructed scenario [that] must be established by context, pattern and purpose.

4) Lastly, in order for the effect to register at all, there must be some element of surprise—even shock—and perhaps momentary confusion, a sense that some prior knowledge of things has been contradicted." [1]

It is what the spectator expects to see that is subverted by an ellipsis and in denying the spectator the satisfaction of what he or she expects to see based on their previously routine television and cinematic experiences, the filmmaker is exerting his artistic vision and purpose through the story. It is how well a narrative ellipsis is used that determines the difference between self-indulgence and artistic purpose. An ellipsis should function to help the spectator see the story from an alternate thematic perspective.

So an ellipsis can be used by a film author to emphasize the theme within the story that would otherwise have been obscured had the particular scene or shot remained in place and fulfilled a spectator's conventional expectation. Yet the act of an ellipsis is a narrative editorial act that ultimately forces the spectator to actively think or become involved in the dynamism of the story. The spectator's involvement in an ellipsis is that he or she must deduce from the subsequent scenes, the exposition that is missing, but is now implied in how the characters behave, appear, and express themselves or the circumstances of the characters that differ or remain unchanged after the omission.

In short, showing a character get arrested by the police in the street and then cutting to a maximum security prison would force the spectator to realize that there was a trial that didn't turn out in the character's favor and that this character was convicted of a serious offense. An ellipsis forces the spectator, not to passively receive 'entertainment' by identifying with a character or set of characters, but to actively engage themselves in the dynamism of how a story is being told.

An ellipsis can have three, if not more, important narrative functions:

1) TIME: the omission of a scene or scenes can signify a gap in chronological time that can reveal hours, days, weeks, months or years that have passed from the preceding scene.
2) MODIFICATION: the omission of a scene or scenes can reveal the modifications of a character's behavior, appearance or circumstance relative to the preceding scene.
3) RESULT: an ellipsis can reveal the result of a character or group of characters actions. This last function is the most important concerning the dynamism of narration.

"For example, in PUBLIC OPINION, [Charlie] Chaplin insisted on the gap of a year, which was not filled by anything, but which we can infer from the new behavior and clothes of the heroine, who has become a rich man's mistress."[2]

The richest and most concise use of ellipsis was practiced by the late French filmmaker Robert Bresson (1901-1999), particularly in his final film, L'ARGENT (1983—MONEY). The film gives us the most purposeful use of ellipsis to concentrate its theme and give the story within the film a narrative dynamism that invites the spectator to contemplate the results of the character's actions.

L'ARGENT was adapted from a short story by Leo Tolstoy called,' THE FORGED COUPON,' also known as,' THE FORGED BANKNOTE.' In Bresson's adaptation, the initial forgery of a single French 500 dollar bill by two high school age youths is passed along and begins a chain of tragic and brutal consequences for the story's main character, Yvon Targe (Christian Patey). Throughout the film we watch as Yvon's life disintegrates and he ultimately becomes a serial killer after his life is torn apart by the duplicity and guile of others and his own stubborn pride.

Bresson himself has said that what intrigued him about Tolstoy's short story, THE FORGED COUPON, was," the idea it is based on, which is an account of how evil spreads."[3] Yet, Tolstoy's," narrative, which takes place over the course of roughly fifteen years and in a variety of city and country locations, is dispersed among twenty-four separate characters . . ."[4] Bresson concentrates his adaptation on the main character, Yvon Targe and four supporting characters. What is striking, besides the reduction of characters between the short story and the film, are the major elisions that Bresson makes in his screenplay adaptation to focus Tolstoy's wide ranging characters, locations and philosophizing into a tightly unified thematically controlled linear narrative structure.[5]

"FALSE COUPON is a magnificent short story, but right at the start Tolstoy refers to God, to the Gospels. I couldn't go down that route because my film is about today's unconscious indifference when people only think about themselves and their families."[6] The most strategic and thematically purposeful ellipsis in L'ARGENT occurs concerning the actions and circumstances of its main character, Yvon Targe. Once Targe is passed the forged money from the camera shop owners who are customers of the heating oil company that he works for, Bresson begins a concise and breathtaking series of elliptical sequences that invites the spectator to contemplate the results of all the characters actions. In short, it is with elliptical narration that Bresson is truly able to,' account how evil spreads.'

We will look at a brief example from early in the film to illustrate the whole of this narrative editorial strategy. After Yvon Targe is deliberately given several counterfeit bills from the shop owner, including the initial bill forged by the students, he leaves and is seen going into the door of a restaurant for lunch. Bresson then cuts to Yvon sitting at a table being confronted by the waiter about a counterfeit bill. Targe offers him another, but the waiter says that one is counterfeit as well as yet another bill Targe offers him. Targe asks for the bills back so that he might return them to where he got them from, to which the waiter replies," No." He intends to keep them as evidence. The waiter then insults Yvon who stands up face to face with the waiter. Here, Bresson cuts to a tight close up of Yvon's hand grabbing the waiter and pushing him away with great force by releasing his hand. The waiter falls back into a table, which falls over, crashing to the floor. The sound of a car's motor is then heard overlapping the image of the fallen table. We then cut to a medium shot of a police car arriving at the camera shop. Yvon gets out of the police car, followed by a detective, and both enter the shop. The next shot is a tight medium shot framed on the left by Yvon and the detective as the shop owner says," I'll ask my assistant if he remembers him."

This brief sequence of events is representative of the startling use of ellipsis that concisely and purposefully illuminates Bresson's theme and dynamically drives the narrative. The first ellipsis is from Yvon's entrance to the restaurant to the waiter confronting him about the counterfeit bills. Here, Bresson has omitted the ordering and eating of the meal. The entire duration of these mundane events is discarded, but we can see that Yvon has finished his meal from the empty plate in front of him as well as the waiter who holds what Yvon had tried to use to pay for his meal. This omission is thematically justified, as all omissions must be to function properly, since it forces the spectator to concentrate on the issue, which is the false money.

The second ellipsis is from the fallen table to the police car, which stops in front of the shop. Here, Bresson has cut away great chunks of narrative exposition like: the police arriving at the restaurant, the waiter's complaints, the examination of the bills, the preliminary questioning of Yvon and any witnesses who might have seen the events. By cutting from the fallen table to the police arriving with Yvon to the camera shop, we as spectators are invited to assume all that must have happened to *result* in the subsequent events we are now seeing. Our own knowledge of laws, police custom and procedural steps is brought into play to move the story along; to present the events with a dynamism that involves the spectator as opposed to placating them with passive entertainment filled with the routine exposition thought necessary for a story to be understood.

The third ellipsis occurs after Yvon and the detective are seen entering the camera shop to the tight medium shot where the shop owner says," I'll ask my assistant if he remembers him." We are conscious of the fact that Bresson again has omitted the initial introduction between the detective, Yvon and the shop owner as well as Yvon's restatement of the circumstances of his situation. The first reason for this omission is the fact that we already know why Yvon is there and it is unnecessary to have to show this explanation. It would only be dramatically unsatisfying exposition. The second reason for this third ellipsis is that it presents us—unequivocally—with the shop owner's lie. By showing us the very end of the moment where the shop owner says he will ask his assistant if he remembers Yvon, this ellipsis gives us the actions that follow a lie: the spreading of evil. Since now the shop owner is compelled to bring his young assistant into the lie that he has been telling ever since the moment he gave Yvon the counterfeit bills as if they were real.

It must be said again that for an ellipsis to work, to drive a story dynamically, it must be thematically justified. The idea of simply omitting a scene because one does not have the money or the imagination to shoot it is not elliptical storytelling—it is simply lazy storytelling. The narrative ellipsis, when concisely used with thematic purpose, must circumvent a spectator's conventional expectations and reveal an alternate perspective that would not have otherwise been clearly understood without the ellipsis; anything less is just an incomplete film.

At bottom, an ellipsis is an assumption presumed by the filmmaker(s) about how an audience should perceive the events or circumstances of a story as it advances to its conclusion. It is a perceptual narrative leap that can usually be noticed only when it is used unconventionally. The most common ellipsis occurs generally due to time constraints accepted by the audience and practiced by the filmmakers (e.g. a single movie is usually 2 to 3 hours in length). An ellipsis for time is the ellipsis that is the least disruptive because it is so widely understood. Hopefully, this chapter has revealed that the other uses of an ellipsis are valuable narrative tools to shape a story to illuminate theme as well as to place emphasis upon circumstances and events that might have otherwise been obscured or overlooked had they have been presented conventionally.

NOTES

[1] Pgs. 208-9, RULES OF THE GAME: On Bresson's LES ANGES DU PECHE by Tony Pipolo in ROBERT BRESSON edited by James Quandt, 1998, Toronto International Film Festival Group.

[2] Pg. 160-1, CINEMA 1 THE MOVEMENT-IMAGE by Gilles Deleuze. 1991. University of Minnesota Press.

[3] Pg. 499, I SEEK NOT DESCRIPTION BUT VISION, Robert Bresson on L'ARGENT, interview by Michel Climent in ROBERT BRESSON, ed. James Quandt, Toronto International Film Festival Group, 1998.

[4] Pg. 25, L'ARGENT by Kent James, BFI Publications, 1999.

[5] For clarity's sake an elision is something that is taken out of a story or treatment in preparation of the screenplay and an ellipsis is the actual performance of the elision as it is perceived during the viewing of the actual film. Both the elision and the resultant ellipsis are acts of faith between the writer and the reader and the filmmaker and the spectator. Elision is how one might see religious texts prepared. In the Bible a whole story with complete exposition is rarely supplied, but the faith of the reader in 'the hand of God' supplies what exposition has been elided. Thus, filmmaker Robert Bresson, who was notoriously against psychological explanation, uses the ellipsis to guide the spirit of his characters and by extension the faith of his spectators.

[6] Pg. 503, Michel Climent Interview, Ibid.

THE NIHILIST'S ERECTION
The Male Admiration for Nihilistic Characters in Cinema

"Nihilism, then, is the recognition of the long waste of strength, the agony of the "in vain," insecurity, the lack of any opportunity to recover and to regain composure—being ashamed in front of oneself, as if one had deceived oneself all too long."

-Friedrich Nietzsche, Book One: European Nihilism, The Will To Power

Perhaps we've noticed it ever since the charismatic outlaw made his appearance in black & white Westerns or just after James Cagney pushed a grapefruit into that woman's face in PUBLIC ENEMY (1931)—but there grows a genuine and palpable admiration in the male spectator for male characters who do whatever they want at all cost to themselves and others. This is not mere hero or anti-hero worship, for the male characters that are being admired are flawed, irredeemable characters of a despicable and/or despotic nature. These characters shoot, rape, burn, terrorize, loot, maim, wound, disrupt, and destroy anything and everything that stands in their way. Upon first glance these villainous characters seem to commit evil acts without any higher purpose, goal or mission other than just being able to commit them. They are the bandit characters who," *don't need no stinkin' badges*," to inflict violence on the innocent and guilty alike. Beyond bad guys, this nihilism is what hides inside the psyche of all men if pushed too far.

No matter if the filmmaker attempts to cast these characters in a dark and irredeemable light, the legacy of their egoism and disregard for right and wrong lives far beyond their own self destruction and condemnation. We've witnessed just such a nihilistic legacy and admiration for Al Pacino's livid characterization of Tony Montana in DePalma & Stone's SCARFACE (1983). The final battle, where he is killed after destroying the lives of his best friend, his sister, his mother and murdering countless others, does nothing to tarnish the admiration of his will to fight a battle he could never win, against all odds. Moreover, his character is ennobled by the very outrageous gestures and phrases he performs in the process of his destruction. The snorting of a mound of cocaine, the guns and weaponry, the," say hello to my little friend," mantra—all fueled the mystique, the passion for his own undoing, the nihilism at the heart of his demise. Montana, like Cody Jarrett (James Cagney again) in WHITE HEAT (1949) dies personifying the creed of the nihilist: *They'll never take me alive!* The reverence and male admiration for Al Pacino as Scarface has endured for more than Twenty years as a recent re-release on DVD, and images from the film on everything from tee-shirts, leather jackets, coffee mugs and framed posters have proven.

So we can say that, undermining the heroism of contemporary cinema is a nihilist who opposes the hypocrisy of the righteous and the avarice of the wrong. He is the character who, if left unchecked, will take it all (the entire drama and the spectators who are watching it) to its bitter and bloody end. And like the hero, this nihilist has a thousand faces. We saw him briefly as Sonny Corleone (James Caan) in THE GODFATHER (1972) and we got an extended study of him as Travis Bickle (Robert DeNiro) in TAXI DRIVER (1976). He was revealed as Leonard Lawrence/Private Pyle (Vincent D'Onofrio) in FULL METAL JACKET (1987) and Bishop (Tupac Shakur) in JUICE (1991). This nihilist returned again as John Doe (Kevin Spacey) in SEVEN (1996) and as Sam Bicke (Sean Penn) in THE ASSASSINATION OF RICHARD NIXON (2004). Yet his most ecstatic appearance, even extended portrait, comes as the character of Li'l Dice/Ze (Douglas Silva/Leandro Firmino Da Hora) in the Brazilian drug epic CITY OF GOD (2003) directed by Fernando Meirelles.

No singular character has inspired such blood lust and admiration in contemporary cinema since, maybe, a few characters in the early work of John Woo or Takeshi Kitano, than Li'l Dice, who after a voodoo ceremony becomes Li'l Ze and continues on a socio-pathic path of destruction for destruction's sake. He is at once the antithesis of idealism and the transgression of cynicism when he shoots his way to the top as a drug kingpin and then shoots his way to the bottom as a gangster bent on revenge. Here is a character whose actions and their tragic consequences would lead us to believe that he could never be admired by any spectators who are witnessing the drama. Yet many male spectators are fascinated by Li'l Dice/Ze and the unmitigated carnage he leaves behind himself in this film.

Our first introduction to this character comes as he is a very young delinquent who provides the idea for a motel robbery to some older youths who call themselves," The Tender Trio." Li'l Dice wants to come along and participate, but he is admonished to stay behind as a lookout for the older robbers. He finally negotiates with them to at least leave him a gun to signal them if the cops should arrive. As the film later reveals, Li'l Dice did more than act as a look out, after the robbery he went into the motel and systematically slaughtered all of the people who had just been robbed. The very shot he fired as a signal was a ruse to make the older boys flee so that he could begin his rampage. He does all this with a childish look of glee upon his face.

Rather than simply catalogue the egregious number of horrors this character inflicts, it is important to note how bandits—any bandits whose crimes are witnessed from afar—whether in this country or on a movie screen, can easily be translated into a source of masculine admiration. It is significant here to point out that CITY OF GOD is set in the slums of Rio de Janeiro and two decades in the past. Thus, giving some distance for the male spectator to admire Li'l Dice/Ze safely and without immediate moral trepidation. Yet the essential question must be asked," Why do male spectators admire these male nihilistic characters?"

The Rape of Morality

If as author James Q. Wilson suggests, the source of morality is found in man's innate need to be sociable to others, then these nihilistic characters deny such sociability; some at first for their own gain and reputation, and then ultimately for their own destruction. Tony Montana, in SCARFACE, wouldn't blow up the United Nations official with his wife and children in the vehicle, so he murdered his co-conspirators and thus began his death spiral to his own bloody demise. It's almost as if these nihilistic characters start out with too great an unbending sense of justice—an absolutism that when it is confronted with the pragmatism and gray areas of real human co-existence, these characters snap and release a hailstorm of violence. First, they inflict violence with extreme prejudice, targeting the specific people or places that are unjust for their own gain or reputation, and then later indiscriminately as their perception begins to see everyone and everything as unjust and hostile until their own demise.

This nihilism then, seems to be the penultimate escapist act of dismissing and rejecting everything and doing exactly what you want, when you want, with whom you want without any consideration for another's feelings or circumstances. It is a moral rape couched in the rhetoric of revenge, like the muscular and elongated male actor in hard core pornography. He "fucks" the woman in ways and positions many of us are not allowed to do without legal consequences (and more often than not, without a condom to boot). The rituals, agreements, niceties, laws and reciprocation that manifest the routine sexual indulgences in a marriage or a relationship are thrown away the moment a hardcore pornographic film begins.

It is a masculine fantasy of revenge for many that have been 'forced' to be sociable and accept or buy into all the trappings of a capitalist system to attract the opposite sex and 'get sum'. And yet even this actor—this hardcore porn actor—is a nihilist. His revenge, couched in sexual gymnastics and 'bare bones' interaction with the opposite sex, is a rejection of all the rules governing male and female relationships; it is an escapist's illusion.

The admiration for pornographic actors Ron Jeremy, John Holmes, Jake Steed, and Lex The Impaler, is ultimately masturbatory; with the woman replacing the hand—the real object of pleasure is oneself, getting what one wants regardless of the consequences. The erection of this nihilist is based in a denial of man's sociability and interdependence for self-gratification. The same can be said of the nihilist in non-pornographic film. Perhaps the source of admiration in both genres is a self-gratifying revenge fantasy of total destruction: one against sexual reciprocity and the other against the perceived weaknesses of mankind.

In SEVEN, John Doe's strict adherence to his own rules and methodology reveal that he too had an absolute and exacting sense of morality. When he was questioned in the back of the police car, he spoke of,' the AIDS ridden whore,' who continued prostituting herself and spreading her disease. Even Li'l Dice when he was asking 'the tender trio' to allow him to fully participate in the robbery he had set up for them, was only voicing his own absolute sense of fairness that would be twisted and destroyed by the end of his life. Sonny Corleone, when he was confronted by Tom Hagen (Robert Duvall) about not being able to "kill everybody" was outraged by what he felt was an unfairness in 'war' caused by an adherence to morality and business ethics by his *consigliere*. Sonny did not care about business as he said;" Business will have to suffer!" He wanted to avenge the attempted murder of his father whether or not it caused the annihilation of all the mob families. Sonny was killed because the other families knew he was a nihilist, even his own.

Over and over again we see that the structure of a nihilist's paradigm in narrative film develops from an absolutism that breaks when it is confronted by the interdependence of mankind. (See: Fig.4 below) This first break is the "lucky break" where the character, usually at the urging of his pragmatic compatriot, attempts to abide by whatever rules of his chosen enterprise or expertise. This is where he tries to become a respected hero, mercenary, gangster or businessman. But, he always fatalistically encounters a second "bad break" that destroys his adherence to the rules and/or reveals an underlying hypocrisy he is compelled to violently rebel against. The end result is a violent orgy of revenge once the character or those around him are unable to live up to the strict standards he has set for himself and others. The outrage at hypocrisy (his own or others) is the fuel of every nihilist. And since modern society is full of hypocrisies, society and the silver screen will always have its nihilists and their admirers.

FIG.4 Dramatic Paradigm of the Nihilist

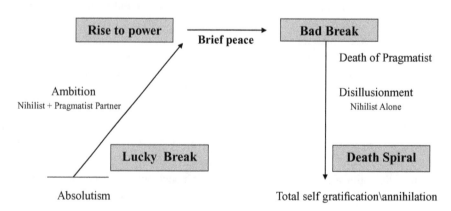

NOTE: The brevity of peace, the steep decline after the death of the pragmatist and the fatalism of the lucky break and the bad break.

The source of the final desperate acts of the nihilist can be found in how the character attempts to reconcile his shift from an absolutist to a pragmatist either through his own observations or the encouragement of others or both. For instance, Li'l Dice/Ze's love for his compatriot, Bene (Phellipe Haagensen), was absolute. Yet when Bene had decided to take a wife and get out of the drug business, Li'l Ze was devastated and distraught. Once Bene was accidentally killed by a bullet that was meant for Li'l Ze, he began a rampage that would ultimately lead to his demise. Ironically, only the audience is shown that the man who killed Bene was the same man that Bene had stopped Li'l Ze from killing earlier in the film. Bene was the only person who could soften Li'l Ze's absolutism. He understood man's interdependence; he was a pragmatist, whereas Li'l Ze could not grasp such a notion without him.

The masculine archetype of the nihilist is almost always complimented by a pragmatist.[1] In WHITE HEAT Cody Jarrett's pragmatist compliment was his mother; to whom he was nearly incestuously devoted. For Sonny Corleone it was obviously Tom Hagen. And finally, for Tony Montana it was the friend he killed in a jealous rage, Manny Rivera (Steven Bauer). These pragmatists, so well schooled in the art of interdependence, mercy, trust, loyalty, and calculated thinking, are often betrayed by their own virtues. They die the most unjust and incendiary deaths, whether caused by the nihilists themselves or by the contracts and obligations wherein the two are immersed. The nihilist, unchecked, nullifies all social, business, familial and ethical contracts for the sole purpose of self-gratification. Without his pragmatist, he is free to go out in blaze of glory.

The pragmatism to which Li'l Ze had subscribed to put himself on top, at his friend's urging, was the very bullet that returned to take from him what he loved most: Bene. Rather than see this as a displaced homosexuality, we should not distract ourselves so easily. Li'l Ze could not reconcile the indiscriminate violence that he had delivered as a consequence to his friend's murder. Nothing really mattered anymore after Bene's slaying and so he began a nihilistic rampage that would win him many male admirers as distant witnesses to his rapid fire death spiral. Including, but certainly not limited to, the film's narrator, Rocket who profited in spite of Li'l Ze carnage and death by becoming the only newspaper photographer capturing the drug war in the slums and the voice who brought the true story to the screen.

Each one of the characters we identified (Tom Powers, Sonny Corleone, Scarface, Mouse, Li'l Dice/Ze) have participated in a rape of the drama by taking what they want at all costs to themselves and others. Drama, if we might define it, is a nexus of characters with competing wants, needs, and ideas, interacting with one another to acquire or express these wants, needs, and ideas. So you can see that the drama is a mirror of real life—with all of its pragmatics, contradictions, rights and wrongs. The dramatic paradigm of the nihilist is essentially a modernized version of the Tragedy story archetype where we witness a hero or heroine," slip into ever greater egocentricity and lack of feeling for others, we see how their judgment, their ability to see the world straight and whole, becomes increasingly clouded." (Page 258, Booker, Seven Basic Plots) The banditry of the nihilist suspends this interdependence for the narrative life of the character and returns the spectator to an absolutism of childhood fantasy or experience. A time when right was what you got away with and wrong was when you got caught. No gray areas, no exceptions. No rules to protect those who cannot protect themselves.

These nihilists and their admirers share a certain giddiness in their destruction. A joy in counting how many bullets it took to bring him down; a last guffaw in the face of all the rules, laws, and hypocrisies of modern life. Thus, maybe clinical evidence may find that those male spectators who most admire these nihilistic characters in movies are those males themselves who are confined, sequestered, or castrated by the rules of a society whose *interdependence* seems to stifle their own *independence.*

THE ASSASSINATION OF RICHARD NIXON
Written by Niels Mueller & Kevin Kennedy
Directed by Niels Mueller

Another chilling example of the nihilist paradigm in cinema is found in Niels Mueller & Kevin Kennedy's film, THE ASSASSINATION OF RICHARD NIXON (2005). This riveting true story of Sam Bicke (Sean Penn), an office furniture salesman, whose unsuccessful attempt to highjack a plane and have it flown into the White House during Richard Nixon's beleaguered second term, is yet another profound portrayal of the nihilist in modern society that ultimately broadens the narrative structure we have identified as nihilistic. We only have Sam Bicke's true story because he left a series of taped confessions that he mailed to conductor Leonard Bernstein. Mueller and Kennedy were able to reconstruct a portrait of Sam Bicke through these recordings of Bicke venting his tormented soul. *"Is independence too much to ask, Mr. Bernstein? I mean, you're your own boss, right? You don't have any idea what its like to work for somebody else like some kind of slave. But I'm telling you slavery never really ended in this country. They just gave it another name: employee."* It is the tormented soul of an idealistic everyman caught in the ever changing circumstances of life's unfairness.

The character of Sam Bicke as so uniquely portrayed by actor Sean Penn contains the familiar anti-pragmatic trait of a child-like absolutism expressed in his disdain for lies or deception in business. As he states unequivocally to a small business loan administrator," I don't believe that someone should have to lie to make a living." It is this ethical absolutism, we find out, that had led to the estrangement between Sam Bicke and his older brother, Julius Bicke (Michael Wincott), who owns a tire shop.

The crisis of Sam Bicke is a poignant demonstration of an observation suggested by psychiatrist William Sargant. "People who hold minority opinions, even though these may be posthumously proved correct, are often called "madd", or at least "eccentric" during their lifetime. But that they can hold either advanced or demoted views distasteful to the community as a whole, shows them to be far less suggestible than their "normal" contemporaries; and no patients can be so difficult to influence by suggestion as the chronically mentally ill. Ordinary persons also have much greater powers of adaptation to circumstance than most eccentrics or psychotics."[2] Bicke's problem, typical of most nihilists, is his refusal to remain pragmatic; as business, familial and employment interdependencies encroach on his "idealistic" sense of independence, he fatalistically heads towards the bad break that begins every nihilist's downward spiral into violence and self destruction.

The lies and deceptions that must be played on unwitting customers to sell office furniture by his boss, the boss' son and himself are begrudgingly tolerated by Sam as long as his position as top salesman allows him limited access to his estranged wife, Marie (Naomi Watts) and their three children. Within an introductory scene of precise economy, Sam's boss, Jack Jones (Jack Thompson) draws an analogy of great salesmanship from the disingenuous 1968 and 1972 campaigns of Richard M. Nixon.

Jack: You wanna know who the greatest salesman in the world is? That man right there. Right there. He sold the whole country, 200 million people, on himself twice. What was Nixon's sales pitch in '68?"

Sam: In '68 it was . . ."

Jack: He said he would end the war. He would get us out of Vietnam. And what did he do? He sent another 100,000 troops in and he bombed the shit out of them, that's what he did. Now what did Nixon run on last year? Ending the war in Vietnam. And he won, by a landslide; that is a salesman. He made a promise. He didn't deliver and then he sold us on the exact same promise all over again. That's believing in yourself.

The key to understanding Sam Bicke in particular and every nihilist in general is found in the kind of hypocrisy demonstrated in this scene that corrupts their absolute idealism for the sake of maintaining their pragmatic circumstances. Such hypocrisy is tolerated only in so far as the would-be nihilist is satisfied in other areas of their lives (love, family, friends, money, independence etc.). Ironically, it is this job, as a deceptive office furniture salesman, that is Sam Bicke's lucky break. He excels as a top salesman and is able to give his estranged wife more money for their household and children.

If we look for a singular pragmatist character in Sam Bicke's story, we find not one character, but two characters whose pragmatist situations and ways of making a living weigh heavily upon him to keep him inter-dependant. 1) his estranged wife, Marie, who dresses in skimpy waitress uniforms and allows her customers to "feel her up" for extra tips to support her family; and 2) his African-American friend, Bonny Simmons (Don Cheadle), who has a family and his own auto repair business while tolerating the daily indignities thrown at him from his White customers.

The central conflict in the first act of the film is between Bicke and the absurd power and control exercised upon him at his work place; even to the point of making him shave his moustache. His boss tells him after he cuts it off," *I know it was important to you*

Sam. And I wanna thank you for the sacrifice. I think it was a good decision. Now you can smile. You look like a family man, not some schmuck with a pussy on his face." As Bicke tolerates his humiliation and the deception at work, his wife and his best friend attempt to reason with him so that he might keep his job, since apparently he has quit several before in indignation. Unable to get either his best friend or his wife to empathize with his views about the individual rights of the working man, Bicke encounters two double-sided bad breaks that are attached to each of his pragmatists and destroy his ideals and his heart; these bad breaks occur in devastating succession.

First, after applying for a small business loan for an idea he and Bonny had about a mobile tire store, he searches his mail day in and day out for an approval letter. Instead, he receives an," Official Notice of Dissolution of Marriage Decree of Divorce." His estranged wife, Marie, has divorced him and this binds his emotions into a Gordian knot of desperation. It doesn't help matters, that his boss expects and demands all of his salesmen to be married men. *"As I told you I only hire married men. A single salesman is distracted. A divorced salesman fails at selling the same as marriage."* In lieu of his loss of Marie, Sam unceremoniously quits his job while Nixon is on television defending himself against criminal accusations. The loss of Marie and his family renders his tolerance of the hypocrisy, subservience and deception at his job meaningless.

The second bad break concerns a large tire order that Sam placed on the behalf of his Brother Julius' tire store in preparation for the approval of a small business loan for the mobile tire business he wanted to start up. After quitting his job, Sam searches day in and day out for an approval letter (totally isolated from friends and family) in the mail, but when the letter finally arrives it announces that he has been denied. Moreover, the same evening he receives an eviction notice, his brother Julius is waiting for him. Julius accuses him of stealing from him and informs him that because of the unauthorized tire order he had to bail Bonny out of jail for receiving stolen goods. Julius disowns Sam and washes his hands of him. Admonishing him never to steal from him again or," brother or no brother I will send you to jail."

Each one of the bad breaks is double sided:

Loss of wife/Loss of Job

Loss of loan/Loss of friend

The final dismissal from Julius is a continuation of their pre-existing estrangement. The sheer wretchedness of Sam Bicke's condition, the lack of empathy for his ideals of independence and integrity in a world of corruption, hypocrisy and lies (all typified by the turmoil of Watergate and the Nixon Administration) gives Bicke's nihilism a disturbing martyr-like quality. It is this martyr-like quality that sets this portrait of a nihilist apart from our previous examples; not many male spectators will admire Bicke, but many can feel his pain. Moreover, the character of Sam Bicke is a terminal point in the Seventies to the idealism and activism that was started in the Sixties.

It can be surmised from his friendship with Bonny that their relationship began during the civil rights movement. Since Bicke himself was a Jew, it stands to reason that like many other Jews (the most famous being, Michael Schwerner one of the three murdered Freedom riders in 1964) there was a fraternal bond around the idea of civil rights and liberal ideals of a color blind society. Of course those ideas and ideals get tested during the film and culminate in Bicke's decision to check the Negro Box on the loan application when asked about the race of his business partner, which Bonny didn't think was such a good idea.

The deteriorating relationship between Sam and Marie can also be seen as a terminal point in the Sixties idealism that perhaps brought the two together, but by the Seventies was tearing them apart. The demurring mannerisms of Naomi Watts characterization of Marie and her impatience with many of Sam's arguments reveals that the qualities in Sam that first drew her to him in the Sixties are now the very same qualities that are causing her to revile him in the Seventies. The fate of Sam's pragmatists deviates from the usual structure of a Nihilist paradigm in that neither Bonny nor Marie physically die, but Sam's relationship with them is certainly destroyed; their ignorance of his terrible fate is shown as inconsequential to their day to day lives in the profound finale of the film.

Bicke is not one of those "ordinary" persons who can adapt to the changing circumstances of the times. Bicke is a man whose nihilism is caused by the turbulent and disingenuous tenor of the changing times from Sixties idealism to Seventies hypocrisy. Nihilism itself might be the horrific corollary to Nietzsche's famous maxim," He who attains his ideal by that very fact transcends it."[3] For the nihilist the maxim might be, "He who loses his ideal by that very fact is destroyed by it."

NOTES

[1]   I am using the definition of pragmatism given by sociologist Gerhard Lenski in his book POWER & PRIVILEGE: A Theory of Social Stratification," Pragmatic morality is the basis of all popular moral codes, and is based on the recognition that men need one another, and therefore condemns many kinds of harmful actions, especially those which threaten to undermine the social order." (Cf. page 30)

[2]   Pgs. 66-7, THE BATTLE FOR THE MIND by William Sargant. 1957. New York. Doubleday.

[3]   Pg. 91, BEYOND GOOD AND EVIL by Friedrich Nietzsche. Trans. R.J. Hollingdale. 1990. New York. Penguin Books.

BOOK ADAPTATIONS:
Faithfulness Does Not Always Mean Fidelity

In a previous chapter I laid some theoretical groundwork concerning the right of the film author vis-à-vis the right of the literary author that was based on the fundamental difference between the two mediums. In short, the isolated film image is more expressive than the isolated word. This expressive advantage is the first thing that must be considered concerning adapting a novel or literary text to the screen. It is the expressive advantages of the film image over the written word that leads us to the most difficult edict to suggest for film adaptations:

The Film Author (screenwriter/director) must lose his or her inhibitory reverence for the literary artist without losing their faith in the material.

I must qualify this immediately by stating that I do not mean this in any kind of a derogatory or pejorative fashion against writers or playwrights. It's just that the reverence for a literary author and his or her work can often become inhibitory to the film author's creativity and diminish the authorial right of the film author to re-assemble the material in the medium of cinema. I know this from my experiences in attempting to adapt Franz Kafka's THE METAMORPHOSIS and Albert Camus' THE STRANGER several years ago. The fact of the matter is that often the reasons why you like a novel may not be translatable verbatim into the medium of film. To be even more specific, you cannot be afraid to disturb the oyster to get at the pearl.

To get what you want you will have to change, adapt, cut out or reinterpret the text to accommodate the expressiveness of the cinematic image, the dynamism of cinematic editing and the running time of your final film. It is an unavoidable form of the collateral damage of translation. If the film artist does not divest him or herself of their reverence for the literary author, then they can easily become inhibited in their attempts at adapting the novel. In not wanting to disturb or desecrate the material or piss off the original artist and the fans of the work, the book is not actually translated into the cinematic medium, but it is rather transposed and that is actually a greater disservice to all. Because a literary work cannot be transposed into the medium of film verbatim, it must be translated (unless one were to adopt the surrealistic approach and simply photograph the actual pages in close up so that we can read the words). Translation is a matter of remaining faithful to the spirit and content of a work without slavishly and unerringly being in total fidelity to the work itself.

This inhibitory reverence of the film author for the literary author is actually a consequence of the fact that the film author has first encountered the story in the medium of literature—in the written word. Thus, in that initial discovery, lay the fatal impetus to try to simply transpose the style of written words to the screen instead of translating the story to the screen. "The [filmmaker] does not subordinate himself to another author; his source is only a pretext, which provides catalysts, scenes which fuse with his own preoccupations to produce a radically new work."[1] So the edict to obey when translating a novel or written work to the screen is to forgo one's reverence for the literary author and the material without losing faith in the material.

The real work to bring a literary text to the screen might entail various surgeries, amputations and transfusions; as long as the patient survives we can call the operation a success. Before moving on to some specific tools that are necessary for adaptations we will return to another simplification process that may aid in preparing literary material for cinematic adaptation.

THE CHAPTER OUTLINE

Congruent with the step outline of the story simplification process suggested for original screenplay development, a chapter outline is the first simplification process advised for literary adaptations. A chapter outline should be a brief and extremely subjective impression of the events, actions, objects, and characters of each chapter. If the work does not have chapters, then one can make chapters at ten or fifteen page intervals. In the chapter outline you only note the events, actions, and objects that stand out in your mind as significant and the characters who are significant to the story in your own opinion. Each section of the chapter outline should be no longer than 4 or 5 sentences, depending upon the complexity of the work or the importance of the chapter in your own subjective opinion.

The chapter outline allows the filmmaker to better see the potential cinematic or dramatic structure that is "in vitro" within the literary text as well as determining which of the seven basic story archetypes best describes the material to be adapted. The chapter outline allows the film author to better decide what events, characters, objects and actions are integral to a cinematic adaptation and what is superfluous. But most importantly, the function of the chapter outline allows the film author to find a way to elicit his or her own cinematic voice to tell the story. Below is a sample of a chapter outline for the screenplay adaptation of Bill Coleman's novel, TRAILER PARK HIPPIES, which was composed by filmmaker Sean Hodgson:

(Example Chapter Outline)

Trailer Park Hippies
Section 1964-1960

Chapter ONE: Mother is raging from schizophrenic delusion. The Son, father and mother (Mona) take a ride in Red 1955 Buick.

Chapter TWO: The Son, father and mother travel looking for a spot the mother will call safe. Son remembers the first time he realized his mother was crazy. The car stops near an airfield. Mother gets out of car in nightgown, brandishing a rusty tire iron. She runs across airfield towards a pilot, driver and a fuel truck.

Chapter THREE: Green 1952 Chrysler. The Son is nine years old. Father and Son go to Soul Brothers Lounge in Downtown Cincinnati looking for mother. Father smacks mother. Son hates mother's smell of Tabu [perfume] and alcohol. Introduction of Cookie, tight white jeans and Jackie Wilson "Lonely Teardrops."

Chapter FOUR: Father and son pull up to airport gate. Farmcrest police show up at gate. Son wished Mona would have stayed in the car and refused to speak.

Chapter FIVE: Cookie fixes the Son's pants. Cookie and son listen to records in Cookie's trailer. Cookie leans over and gives the son a small kiss.

Note the brevity of chapters 1, 4, and 5 relative to the length of chapters 2 and 3. This reveals the subjective importance these longer chapters will have for the filmmaker and will play a great importance in the story within the subsequent screenplay. Also in this chapter outline there are clues to the non-linear structure of the novel, particularly in chapter 2 and 4 which might allow the film author to find a thematic structure to justify presenting the film in a non-linear structure. Again, this simplification process allows the film author to find his or her own voice within the material as opposed to coldly attempting to replicate what the literary artist has done in literature. The other advantages of an outline is that it can allow you to identify conflict dynamics (such as the one between the son and the mother in the previous example) and other adaptation possibilities like, perspective, compression and condensation, which will we discuss individually below.

PERSPECTIVE

Perspective is best understood as who is telling the story as opposed to who is this story about. We know that who is telling the story need not be the same as who the story is about. In the synoptic gospels (Matthew, Luke, John, and Mark), it is the apostles who are telling the story, but the story is about Jesus Christ. Yet perspective in adapting a literary text is not as simplistic a decision as one would immediately assume. The perspective delivered in the novel is not sacral to the perspective delivered in the screenplay adaptation. Who is telling the story can be changed in the screenplay adaptation.

The most famous example of perspective change in a screenplay adaptation of a literary text is Laurence Hauben and Bo Goldman's screenplay of Ken Kesey's novel, ONE FLEW OVER THE CUCKOO'S NEST (1975). In the novel the anti-establishment/anti-authoritarian themes are delivered through the detailed observations of Chief Bromden, a brawny, but silent Native American who has been "passing" as a deaf/mute since he was twelve years old. The story of R.P. McMurphy, the wild-card prisoner who was transferred to the mental institution is given to us more or less from Chief Bromden's perspective. McMurphy ends up liberating the patients from the bureaucratic and authoritarian rationalism that was typified by the cold and cruel Nurse Ratched. He does this at the cost of his own freedom and another patient's suicide. By the end of the tale, Chief Bromden has found his voice and commits a sacrificial murder of a lobotomized and neutered R.P. McMurphy before he escapes the asylum; it is Bromden who tells this story.

Both the stage adaptation of the novel by Dale Wasserman and the screen adaptation by Laurence Hauben and Bo Goldman change the perspective of who is delivering the story. Chief Bromden (William Redfield) becomes just another character in the ward of mental patients, until he raises his hand to vote for watching the World Series on TV and finally reveals to McMurphy that he can hear and talk. After the revelation, the perspective of the screen and stage adaptations remains omniscient; that is the story is observed from the singular perspective of the "sane" audience watching the characters. Author Ken Kesey was never enamored of either adaptation of his work since he was trying to do, as he told his friend Ken Babbs," something that will be extremely difficult to pull off, and, to my knowledge, has never been tried before—the narrator is going to be a character."[2]

But both commercial reasons and dramatic reasons compelled the change in perspective for the screenplay. Obviously, to reach a wider audience the shift from the Native American perspective to an omniscient perspective that highlighted the antics of the White male R.P. McMurphy was perhaps the most rationalized difference between the novel and the film. This shift had the potential of increasing the box office attractiveness of the material. The prejudice and stereotypes that existed about Native Americans sustained in the 20th Century by decades and decades of Western films would have constricted the box office potential of the film if the film had been delivered solely from Chief Bromden's point of view. Of course, there is room for argument here; given the fact that the novel was successful without the perspective change—but reading about a kind of man and seeing a kind of man are qualitatively different experiences.

The dramatic reasons for the shift in perspective are inextricably linked to the fundamental aspects of the cinematic language: that is it records reality through images and sounds. Thus, the most dramatically concise method of presenting Chief Bromden as a deaf/mute was to have the actor perform the character as a deaf/mute and remove the internal monologues of the novel. This shift in perspective allowed the dramatic surprise and elation of R.P. McMurphy, when he discovered that Chief Bromden could hear and speak to also be a surprise for the audience as well. This is a very, very significant point and it relates directly to our previous observation about Native American stereotypes and the character of "White" moviegoers at that time.

If Chief Bromden, in the novel, had been passing as a "deaf/mute" because of the mendacity and indifference of White America, the dramatic corollary to this in a film is to shift the perspective so that White America as a film going audience at large would accept his passing as deaf/mute also. This is really the key to the film's success and its enduring legacy as a cinematic classic. This film, though greatly different from the novel in perspective, is faithful in the meaning and insightfulness of its critique of the sanity of American society.

This is what the film author must keep in mind when adapting a literary text to the screen: that a shift in perspective is permissible as long as the ends justify the means. Faithfulness to a novel does not always mean fidelity to the novel.

COMPRESSION

"Expression through compression. To put into an image what a writer would spin out over ten pages."

-Robert Bresson, pg.86 Notes On The Cinematographer

Compression is a wholly editorial process whereby information, time, situation, and/or characters are modified in the film from where they occur or are positioned within the novel. THIS IS THE MOST IMPORTANT ASPECT OF ANY CINEMATIC ADAPTATION OF LITERARY MATERIAL and it cannot be underestimated. It is achieved primarily by two means: 1) The Narrative Ellipsis (for a detailed discussion please see the previous chapter on Narrative Ellipsis) and 2) Dramatic Economy.

Since Narrative Ellipsis already has a separate chapter I will only briefly detail it here.

1) NARRATIVE ELLIPSIS

An ellipsis is a narrative editorial strategy whereby a specific shot or scene is omitted but clearly implied and chronologically consistent with the rest of the story. An ellipsis can have three, if not more, important narrative functions:

TIME: the omission of a scene or scenes can signify a gap in chronological time that can reveal hours, days, weeks, months or years that have passed from the preceding scene.

MODIFICATION: the omission of a scene or scenes can reveal the modifications of a character's behavior or circumstance relative to the preceding scene.

RESULT: an ellipsis can reveal the result of a character or group of characters actions.

A film author might consider using a narrative ellipsis or several to move the story along at a greater pace than the novel and focus the audience's attention on the themes within the material. An ellipsis allows the film author, through a basic tool of the cinematic language (editing), to cut out unnecessary exposition, cut out lengthy transportation sequences, and make emphatic transitions and contrasts in the circumstances, looks, or behaviors of characters.

2) DRAMATIC ECONOMY

Our best example of dramatic economy returns us again to that rich and incomparable adaptation, Coppola and Puzo's THE GODFATHER. We witness the fact that the first 25 minutes of the movie are the first 80 pages of the novel. Dramatic economy is the editorial means by which a film author shifts and compresses dramatic events, characters, back-story, and character introductions to get the most out of a single scene that a writer would take several chapters to build.

Working in intimate collaboration with literary artist Mario Puzo, film author Francis Coppola achieved this economy with the extraordinary narrative decision to use The Wedding Scene as the single scene to introduce the bulk of all major and minor characters and their back stories that were originally spread out throughout the entire novel. From famous family friends, the capo regimes of Tessio and Clemenza, the competing mafia family of Don Barzini, the brothers Sonny, Fredo, Michael, and Tom, the mother and sister Connie and her new husband Carlo, all are introduced in this one single opening scene. [3] This was the masterstroke; Coppola could see that the wedding was the key to the entire story as well as a powerful demonstration of the theme: the wedding of crime and family- "La Cosa Nostra."

"No Sicilian can refuse any request on his Daughter's wedding day."

As Michael Corleone is telling his girlfriend Kay Adams about the members of his family and his father's dark past, he is also telling "us" the audience and in so doing Coppola and Puzo are instantly compressing pages and pages of narration from the novel into single lines.

185

"Michael, you never told me you knew Johnny Fontaine!"
"Sure, you want to meet him?"
"Huh, oh, uhmm, sure."
"My Father helped him with his career."
"He did? How?"

Dramatic economy means getting the most out of every scene, particularly in a film where time constraints inhibit the total translation of the languid or laconic style of a novel. The film author has to look for the opportunity to compress. But in order for compression to be successful it is important that the opportunity to use it be found within the material. Again, the wedding scene was already within the novel of THE GODFATHER, thus it was a thematically justified opportunity to introduce most of the major characters in this scene to strengthen the dramatic impact of later tragic events in the story.

If the opportunity is found within the material one is still being faithful to the spirit of the book without committing an infidelity that destroys the author's original intentions. But let me warn here, the opportunity to compress does not mean making a scene overwrought with characters; it is a delicate balance that is not so much an exact science as it is an exact intuition. For instance, although Coppola introduces us to most of the major and minor characters in The Wedding Scene, the scene itself has a deliberate and respectful pacing that lasts for nearly 25 minutes. So economy does not always relate to the quickening of pace. Dramatic economy is a compression of events, characters, information, and actions to achieve the greatest dramatic impact. To make dramatic use of every scene so that we are not just watching exposition (How a person got from point A to point B) but dramatizing why they are going there, what circumstances or who made them go there and the effect of their decisions or actions.

CONDENSATION

If compression is the modification of events, then condensation is the modification of characters. The combining of two or more characters into one character is another side of dramatic economy, but more importantly it is the recognition of similarities within two or more characters that make it dramatically expedient and concise to condense these weaker characters into one powerful dramatic characterization. It is the recognition of the same "soul" in two similar beings.

Condensation may also be the simple elimination or diminishing of a character whose dramatic redundancy is unnecessary. Returning again to ONE FLEW OVER THE CUCKOO'S NEST, there were originally two authority figures in the Novel: Doctor Spivey and Nurse Ratched. But in the film Doctor Spivey's part is diminished and more sympathetic and much of his vile authority is given over to Nurse Ratched. This condensation of Doctor Spivey allowed the filmmakers to focus the themes of authority, bureaucracy and sexual politics through R.P. McMurphy and Nurse Ratched. Here again, fidelity is sacrificed for faithfulness.

It is rare, but worth noting, that one could perhaps expand one character into two or more characters, but I do not have any reference films to support such an idea. Perhaps, the dual roles performed by a female actress in David Cronenberg's NAKED LUNCH adaptation. It is conceivable that a difficult major character could be expanded into two characters (a domineering mother split into an equally domineering pair of parents), but such expansion would have to be compensated for elsewhere in the narrative in terms of time or dramatic impact. Expansion would seem to dilute the dramatic impact of a scene, by multiplying the characters within the scene, where as condensation is a matter of combining two weaker characters into one stronger character.

To reiterate, for condensation to be effective the film author must recognize the opportunity within the material to do so. It is the recognition of "similar" souls in different characters that determines the opportunity for condensation. The dramatic redundancy of two or more characters saying or doing the same things, if not an overall thematic concept, provides a clear cut opportunity to condense the two characters into one. Condensation must be judged by its potential dramatic impact. If condensation does not increase the potential for a story's dramatic impact then condensation should be avoided.

CONCLUSION

So once the film author loses his or her inhibitory reverence for the literary author, a cinematic adaptation can begin in earnest. The first step to reducing the inhibition is the grasping of the story within the novel and judging whether or not the perspective within the material can be maintained in a cinematic context for maximum dramatic impact (seeing and hearing as opposed to reading). Secondly, by means of dramatic and narrative economy the film author has the right to modify and condense characters, events and actions to achieve the greatest dramatic use out of every single scene and focus the thematic explorations. One of the greatest missteps in adaptations of literary material has to do with using the cinema to make literal everything that was imagined in the novel; that is, to show shot for word and word for shot what the novel tells. Reading fires the imagination if simply because words are symbolic and the mind must complete the picture those words suggest. "For the experiencing of, say, a novel is in large part the experiencing of imagined images and sounds. The film presents actual images and sounds to the spectator . . . unless these actual pictures and sounds appeal past the eye to the inner eye of imagination they tend to become dull and uninteresting."[4]

Cinema can render the images of a novel with great explicitness, but in doing so the film author is better served if he or she uses sound to fire the imagination of the spectator. As Bresson has noted," When a sound can replace an image, cut the image or neutralize it. The ear goes more towards the within, the eye towards the outer."[5] Thus, another expressive advantage that the cinema has over the novel is sound. Moreover, the use of sound in the cinema is arguably more important than what has been rendered visible for the eye. Without an expressive use of sound would the Kung-Fu movie even exist as a genre? Who can forget Kubrick's daring use of 'breathing' to build and sustain suspense in the space walking sequences of 2001: A Space Odyssey? Sound adds an expressive advantage in literary adaptations that should not be overlooked.

Faithfulness to a novel does not always mean total fidelity with how the events or characters were presented in that novel. Of course this does not mean that the film author's interpretation will be accepted by the literary author or the fans as Tarkovsky's adaptation of Stanislaw Lem's SOLARIS (See: Collapsing of Back-story into Story Proper) and Stanley Kubrick's adaptation of Stephen King's THE SHINING demonstrate. Although time has gracefully placed the patina of classic status upon both of these works and allowed us to see the film authors accomplishments beyond the page of the literary author. You remain faithful in spirit and the spirit is what matters the most in any adaptation.

NOTES

[1]   Pg.113, SIGNS and MEANING in the CINEMA by Peter Wollen, Indiana University Press, Bloomington. 1972.

[2]   Pg.337, ONE FLEW OVER THE CUCKOO'S NEST by Ken Kesey, Viking Critical Library Edition, New York. 1996.

[3]   Robert Towne also worked on the screenplay adaptation of THE GODFATHER, given his obvious gifts of building and sustaining the 'state of mind' of characters and his long history of polishing scripts and solving problem scripts it is no surprise. (C.f. Chapter Ten, THE GODFATHER LEGACY, by Harlan Lebo. New York. Fireside Books. 1997.)

[4]   Pg.64, LITERATURE and FILM by Robert Richardson, Indiana University Press, Bloomington. 1969.

[5]   Pg.51, NOTES ON THE CINEMATOGRAPHER by Robert Bresson, Quartet Books, London. 1975

THE BREAKTHROUGH SCENE
Discussion and Analysis

E very film of high quality, classic status, or subversive notoriety contains what I'd like to define as a breakthrough scene. The breakthrough scene is a scene that exists beyond the mechanics of the plot, the standard limits of character development and sometimes even the boundaries of the story. In other words, the breakthrough scene is a scene that usually transcends every aspect of the fiction it is bound within and seems to let us peak behind that fictional veil to see real life, if only for a few fleeting moments. Although the breakthrough scene itself is shocking it is not a scene that is written with the sole intent to simplistically shock an audience through unmitigated violence, sex, coarse language or otherwise. This scene is also shocking because it usually eschews the conventional representation of reality to get dangerously close to an alternate or heightened representation of reality.

The writer/director of high quality films (irrespective of the budget) seeks to present a breakthrough scene to his or her audience not explicitly for their entertainment, but more so because the writer/director is obsessed with some aspect of real life or some emotional or mental state that they must demonstrate. In this obsession, the writer/director may not even know that he or she has created a breakthrough scene until they are directing it or until the final film is organized and presented. The reason for this 'blindness' is perhaps because the director's unique vision has caused him or her to push the envelope of conventional representation in chasing a truth in reality that fascinates them. The breakthrough scene is usually the scene that would be cut out, cut short or not even filmed under conventional standards and wisdom.

Of all the American directors, Martin Scorsese has made the breakthrough scene a hallmark of his films. Scorsese is always in pursuit of a realism beyond conventional representation and practices. In TAXI DRIVER it was the "You talkin' to me?" improvisation by Robert DeNiro that has gone on to be the most beloved movie quote in history. Yet this scene is more than just a titillating quote, it is a moment of daring introspection; the unveiling of a disturbed individual rehearsing a violent fiction within his mind. The list of Scorsese's breakthrough scenes is varied and long: the intimate and seductive conversation between Max Cady (Robert DeNiro) and Danielle Bowden (Juliette Lewis) in CAPE FEAR (1991), the "What's so fuckin' funny about me?" scene between Tommy (Joe Pesci) and Henry Hill (Ray Liotta) in GOODFELLAS (1990) and of course the emotionally horrific "I am not an animal", knuckle breaking scene in RAGING BULL (1980). For Scorsese it is clear that his approach to a breakthrough scene is dependant upon the controlled improvisation of his actors and the state of mind he is trying to represent that forces him to go beyond a conventional presentation.

But there are other filmmakers who create breakthrough scenes beyond the boundaries of the emotional world reproduced on screen. If the breakthrough scene gives us a heightened presentation of reality it does so only by breaking our conventional expectations of how reality is usually presented to us in modern commercial films. The breakthrough scene is the scene that gives us an uncommon view of what we often view as common. It is a certainty that all artists who find themselves penetrating such boundaries must always have some level of control over their work so that that breakthrough scene can remain in the final film.

We will look at three very different filmmakers and three very diverse approaches to a breakthrough scene: Michael Mann's HEAT (1995), Gaspar Noe's IRREVERSIBLE (2003) and finally Carl Franklin's DEVIL IN A BLUE DRESS (1995). But I must caution the reader again: most breakthrough scenes occur while in pursuit; that is, during production or post-production. These scenes are 'discovered' in the act and without much preparation. The breakthrough scene is usually that which is unexpected; an unplanned magic or thematic obsession that materializes on screen and must be pursued and protected by the film author.

HEAT
Written and Directed by Michael Mann

The epic crime saga HEAT has been acclaimed for its first time simultaneous on screen performances of Robert DeNiro and Al Pacino. Of the many things to admire in this layered and richly themed masterpiece is the scene where reality threatens to overtake the story and present to the audience the terror of random street violence. Of course I am referring to the bank robbery getaway scene where the crew of professional criminals go bullet for bullet with the L.A.P.D. in the middle of the street in the middle of the day. For this single scene (a set piece or sequence really) is the scene that brings the film 'closer' to reality by bringing the violence out of its tightly framed fictional context. Instead of the violence being solely between criminals and the police, the "plein air" street battle has the potential to harm innocent bystanders.

In contrast to 1940's Western shoot outs where the bad guys and the good guys pace off against each other in a ritual that has the streets cleared and onlookers carefully out of harm's way; this gun battle in HEAT is sudden, unplanned and explodes in the unguarded center of civil society. So unlike the gun fight at the O.K. Corral in John Ford's MY DARLING CLEMENTINE (1946) where everyone in town knew of the coming event and anticipated the outcome. HEAT delivers the gunfight 'sans ritual' bringing the battle between bandits and the law out of the limitations of its conventional fictional representation; it is in this way that the realism of the scene is heightened.

The other aspect of this sequence that truly makes it a breakthrough scene is purely technical: the uncompressed sound of the gunfire. This was the actual sound of blank firing rounds captured on the set of the film during production. The story goes that Mann was truly enamoured of this "terrifying" cacophony of gunfire that reverberated off the walls of the skyscrapers and created a symphony of banditry and death. Yet the sound technicians in Hollywood, following their standard procedures, re-recorded the gunfire and discarded the actual sound. It is a standard practice in commercial motion pictures to take the multiple audio tracks of wildly varying volumes and mix them down to its final stereo, 5.1, THX, Dolby, SDDS, or multi-speaker output, with all of the sound levels "compressed" to give a clear sonic picture of what we are hearing.

Voices are distinct; background noise is removed or lowered, etc. It is not uncommon to re-record actor's voices, footsteps, and many other sounds in processes that are alternately called ADR (for Dialogue Replacement or "looping') and Foleying (for all natural sound effects). Indeed, much of what we hear in a motion picture has been significantly processed to remove sounds that would be distracting to the ear.

When Mann first saw a rough-cut of his film, he realized that the actual sound had been replaced and demanded that the original sound be restored. "Nothing artificial could come close to delivering the fear of the sound that the full load made moving through those automatic weapons. The way the sound ricocheted off the walls of the buildings of an empty downtown. You couldn't manufacture that sound and it was quite extraordinary." (Michael Mann, DVD documentary on the making of HEAT)

By recording and insisting upon the restoration and preservation of the actual sound, Mann created a breakthrough scene; a scene of 'heightened' realism that threatened both the fictional characters and innocent bystanders within the film and the conventional representation of violence in the cinema. By simply ignoring or bypassing a conventional practice of Hollywood cinema a new realism was attained. It is a sudden realism captured in the moment when the last bank robber, Chris (Val Kilmer), sees the two L.A.P.D. officers just before he was supposed to climb into the getaway after a perfect job. Without hesitation, he opens fire.

The first officer, who is killed in crossfire, dies with a look of gruesome surprise frozen on his face—as if his bulletproof vest was supposed to make him invincible.

The anxious roar of the getaway driver is cut short within the hailstorm of bullets. His blood and brain matter spraying against the windshield. His death made to seem inevitable in these circumstances. In fact, within this single sequence are many dramatic vignettes with their conflicts rising and resolving in between the sound of a firing bullet.

Friendships grow stronger or suddenly end, accuracy and preparation are put on the line. Again, what is most important here is the alternate representation of reality that seems to get us closer to the "real" in this sequence was deliberately caught while in pursuit—or while in production—by the artist. It is an extreme representation that had to be protected by the artist as this terrifying sound caught during the production had to be restored in the final release print of the film. The breakthrough scene is often created by the will of the artist as much as by the imagination of the artist.

IRREVERSIBLE
Written and Directed by Gaspar Noe

The infamous rape scene within Gaspar Noe's IRREVERSIBLE is perhaps yet another obvious choice as being a breakthrough scene. The sheer cruelty and unmitigated brutality of such a rape scene borders on a kind of modern barbarism not recorded in the cinema since the work of Sam Peckinpah or Pier Paolo Pasolini. [1] Yet my interest in it is found not in the nihilistic thrusts of the rapist, Le Tenia (Joe Presia), within his victim, or in the desperate wails of the victim herself. My interest in the breakthrough aspects of this horrific scene lay in how the scene captures an unvarnished look at human nature that pushes it beyond conventional representation.

The rape scene is approached with seemingly audacious simplicity. A woman, Alex (Monica Bellucci), leaves a house party early without her male escorts (her boyfriend and her ex-boyfriend). As she attempts to hail a taxi, a female bystander informs her of an underground passage that's "safer" and will allow her to cross the street, presumably to better hail a taxi. As she walks into the tunnel, a couple comes into view at the other end. When she attempts to pass by them the man viscously assaults his female companion with several punches. Alex is caught off guard by this sudden violence and is noticed by the attacker. He quickly loses interest in his companion and turns his attention to Alex. His companion scampers away and out of the tunnel. Alex is brutally raped and savagely beaten in a scene that has been designed to appear as a single unadulterated long take. [2]

First and foremost in our consideration of this scene as a breakthrough scene is the straightforward presentation of the criminal act "sans musique" and in long take. The long take, in and of itself as a cinematic device, retains the "temporal" integrity of a scene in that it seems to have not been manipulated through cutting (the linear conjoining of one shot to another). The long take is a form that mimics the temporal nature of reality. As the late Russian filmmaker Andrei Tarkovsky had repeatedly stated," The cinema image, then, is basically observation of life's facts within time, organized according to the pattern of life itself, and observing its time laws." [3] Thus, in IRREVERSIBLE, the set up and presentation of the rape scene as if it were a single unadulterated long take gives the entire sequence a heightened (and to a certain extent, nauseating) realism. It is the timing of the events within the frame that gives a long take its realism; the events are organized according to the temporal pattern of life itself (or at least life under the subjective eyes of the artists participating in the scene).

In this sequence we see the rapist, Le Tenia, become aroused as he verbally denigrates his victim. His use of the knife against Alex's face is both a threat to encourage her obedience and a symbol of his power over her. That he penetrates her anally and the camera unflinchingly captures the experience from insertion to withdrawal gives us what amounts to a sociological document of the crime of rape. The power dynamics, the denigration of the female and what she symbolizes, the nihilistic pride of the rapist, who gratifies himself without any thought of reciprocation, is revealed in all of its sadistic glory. Another disturbing aspect of the rape scene is that Le Tenia is defiling what the woman symbolizes in modern society: the bourgeois ideal, her class object status as another man's trophy of social conformity and economic success. He defiles the ideal of feminine beauty that she epitomizes, the vagina as a symbol of masculine enslavement and feminine power, and finally her humanity as he ignores her muffled screams and physical suffering.

And yet, were the sequence comprised of only these briefly mentioned attributes it would only be a breakthrough scene because of its graphic nature and could soon be surpassed by other self-indulgent filmmakers with sadistic predilections. Instead, there are three seemingly small events that push this scene beyond its sadism and into the "heightened" realism so characteristic of the best breakthrough scenes.

1) The female bystander who advised Alex to use the underground tunnel because it was safer.
2) The "female" companion who was first assaulted in the tunnel by Le Tenia.
3) The stranger who came into the tunnel and saw what was going on.

Let us look at these three minor events separately and learn how they impact the dramatic presentation of the breakthrough scene's 'heightened' realism.

Ladies of the Night

The woman who advised Alex to use the underground passage, at first appears to be just an innocent bystander giving helpful advice. But as Alex walks the few meters to the passage entrance other women are seen standing on the street and on display as they wait for passing customers. It becomes evident that all the women standing on this street, including Alex's helpful bystander are prostitutes looking for their night's earnings. It is perhaps the casual tone and civil nature of the woman who advised Alex that does not raise our (and her) suspicions about her profession.

It is not until Alex walks further down the street, that we notice the other women and put two and two together. There is a speculation that can be advanced here that the woman may have told Alex about the underground passage as a way of ridding herself of unwanted competition. Alex was standing right next to her and could have drawn attention from the potential customers of the prostitute. She could have simply been telling Alex a lie to get her away from her pick up zone. Over and over again in this film, people and their actions are not what they are first presumed to be.

Guillermo Nunez

This 'double entendre' aspect of the film is no more clearly evident than when Le Tenia enters the tunnel with his 'female' companion. This character is the male transvestite prostitute named Guillermo Nunez we encountered earlier in the film and his/her role is significant because once Le Tenia sets his sights upon Alex, Nunez immediately exits—apparently to get back to work on the streets. This is revealing because Alex literally becomes a replacement victim for Nunez. Like a vampire's victim who must find another fresh body to replace himself before he can escape his master's servitude, Nunez thinks only of his own survival. He runs away, leaving the new victim, Alex, to a fate worse than what he was ever going to receive.

It is also significant to point out that during Nunez's brutal attack he/she was screaming for help from Alex as she was seen in the tunnel passing them. Yet once Le Tenia turned to Alex it was Nunez who disregarded Alex's pleas for help. What does this reveal about human nature? This victim exchange, this passage of souls underneath the ground might suggest that we are not as morally reciprocating as we would like to believe. Could it be that a cry for help might be a ruse to gain one's freedom at the expense and victimization of someone else? The long take allows us to observe these behaviors from an objective distance, but their meaning is withheld until we understand what has caused these behaviors and actions in the story.

The Stranger

Our third event is the hapless male stranger who enters the underground passage just as the rape is about to begin. He cautiously waits for a few seconds and then turns away and exits with nonchalance. This shadowy figure who takes a moment to appraise the situation is perhaps not as callous as we would like to presume. He came in on something that from his vantage-point was not so much a rape as it might have been a kinky form of public sex. Unsure of what to do, he chose to give the 'couple' their 'privacy' and find another route. Sure, in Paris, he has probably seen it all, but he had no way of fully grasping the true nature of the situation unless he risked acting on his own voyeurism and extending the time he watched what was going on. He is jaded, perhaps, but not callous. Certainly no more callous that anyone on a Saturday night at one in the morning who just wants to get home.

He leaves the scene, no doubt chalking up what he had seen to another bizarre event in Paris after dark. His position is also reflective of a theme running throughout the film of actions, events and characters not being what they initially seem. His action of leaving the scene and not trying to help the victim seems to contradict the so-called 'Kitty Genovese' effect of social psychology which was," named after the 1964 incident in which no one even called the police, much less tried to help, when Genovese's cries were heard as she was being stabbed to death in a New York City neighborhood."[4] Subsequent experiments and investigations by social psychologists found that," When in a group we experience a social inhibition against helping, that probably derives from a diffused sense of personal responsibility. It is as if each person in a group says to himself or herself," Maybe somebody else will do it . . . In every case, a lone bystander was more likely to help the "victim" than was a group of bystanders."[5] Yet our bystander here in IRREVESIBLE does not try to help and the reason for this is as simple as it is tragic: He did not have enough information to discern whether or not Alex was an innocent victim or a willing participant. Moreover, he did not have enough information to discern that a rape was about to be committed. The event from his vantage-point was not a sadistic crime, but perhaps just an inopportune moment between two reckless lovers. He had no way of knowing what had just happened or what was about to actually occur.

So we can see how the inclusion of these three minor events in the overall long take sequence adds to the heightened realism that Gaspar Noe was pursuing in this scene and turned what at first seemed to be a sadistic exercise in misogyny into a perceptive, albeit uncompromising, commentary upon human nature. Even the digital penis, a computer added artifact that shows the rapist's waning erection after the act, was a post-production decision. This was an artifact that Noe fought for to advance the realism of what he was pursuing, though many would say that what he was pursuing was a new type of graphic pornography posing as an artistic inquiry into the human condition. The breakthrough scene may not be what we want to see, but instead what we need to see; the challenge is within the artist that is brave enough to risk his or her reputation to show it.

DEVIL IN A BLUE DRESS
Written and Directed by Carl Franklin
Based on the novel by Walter Mosley

About The Novel

Walter Mosley's 1990, Devil In a Blue Dress, was a strong, yet malleable novel and fully capable after modification of retaining the shape that its author envisioned: that of 1940's Southern California and its post-war African-American culture. This screenplay adaptation by Carl Franklin is an exact example of all the points discussed in the preceding chapter on book adaptations: faithfulness does not always mean fidelity.

The novel concerns the recently unemployed ex-GI, Easy Rawlins (Denzel Washington), who has been hired by an unsavory White underworld criminal named, Dewitt Albright (Tom Sizemore), to find a missing White girl named, Daphne Monet (Jennifer Beals). Throughout the course of the novel, Easy Rawlins is drawn into an ever-increasing web of deception which culminates into a mysterious series of murders of almost anyone Easy questions during his search. Added to this, Easy receives quite a few knocks on his head from various thugs and police officers every step of the way.

The novel continues with Easy finding and falling in love with Daphne Monet only to discover that she is not White, but a biracial woman passing for White. When Dewitt Albright and the notorious Black gangster, Frank Green (Joseph Latimore) threaten his life, Easy calls in an old friend from his home town of Austin, Texas named Mouse Alexander (Don Cheadle). Mouse is a man whose trigger-happy demeanor is matched only by his love for money. Easy rescues Daphne Monet from the hands of Albright and uncovers an extortion scheme by two rich and powerful Whites who were involved with Monet. One is a powerful man named, Todd Carter (Terry Kinney), who loved her and wanted to expose the mayoral candidate, Matthew Terrell (Maury Chaykin), as a pederast. Of course, Matthew Terrell is the other man who wanted to kidnap Daphne to keep Todd Carter from exposing his perversion and forcing him out of the mayoral race; politics, sex and race are always familiar bedfellows.

About The Adaptation

Anyone who has read this novel and seen the film can discern immediately the extensive changes writer/director Carl Franklin made to bring the story within the novel to the screen. Many of the changes were slight, but substantial. Mosley's novel is full of flashy and superfluous prose that just simply could not be translated to the screen. Most importantly, the subjective chapter in the book where Easy has a conversation with a voice in his head to bolster his ego and stand up for himself is cut out of the movie. This chapter and the references to the voice in his head throughout the novel are distracting and ultimately unnecessary for the film adaptation. Carl Franklin beautifully translates, modifies and reinterprets some of these passages as insightful voice-overs in the subsequent film and the achievement is no less sublime than it is merciful. Where Mosley's Easy Rawlins relentlessly gives tiring and obvious descriptions of Black, White and even Mexican race relations within post-war Southern California, Carl Franklin's Easy Rawlins is content to simply make matter-of-fact observations: a subtle and paramount change.

We no longer have to see Easy Rawlins as a Phillip Marlow in Blackface, but rather as a fully fleshed out Black man living in a realistic historical period. Where the last three chapters of Mosley's novel reads like a disinterested coroner's report of long dead body, Franklin's script and film brings sweeping dramatic changes in the characters, their motivations, clues and resolutions too numerous and too brilliant to go into detail about within this chapter.

What all this is building towards is the obvious, but rare conclusion that the movie was far superior to the book. "Where a book is unfulfilled a frightful problem arises. The film, if successful, is a critique of the author's failures."[6] One of the few historical instances where a so-so novel was transformed into a brilliant film was when Orson Welles re-wrote and filmed his, TOUCH OF EVIL (1958), from an earlier script by writer Paul Monash and the so-so novel upon which it was based, Badge of Evil, by Whit Masterson. Although TOUCH OF EVIL and DEVIL IN A BLUE DRESS have a myriad of differences in structure, tone and content between them, there is one interesting similarity: both films have themes of miscegenation.

We know that Orson Welles' decision to change the American detective character in the novel to a Mexican male (Mike Vargas, performed by Charlton Heston) with a White wife," adds a new dimension," to the entire film.[7] TOUCH OF EVIL observes American racial prejudices and double standards from a strategic and intense point of view. The film observes these racial tensions from the border town in-between the United States and Mexico where such relations were apt to be more distinct and intolerant.

Carl Franklin's DEVIL IN A BLUE DRESS deals with miscegenation among Whites and Blacks from a less hostile point of view. It observes the issue as sort of a pre-existing social condition that created its own sub-culture rather than as an attempt to point out an injustice or promote a message of indignation. The separation of Whites and Blacks in daylight and open society was an accepted fact of life. But in the underworld of juke joints, after hour's clubs and gambling halls this segregation was easily forgotten at night in the closed world of vice and crime.

For instance, Dewitt Albright, a White man, travels within the semi-legal Black social milieu without the prejudice or racial vilification we have come to expect of such White characters in that historical time period. Clearly, Daphne Monet's ability to pass for White in both the Black and White social circles says something incredible about the prejudice inherent in Americans (yesterday and today): Her existence is a consequence of this crossing into 'mixed' racial company by her own parents. Throughout the novel, it is unclear whether Easy is sexually attracted to Daphne Monet because he believes she is White or in spite of her race. If there is any flaw in Carl Franklin's film adaptation, it is the omission of a sex scene (implied or explicit) between Monet and Rawlins that would have 'fleshed out' the racial and sexual ambiguities that surrounded his attraction as was drawn in the novel.

If we are to understand how a so-so novel can be transformed into a brilliant film, we must understand that the writer/director approaching such work always reshapes the material to fit his own obsessions. For both Orson Welles and Carl Franklin, the theme of miscegenation played an important part in their approach. For Welles the inclusion of miscegenation brought dynamic changes to the script and made the film an incredible statement about American sexual/racial stereotypes. For Carl Franklin, miscegenation was only one theme in DEVIL IN A BLUE DRESS that attracted him to the project. We know this because his previous film, ONE FALSE MOVE (1987) contains a subtext of miscegenation between a Black woman and a White small town sheriff. The real obsession that seems to have drawn Carl Franklin to the DEVIL IN A BLUE DRESS was the psychopathic character Mouse. Many of the substantial changes in the film from the novel are made to explore, develop, and highlight this sick, trigger happy and frighteningly consistent character. It is within the writer/director's obsession with this psychopath that we are given a breakthrough scene.

MOUSE ALEXANDER

"Conscience depends not only on the ability to imagine consequences but on the capacity to mentally 'talk to oneself'."

-Without Conscience, The Disturbing World of The Psychopaths Among Us, Robert D. Hare, pg.77

Our introduction to the character of Mouse in the movie is much more dramatic than in the novel. In the novel, Mouse writes a letter to Easy and later Easy telephone's Mouse's girlfriend, Etta, to get Mouse's help. In the film, Easy tells us in a voice over that he 'placed a call' to Etta to ask for Mouse's help and Mouse suddenly appears in the film while Frank Green is about to cut Easy's throat in his own house. So with much less dialogue than in the novel Mouse intimidates Frank Green by suddenly shooting him—point blank—in his shoulder. This introduction scene establishes the trigger-happy nature of Mouse and further establishes his single-minded concern for money when Easy tells him of his search for Daphne Monet. But it is not until just near the finale of the film that Carl Franklin delivers his breakthrough scene.

The scene itself concerns Easy's search for a letter that a recently murdered woman named, Coretta (Lisa Nicole Larson), was keeping for Daphne Monet. Earlier in the film, Coretta was Easy's friend, Dupree Bouchard's (Jernnard Burks) woman and Easy had had a sexually intimate one night stand with her in her home while Dupree was drunk and asleep in her home the night before her demise. Easy and Mouse go to Dupree's sister's house where Dupree, just recently released from police questioning, is grieving over the loss of Coretta. As the night wears on Dupree and Mouse get drunk and fall asleep while Easy finds the letter and pictures in a bible Coretta had asked Dupree to keep for her just hours before her death. The following is a transcription of what I identify as the breakthrough scene in DEVIL IN A BLUE DRESS:

Easy Rawlins enters the kitchen area from another room after having found Daphne's letter to Coretta. Mouse and Dupree are drunk and sleeping at the dining table. The hand held camera pans and tilts up from Easy's waist and moves in behind him, holding a medium two shot.

EASY

(To Mouse, touching him to wake him up)

I got it come on, let's go.

[Mouse jumps up and draws his gun on Easy]

EASY (Con't)

Boy is you crazy or is you drunk? Come on!

MOUSE

Am I drunk? You saw me draw that gun!

[He cocks the pistol and aims it at Easy's chest]

MOUSE (Con't)

Ain't no man in Texas can out draw me!

EASY

Mouse put the gun down!

MOUSE

Naw, I'm drunk. Naw, I'm drunk, you right.

[He places the gun on the table]

MOUSE (Con't)

I'mmo put that gun right there—we gone see whose drunk.

[Easy moves to reach for his coat. Mouse draws another gun from his back]

MOUSE (Con't)

Naw, watch it now, watch it goddammit!

[The gun is pointed at Easy's chest]

MOUSE (Con't)

Right there now! Oh yeah, now how this fool gonna call me out and he ain't even got no gun?

I'll kill that mutherfucka!

EASY
No ah . . . Let him go.

MOUSE
Uhhm?

EASY
Let him live and he'll be scared of you every time you walk into a room.

MOUSE
Shit, he better be scared goddammit—I'll kill'im!

EASY
He will . . . If, if, if he ain't-

MOUSE (Over)
You better tell'im!

EASY
I will. Trust me, I'll tell him.

[Mouse takes the gun away from Easy's chest. They both laugh and sit down]

MOUSE
(He draws his gun on Easy again)
Right there, goddammit!

EASY
No, no keep an eye on him.

[Easy gestures to Dupree who is still sleeping]

MOUSE
(Turns his gun towards Dupree)
Where you goin'?

EASY
That's right.

[Easy puts on his coat as Mouse falls back to sleep. He takes the gun from Mouse's hand and leaves.
CUT TO THE NEXT SCENE]

In the novel the scene is not as shocking and it appears seven chapters before the conclusion and seems to function as one more loop in the labyrinth that Easy is running through on his search for Daphne. But Carl Franklin makes this scene his breakthrough because it is placed very late in the narrative. It is placed well after Mouse has been firmly established as trigger-happy and after it is known that he is an old friend of Easy's from his hometown. Indeed, in an earlier scene it is Mouse who convinces Easy that he will need someone like himself—"at yo back"—to keep thugs like Frank Green in check. But in this scene where a drunk Mouse pulls his guns on Easy with the intent to kill, the shock effect exists beyond the demands of simple character development, beyond the story and most certainly beyond the plot.

As aforementioned, the dramatic changes in the film from the novel concern the Mouse character. Franklin explores the unpredictable psychopathic nature of Mouse and he does this by offsetting him against the rational and predictable Easy Rawlins. The 'polite' switching of guns during the shooting of Frank Green and the switching of guns here in this scene increases the unpredictability of Mouse. But it is the effect of alcohol on the character of Mouse that provides the breakthrough in this scene and allows Franklin to give us a glimpse into an alternate realism for a few fleeting moments.

The study of the effects of drugs and alcohol has been widely documented, but rarely filmed without cliché. What we are witnessing in this scene is both how alcohol increases aggression and how alcohol brings past unresolved conflicts to the surface in this aggressive and uninhibited state. Mosley tells us in his most concise subjective prose that Mouse saw," some demon he carried around in his head." [8] But in the film this subjective state of mind is given a richer exploration that makes the scene capture a heightened realism.

On the urban streets, the term for this type of latent, semi-conscious behavior brought about by drugs or alcohol is called an 'out of body,' experience. The inebriated person reacts violently to a past experience or a violent fiction rehearsed in their mind, in the calm of a present tense situation. The people (friends/family members/peace makers) around him or her become the faces and voices of enemies from the past and unresolved conflicts that have been suppressed, but are suddenly released with the aid of alcohol or drugs. These threatening phantoms reoccur when the semi-conscious victim hears a similar phrase, sees a similar gesture, or feels a similar pain in the harmless present tense that reminds them of the past. This is like the past erupting inexplicably into the present. Perhaps no different than when Macbeth, with the aid of plentiful ale, saw Banquo's ghost at the dining table with," twenty mortal murders on their crowns." [9]

This state of mind is usually calmed by trying to convince the person that he or she is drunk; but for Easy, telling Mouse that he was drunk is what ignited the latent aggression in the first place. It is clear that when Mouse draws his gun he does not recognize Easy as his friend, but rather as an enemy from his past. **"Oh, yeah, now how this fool gonna call me out and he ain't even got no gun? I'll kill that mutherfucka!"** The use of the third person invectives by Mouse indicates the psychic or internal nature of the conflict. If it is true, what philosopher Henri Bergson has suggested, that the past," gnaws into the future," and swells as it advances, then Mouse demonstrates that given the right circumstances the past can over take the present mental state as a kind of paranoid delusion induced by chemicals, alcohol and/or exhaustion.

Easy must jump into 'the third person' to talk Mouse out of shooting him. **"Let him go."** In effect, Mouse is 'out of his body' from the alcohol and Easy has to come 'out of his body' to convince Mouse not to shoot him. Paradoxically, it is the dramatization of a phantom third person induced by alcohol that brings this scene closer to reality. The effect of the scene is enhanced by the handheld camera shot that introduces it. The unpredictable nature of the event is aided by the terse interplay between the brilliant actors and the hand held camera that seems to capture the event as if it were not planned.

Carl Franklin on the DVD commentary for this specific scene succinctly expresses why breakthrough scenes enrich characters and theme and must be protected by the film author: "I was under a lot of pressure to get rid of this scene; not to use this scene. They felt that this scene didn't add anything to the movie; that it wasn't moving the story forward. My feeling was that *it was a centerpiece of who Mouse was* in a lot of ways . . . [My emphasis] Because I was concerned about a character like Mouse being too attractive and I wanted to make sure that we could see how dangerous he could be—even though it's comedic. We wanted to make sure you realize that this man is outta control. And this spells their relationship. This has been their relationship all their lives: Easy finding some way to somehow be friends with a rattlesnake."[10] Here Carl Franklin also reveals a similar moral concern as Francis Coppola did in THE GODFATHER films. Both artists are concerned that their negative characters are not taken solely as a source of admiration. Yet in constructing vicious or immoral scenes to repel an audience, these scenes actually attract a certain 'male' audience towards the character. (See chapter: THE NIHILIST'S ERECTION)

We can sense a lesser writer/director attempting to remain in total fidelity with novel, having no use for such a scene and cutting it out because it does not 'advance' the story. But this scene adds depth to the characters and gives the film an intense and heightened realism that suspends the plot and the story as the filmmaker and the actors pursue this breakthrough moment. Because this scene comes so late in the film, the spectator is caught off guard with the potential irony of the situation: that Easy, after having found a major clue (the letter and pictures), might suddenly be killed by his trigger happy friend in a drunken paranoid state.

Carl Franklin seems to have been drawn to the novel through the Mouse character and his unpredictable behaviors. This scene brings together the search for Daphne and the unpredictable behaviors of Mouse into a highly charged dramatic context. Is Easy fighting to defend himself from his old friend or from the people who hired him to find Daphne? This is miles away from the chivalry and romantic fatalism of Raymond Chandler and James Cain. DEVIL IN A BLUE DRESS is about one man's attempt to retain control of his own destiny in a politically corrupt and racially contemptuous post-war America—against all odds.

The characterization of Mouse by actor Don Cheadle has already been noted by audiences and critics who have seen the film, but the effect of his character was brought out by Carl Franklin's substantial changes made to bring the novel to the screen and contrast the behaviors of Mouse and Easy beside each other. But again as discussed in an earlier chapter, faithfulness to a novel does not always mean fidelity to a novel. The breakthrough scene in this film is the dramatization of a rarely seen subjective state that pushes the scene closer to reality by enriching the characterization beyond the context of the immediate story and plot.

Approaching The Breakthrough Scene

So we have read how three major film artists have presented breakthrough scenes in their films. These are scenes that seem to lift the fictional veil and let us take a glimpse at a heightened realism so often obscured in conventional entertainment. The scenes are often threatening in the sense that the 'realism' of their approach threatens to destroy the safe and comforting boundaries of the spectator. For Michael Mann it was the terrifying sound of gunfire reverberating off of the walls of empty skyscrapers in a scene of sudden street violence. The uncompromising long take presentation of a rape scene in Gaspar Noe's IRREVERSIBLE becomes an unsettling document on human behavior. And finally for Carl Franklin, it was the pursuit of a subjective state of mind that threatened to destroy the very characters it sought to enrich.

I am perhaps doing the reader a disservice by only highlighting violent breakthrough scenes in this discussion so it might be considered too little too late for me to mention a subtler breakthrough scene in Ingmar Bergman's, THE PASSION OF ANNA (1970). In this incredibly precise and powerful film Anna (Liv Ullmann) a beautiful widow becomes romantically involved with Andreas (Max Von Sydow) a gruff and dour loner. Both are so obsessed with the past events of their lives that their relationship is devoured from the inside out as neither can escape from their scarred past and their bleak future. The breakthrough scene in this film is done in a single long take in close up as Anna recounts the horrible car accident that destroyed her previous family and crippled her with unbearable guilt and emotional foreshortening.

Liv Ullmann, with a face without make up, delivers the years of anguish of this character in simple unassuming voice that never shouts or betrays its submission to the truth. There is a commitment here between the actor and the filmmaker to get at the naked truth without resorting to cinematic subterfuge or theatrics. An honesty circumscribed by a well placed camera that unflinchingly captures a moment of suffering that allows a character to unburden their soul to the audience as if there was no plot or fictional veil to uphold and give us a judgmental distance. In an interview Ingmar Bergman has said about Liv Ullmann and this scene," . . . it's just an actress doing her job—which isn't bad. It's not often one sees that sort of thing. We snapped it up in the first take. **We only rehearsed that scene from the technical point of view** [my emphasis]; ran through it a few times, and then shot it. That shot was made almost six months after the rest of the film was ready." [11]

So how should a screenwriter approach a breakthrough scene? There does not seem to be a deliberate method that reveals how the scene can be written. In fact, most breakthrough scenes are not actually written they are pursued during production and protected during post-production. The breakthrough scene is an intuition that returns to the artist from beyond the written page. I believe if we can learn anything from these examples it is that none of the filmmakers could pursue a breakthrough scene without paying close attention to real life from a very personal artistic, philosophical and/or spiritual point of view.

Most young screenwriters and filmmakers, today, have so completely conformed to the expectations of the marketplace that they have ceased to develop a will to explore the unknown or resist the temptation to rationalize a mystery and render it moot. This new generation of film artists, spectators and their financial backers," prefer a handful of certainty to a whole cartful beautiful possibilities," as Nietzsche once said. [12] The intuition to pursue a beautiful possibility comes from an intense observation of real life and a sublime knowledge of the limits and boundaries of the cinematic language. But the will to protect what has been pursued comes from the artist's ability to retain his vision in the final construction of the work. Whether this is found in the theatrical release or in the DVD director's cut, the breakthrough scene is the scene that contains the soul of the artist and it must be protected at all costs.

But these statements do not bring us any closer to actually writing a breakthrough scene, particularly if it is something that often cannot be simply written—it must be pursued. A writer/director solely concerned with telling a good (and marketable) story will more than likely self-censor himself from following his intuitions during production or worse, cut the scene from the completed work—citing self-indulgence. In fact, today's generation of filmmaker believes, with the gentle prodding of his financial backers, that his own personal obsessions have no business being in the products of the entertainment industry, so he is content to hide behind the expectations of conventional realism. And while there is nothing that the banker can find inherently wrong with such a position, the subsequent films created lack luster and never earn their place as classics except in a temporal sense as opposed to a qualitative sense.

We see in all of the previous examples a sense of discovery, a sense that the writer/directors were in pursuit of something just at the boundaries of the material. So the writer/director must be searching for something that is both within the fictional material and somehow just beyond it in the representation of that material. He or she is driven by their own personal obsessions that should successfully dovetail into the themes already nascent within the material. To make a breakthrough scene, the search is half of the answer; the other half is fighting to keep it within the finished film.

NOTES

[1] I am of course referring to Sam Peckinpah's STRAW DOGS (1971) and Pier Paolo Pasolini's SALO (1975).

[2] There were several digital computer generated effects added to the sequence including the addition of the controversial digital penis. Since these additions were done by interpolating computer effects within the original long take element we may still consider this as a long take, or at least a long take composite. Even the great long take sequences of Orson Welles in TOUCH OF EVIL (1958) had their sound tracks manipulated to add extra spatial depth to the scenes that was not there during the actual shooting. So perhaps we must modify our conception of a long take as not unadulterated, but one whose computer modifications do not require a break in the original filmed (or recorded) visual element to complete.

[3] Pg. 68, Sculpting In Time by Andrei Tarkovsky

[4] Pgs. 36-37, THE MORAL SENSE by James Q. Wilson. New York. The Free Press. 1993.

[5] Ibid.

[6] Pgs. 12-13, Abraham Polonsky's FORCE OF EVIL: The Critical Edition. Northridge. California State University. 1996.

[7] Pg.183, The Evolution of Orson Welles's TOUCH OF EVIL from Novel to Film, John Stubbs the Rutgers University Press book, Touch of Evil, Terry Comito, editor 1985.

[8] Pg. 170, chapter 24, Devil In A Blue Dress by Walter Mosley, Pocket Books, 1990.

[9] Macbeth by William Shakespeare Act 3, Scene 4

[10] Director's Commentary, DEVIL IN A BLUE DRESS, 1995 Tri-Star Pictures DVD.

[11] Pg. 257, Bergman on Bergman—Please note that there was some time spent on the technical aspect of capturing the breakthrough as is often the case when a filmmaker begins to pursue the breakthrough scene.

[12] Friedrich Nietzsche, Beyond Good And Evil, page 40—On The Prejudices of Philosophers.

ATTENTION ALL SCREENWRITERS

O f all the concepts and ideas that have been said about writing for film in this book, nothing is more important than what will be said below:

In the cinema, a story is moved along primarily through editing.

Editing is conceived here as more than just the linear conjoining of one shot to another shot, but also the selection of events, costume, character, sound, image and circumstance that moves a story forwards or backwards in time. The term editing is used to denote the entire narrative rhetorical strategy that is a selection process involved in telling and *not telling* parts of a story to engage the consciousness and spirit of the spectator.

The screenwriter, filmmaker, producer, special effects engineer, key grip and even the best boy who fail to grasp this single simple concept will fail to actually make a sustained contribution to cinema. They might succeed in filming a play, a laborious documentary or news report, but the work will lack that certain dynamism that makes cinema a powerful and important art form. Much of what has been discussed in this book (e.g. narrative ellipsis, story proper and back-story) relate to the fact that how a story is moved along in the cinema is through this type of selection and omission process otherwise called, editing.

Writers who first approach screenwriting often rely upon their experiences in literature or the stage, just as first time filmmakers rely on their experiences of reading a novel to try to approach screenwriting. These approaches are typified by a heavy reliance upon dialogue to move the story, multiple montage sequences to compress large chunks of narrative time, and vivid explanations of events in the written word that ultimately stagnates the story on screen. For evidence of how a story is moved along in the cinema through editing let us look at two revealing examples, one from Stanley Kubrick and another from Roman Polanski.

2001: A Space Odyssey
By Stanley Kubrick and Arthur C. Clark

In Stanley Kubrick's film of 2001: A Space Odyssey, there is a scene where a pre-historic ape man murders another ape man over the territorial rights to a watering hole with the bone of a dead animal. After the murder, he triumphantly throws the bone into the air. The bone flips against the sky and then Kubrick cuts to a Space Station of a similar shape to the bone as it is orbiting the earth. This is," one of the boldest graphic matches in narrative cinema. The cut eliminates thousands of years of story time." [1] The story has definitively been moved along with a dynamism that is wholly cinematic. It is this ability to cut back and forth or continually forward in time that gives the cinema its narrative dynamism and separates it from the stage, book and canvas.

Oh sure, there are other aspects that define the art and we have discussed many of those aspects in previous chapters, but this dynamism, this ability to cut out or omit pieces of a story as a way to propel a story is what must be understood by any screenwriter to maximize the potential of their efforts. "Story time, or the imagined events of the fiction, might cover an entire lifetime, while discourse time is constituted by the time it takes to . . . see the film." [2] Editing between scenes can imply the continuation of a story without actually having to show the scenes that are specific to how a story continues. A montage sequence might not actually be necessary if the changes in circumstance, behavior, or time can be shown by simply cutting to the next dramatically revealing scene.

We often lose sight of this dynamic aspect of cinematic narration because when we are writing for the screen we are writing on a page and this is too reminiscent of what one does when one is writing literature. The similarity of these actions can often blur the distinctions between the two mediums. We inadvertently want the screenplay to read like a novel, but in doing so we eclipse the cinematic potential of the material because what is filmed cannot always be written and what is written cannot always be filmed. Having said this, let us turn our attention to another filmmaker whose narrative editorial strategy consists of a concentration on details that have great "temporal" significance and has allowed him to develop an extraordinary narrative dynamism.

ROMAN POLANSKI: The Devil is in the Details

Roman Polanski's THE PIANIST (2002) follows the life of Poland's acclaimed musician and composer Wladyslaw Szpilman from the Nazi invasion of Poland in 1939, through WWII, until his "liberation" by the Russians in 1945. The film is well deserving of its Academy Award nominations and its Ocsars for it is in this single film that Polanski has focused all of his narrative dynamics that have become the hallmarks of his style.

Anyone who is familiar with the previous work of Roman Polanski, from the beautiful KNIFE IN THE WATER (Noz W Wodzie, 1962) to the enigmatic THE NINTH GATE (1999), knows that Polanski is obsessive about details and their ability to give both characters and audience a certain perceptual clarity regarding the themes of the stories within his films. From Rosemary Woodhouse's (Mia Farrow) noticing that pictures had recently been removed from her neighbor's apartment because there were," clean spots on the walls," in ROSEMARY'S BABY (1968) to the flaw in the iris of Evelyn Mulwray (Faye Dunaway) that would later be exit hole of a policeman's bullet in CHINATOWN (1974), Polanski's obsession with details is more than just what could be pejoratively called artistic egoism. His obsession is the astute placement and reoccurrence of details that are given both an emotive and temporal significance and contribute to the overall narrative dynamism of his work. Simply put, it is the placement, reoccurrence, and modification of particular details that helps to move the story along in the work of Polanski and gives his films multiple layers of thematic depth that makes them rewarding even after repeated viewings.

For instance, in THE PIANIST, when the Jews of Warsaw, including Wladyslaw Szpilman (Adrian Brody) and his family, are moved into what would eventually become known as the infamous Warsaw Ghetto, they notice from their apartment window, the first masonry blocks of a wall being built. In the next shot, we are presented with the same camera angle, but now the wall is completely finished. Several more shots from ground level reveal barbed wire and the ominous length of the walls that encircle the Ghetto and segregate the Jews from the rest of the city's population. Here, Polanski has essentially extrapolated a detail from the story and used it to both compress the passage of time and in doing so, advance the story through a series of "cuts" rather than through time consuming exposition.

But for clarity's sake let us be sure that this dynamism, this speeding up of narrative events is done with thematic purpose and not just to appease the short attention spans of modern audiences. In fact, Polanski reveals in this film how the Nazi atrocities accumulated from one small indignity to the next slightly larger indignity by degrees until The Final Solution. He does this by singling out a specific detail and then cutting back to it to show how that detail has been modified through time. This is a very sophisticated rhetorical strategy that Polanski has been perfecting since his film REPULSION (1965).

In REPULSION, the character of Carole (Catherine Deneuve) is a disturbed young woman who goes on a schizophrenic homicidal rampage after her sister/caregiver leaves their apartment to go on vacation for a couple of weeks. Her rampage is brought about by her paranoid delusions and sexual fears. To show the passage of time as well as her deteriorating mental state, Polanski shows us an uncooked plate of rabbit and some uncut potatoes that as the film and her psychosis progresses, becomes a rotting carcass and the potatoes begin to sprout roots. He said that," the sprouting potato that marks the passage of time as Carol's mind slowly gives way was borrowed straight from my childhood." [3] Thus, the development of this editorial strategy of highlighting certain details to mark the passage of time became a cinematic device to decrease the need for exposition to explain dramatic changes in circumstance.

Returning to THE PIANIST, early in the film, the Szpilman family is reading about the order from the Nazis that all Jews will be required to wear armbands. Some in the family say they refuse to wear such things as the father wonders if the Nazis will supply the armbands or will the Jews have to make them on their own. CUT TO: The very next scene and we see the father walking down the street wearing the previously discussed apparel as two Nazi officers pass by. One of the officers stops him and asks him why he didn't bow as he passed them. The father apologizes, but is smacked into a wall before he can finish. As he walks away he is told to walk in the gutter instead of the sidewalk.

Here again we are confronted with a detail, the armband, that was discussed in a previous scene and is later shown in the next scene to reveal the progressive degradation and indignity the characters have to endure; indignities that little by little dehumanize and ultimately lead towards the Holocaust. In an interview for the German magazine Die Welt in 2002 the Director has said that, "What I wanted to show in the film was the gradual development of the events that ultimately led to the death camps and gas chambers. It began with simple things like Jews not being allowed to sit on park benches. People often ask me," Why didn't the Jews do something to stop what was happening?" But it's an absurd question. At the time we thought," It can't get any worse. It can only get better." [4] Polanski found a method to compress large chunks of story and narrative time through the careful selection and control of details—objects—found within the story itself. His cutting or editorial emphasis upon these details allowed him to tell the story with a certain economy and dynamism that can only exist in the cinema. The phrase that is most apropos for describing the work of Roman Polanski is," the devil is in the details."

What I have identified as cinematic narrative dynamism is a selection process; an editorial strategy that allows one to omit certain parts of a story to both focus the spectator's attention to the theme of the work and modify the duration or pace of the storytelling.

In the cinema, one does not have to tell the whole story for the whole story to be understood.

If screenwriters and potential filmmakers lose sight of this essential aspect of cinema then their resultant films will not have the dynamism that we cherish in the classics we love. Both Polanski and Kubrick—particularly when adapting literary material—were meticulous in their editorial strategies to push the story along without dragging it down with exposition or omitting details of great thematic importance.

THE OUTTHINKING TRAGEDY

It is an impending tragedy that most young screenwriters and filmmakers assume that they must out think their audience instead of getting their audience to think with them. This is perhaps a consequence of the "overnight" success of M. Night Shyamalan's THE SIXTH SENSE and The WACHOWSKI Brother's MATRIX series. Spectators, financiers, and producers have all developed the nasty habit of attempting to out think a film while watching it—both to protect themselves from looking gullible if there is a surprise ending and to wager whether the story is worth their undivided attention.

In expending so much mental effort to out think a film much of the nuances, rhythm, and depth of a story is lost or discarded. A "gist surfing" mentality is pervading film reception as evident from first weekend box office receipts and second weekend drop off at the box office and DVD sales and resales. On the creative side, the effort to 'surprise' an audience far outweighs the effort to satisfy the drama itself. This "gist surfing" mentality might be a direct consequence of the demands on our attention by cable, satellite and network television—coupled with the go anywhere access of cellular phones, video games, internet and work and educational obligations. All of this can constrict undivided leisure time and forces us to quickly 'get the gist' of a story as opposed to enjoying the telling of a story.

Perhaps the last film to enjoy a full appreciation of its storytelling was Peter Jackson's LOTR series but this was due to the popularity of the books upon which the films were based. The decline in novel reading coupled with the need to out think a film does not bode well for tomorrow's filmmakers who are interested in approaching their stories dynamically. Cinema begins and ends with reality; a certain subjectivity contaminates our reproduction of it, from where we place the camera to what the characters say and we must promote, protect, and project this certain subjectivity or the cinema will cease to have artists strong enough to practice its faith. I hope that with all that has been discussed in this book future filmmakers will return to the narrative dynamism and thematic depth that has made the cinema—in spite of the sweeping changes in technology and reception—the most important art form for the 20th and 21st centuries.

NOTES

[1]   Pg.276, FILM ART: An Introduction 4th ed., David Bordwell and Kristin Thompson, McGraw-HILL Publications, New York, 1993.

[2]   Pg.140, REFLEXIVITY IN FILM AND LITERATURE: From Don Quixote to Jean-Luc Godard by Robert Stam. New York. Columbia University Press. 1992.

[3]   Pg.204, ROMAN BY POLANSKI, by Roman Polanski, Ballantine Books, New York, 1984.

[4]   Pg. 203, ROMAN POLANSKI INTERVIEWS, Edited by Paul Cronin, University of Mississippi Press, Jackson, 2005.

APPENDIX

SLAVE CINEMA:
The Crisis of African-American
Independent Cinema

SLAVE CINEMA:

The Crisis of African-American Independent Cinema

"If I could have just convinced more of them that they were slaves, I could have saved thousands more."

-Harriet Tubman

The crisis has a familiar starting point: film is both a business and an art. One cannot ignore one side of the argument without losing perspective and destroying the other. A purely commercial cinema yields extremely high profits for short periods but lacks innovation, originality and a certain cultural diversity by excluding or limiting minorities and ethnicities that are thought negligible to its bottom line. A pure art cinema is daring, original, innovative, culturally diverse and ethnically inclusive, but lacks the steep short period profit margins of commercial cinema.

Other countries have adopted a panacea to this paradox by supporting the art cinema and its practitioners with generous grants, tax incentives and other government funding and tax loopholes. This allows these countries to battle the ever encroaching commercial (i.e. American) cinema that continually overrides their own domestically produced films. This battle is not as vigorously fought as it used to be given the hefty worldwide foreign grosses of American films vis-à-vis the domestic films of foreign countries. In fact, both France and Germany have just recently constricted their government aid to Film producers; Germany in particular was tightening the restrictions of its generous tax shelters as of the Summer 2005.[1] But foreign producers, filmmakers and film festivals still have a collective incentive to protect their ability to create personal visions and stories that exemplify their culture, heritage and people in films that are as radical as they are independent to assert the relevance of their industries as American media conglomerates swallow the global marketplace. Indeed, the idea of a French independent cinema would seem oxymoronic to a country that has a long history of recognizing and celebrating the personal visions of its filmmakers.

Even in America, White filmmakers enjoy a robust independent cinema that acts as a kind of developing grounds or apprenticeship for future commercial filmmakers. These independent White filmmakers are free to experiment, innovate, re-interpret and otherwise explore the unexplored in their films because the equally White audiences their films will reach have come to expect such daring and original visions. Filmmakers like: Christopher Nolan, whose daring film MEMENTO (2001) featured a character whose short term memory disruptions caused the film's storyline to be presented in reverse, was the 'darling' of the independent film market (at Sundance, Telluride, Venice . . .) and other notable independent film festivals. From the sensation caused by his film, MEMENTO, Christopher Nolan was immediately co-opted by the commercial cinema and has gone on to direct multi-million dollar films like INSOMINIA (2002) and BATMAN BEGINS (2005) with A-list actors. This is not to say that there haven't been any African-American independent filmmakers (e.g. Charles Burnett, Julie Dash, Halie Gerima, William Greaves and the incomparable Melvin Van Peeples). Yet, where White American independent filmmakers can create a sensation in the independent marketplace and translate that sensation into a long term position in commercial cinema, the same is not always so with many African-American Independent filmmakers.[2]

The reason for this problem is simple: so-called independent film festivals administered by Whites are often oblivious to the lack of racial diversity and inclusiveness of their accepted films by believing that they have selected the films according their merit when in actuality they have only selected the films that attend to the issues and fantasies of their own White privilege and closely guarded cultural supremacy. (E.g. Sundance, Slamdance, Telluride, etc.) Although if confronted about the 'whiteness' of their accepted films most film festival administrators would go out of their way to disprove such a charge citing a handful of token films and the fairness of their selection process vis-à-vis the magnitude of submissions. Yet such defenses should remind us of the words of Beverly Daniel Tatum from her book, Why Are All the Black Kids Sitting Together in the Cafeteria? "It is important to understand that the system of advantage is perpetuated when we do not acknowledge its existence." [3]

All films by people of color, by dint of their content and the race of their participants and creators, challenge the issues and fantasies of White privilege and cultural supremacy. A few African-American or ethnic films are accepted by these so-called independent film festivals as tokens of inclusiveness, but if we look deeply we find that these films either have the backing of a major celebrity or Hollywood power broker or contain a recognizable star (e.g. John Singleton's backing of HUSTLE & FLOW, starring Terrence Howard). Concomitantly, there is no truly independent African-American marketplace that embraces and celebrates filmmakers with original, independent and innovative visions.

To be specific, there are few independent African-American marketplaces or festivals that celebrate, promote, or expect daring, original, controversial and culturally diverse cinematic visions from filmmakers. This is because many African-Americans, both filmmakers and audiences, believe that filmmaking is solely a commercial enterprise. The artistic aspect of filmmaking is deliberately suppressed and/or disbelieved. Too many of our films lack innovation, originality and diversity because we have become slaves to profit and not the artisans of purpose and prestige. We have effectively created by default a slave cinema that is solely and exclusively concerned with the short term bottom line profit and marketability of a film with little to no consideration for the vision, originality, purpose, innovation or long term profitability of a work. Without this "independent" mandate, a majority of would-be independent African-American filmmakers have been forced to abandon their dreams of making personal, meaningful or provocative films and find themselves making pornographic films (filled with sex or violence or both) to make a quick buck to support themselves; but these 'quickie' films are only dreams deferred. So the grass roots African-American Independent filmmaker is getting the shaft from both ends, so to speak. Film festivals administrated by Whites are oblivious to their lack of racial inclusiveness and privilege and film festivals administrated by African-Americans are often solely concerned with the bottom-line commercial appeal of the film (genre/cast/budget) and not the independent thought, spirit, and creativity behind it.

WHAT IS INDEPENDENT CINEMA?

Noted White independent filmmaker Jim Jarmusch has concisely defined an independent filmmaker as," anyone who makes a film that is the film they want to make, and it is not defined by marketing analysis or a commercial enterprise . . ." [4] At face value this seems like a deceptively severe statement from a filmmaker who is ignorant of the privileges his skin color affords him. Yet, Jarmusch can make this bold statement because there is a network of festivals, distributors and audiences that expect such originality, innovation and personal vision from White filmmakers who call themselves independent. On the other hand, to African-Americans, the word independent means that you made the film with your own money and now you are broke. So we can see how antithetical Jarmusch's words are to the ears of would be African-American filmmakers.

One wishes we could simply dismiss Jarmusch as some kind of idealistic nutcase, but he is a celebrated and significant independent filmmaker whose work is original, innovative, culturally diverse and racially inclusive. (See: GHOST DOG: The Way of the Samurai, DEADMAN, STRANGER THAN PARADISE, MYSTERY TRAIN) It is very, very difficult for any African-American filmmakers to apply Jim Jarmusch's words to their own efforts because we have been taught indirectly by the lifestyles and business dealings of our movie and music stars that films are made to make money and to make money you must pay strict attention to the marketability of your idea, your vision, etc, etc. So if we must answer the question what is independent cinema then we must first understand that independent cinema is filled with films that fulfill the personal vision of the filmmakers without regard to the marketability and commercial expectation of the films. This, of course, is antithetical to the ear of every business and financial person who makes a living in the film entertainment business.

PERSONAL VISION\COLLECTIVE ART

The question should be raised: Can the cinema really be used as a form of personal expression? Although there are literally volumes of writing, classic films, theory and reviews that prove the validity of individuals using the cinema as a medium of personal expression, the general audience, financiers, and producers do not look at the cinema as a means of personal expression. The cinema, in general, is a form of collective expression; collective in the sense that a film is a collaborative art created by actors, editors, a cinematographer and writers and collective in the sense that popular or 'blockbuster' films express the wishes and fulfill the escapism of its mass audience. Often, for a modern individual to force the cinema to express his or her personal vision, he or she must exaggerate or flout a convention of the medium that resonates with a modern audience (often while simultaneously accepting many other conventions). For instance, for Quentin Tarantino it was an unconventional structure and a peculiar use of profanity that made his films stand apart as a personal vision. We know this to be true because there was no reason based on contemporary market analysis (that is the films that were blockbusters at that time) for Tarantino to structure his films so unconventionally; this was the personal predilection of the filmmaker that was supported by his collaborators (by Harvey Keitel and producer Lawrence Bender, John Travolta, Bruce Willis and other subsequent actors).

So perhaps what we mean by personal expression is a view of the world (or cinema) that is not just different from our own, but also different from what we have come to collectively believe and expect about the world (or cinema). Another condition of this ability to use the cinema as a form of personal expression is the acceptance, encouragement and support of like-spirited collaborators who see that view as justified in its artistic integrity and do everything in their power to help get it made and shown. These conditions taken together support the idea that independent cinema or a cinema that preserves, promotes and protects the personal expression of its filmmaker is a form of socio-political heresy that ultimately must be tolerated in a free and democratic society for that society to call itself free and democratic.

INDEPENDENT CINEMA AS HERESY

A simple definition of heresy is when an individual or group goes against the orthodox doctrine and practices of the dominant religious order. Most of us are familiar with the Holy Roman Catholic church's charges of heresy leveled at Italian astronomer and scientist

Galileo Galilei in 1616. The oft repeated story says that he was forced by threat of torture to recant his opinion that the earth moves around the sun," but allegedly muttered,' eppur si muove' ('yet it does move') just after making his formal recantation."[5] Of course, it is a commonly accepted and proven fact that the Earth does revolve around the Sun, but the idea espoused by Nicolaus Copernicus and Galileo in that day was an affront to religious orthodoxy and as such was a direct threat to the authority of the Church which subscribed to the ancient Ptolemaic system of the sun and the heavens revolving around the earth. To the modern reader, Heresy is a religious crime of little relevance. But in the opinion of this writer, there are many other forms or modes of heresy in modern times that contribute both to independent thought and human potential for good. Such heresies endanger the minorities of people who might engage in such thought or the behaviors and practices that are indicative of it. [6]

The great playwright, Henrik Ibsen, once wrote in his play, AN ENEMY OF THE PEOPLE, that," the strongest man in the world is the one who stands most alone." Such a statement can be taken as the quintessence of independent thought. This line is delivered by a key character of truth and integrity in the play, Dr. Thomas Stockmann. For it is Dr. Stockmann who tries to warn the people of his town that the waters of the profitable and popular health spa and public baths that supports the town are dangerous and filled with the raw sewage of the town itself. It is Dr. Stockmann who is nearly driven to ruin by asserting this truth that the townspeople and the sick and invalid that come to the baths are literally and figuratively swimming in their own shit. "When pollution is discovered in the system, the arrogant refusal of the establishment to listen to dissenting expertise in the rush to profits stands exposed." [7]

Ibsen's AN ENEMY OF THE PEOPLE reveals the great difficulty an individual faces when he or she dissents from the generally accepted beliefs, myths, and stereotypes of their community. But most importantly, Ibsen's play presents us with the devastating effects of social heresy; that is to dissent from the generally accepted and profit making opinions and beliefs of the status quo. One risks alienation or economic disenfranchisement at best or physical harm or even murder at worst. Understanding the price of social heresy can only make us admire the strength of those who attempt to exercise it in the effort to augment humanity's potential for good as did Martin Luther King or Rosa Parks during the struggle for civil rights in this country.

Another form of heresy is racial heresy committed in its most visible consequence as interracial dating or marriage. The mixing of the races is a powerful form of racial heresy that is privately frowned upon by more people than those who begrudgingly tolerate it in public. To choose to go outside of one's race for sexual satisfaction or even love is to assert an independence that betrays the tacit bonds that unite a racial group as well as the myths and beliefs that are endogamously circulated to keep the races apart. Racial heresy has a social price exerted through the friendships lost or family members who shun the participants yet it is just one more form of modern heresy that is not tied to a religious order, but instead to the fixed social circumstances that govern our culture. Of course there are other forms of heresy as in the sexual heresy of homosexuality but I have digressed for a reason and that is to help lay the groundwork for the idea that we might lack a large number of African-American independent filmmakers because being an independent filmmaker is a form of intellectual and economic heresy that is extraordinarily difficult to tolerate in the African-American community.

AFRICAN-AMERICAN INDEPENDENT CINEMA as INTELLECTUAL HERESY and THE INTERNAL OVERSEER

"In addition to the general anti-intellectual tenor of American society, there is a deep distrust and suspicion of black intellectuals within the black community. This distrust and suspicion stem not simply from the usual arrogant and haughty disposition of intellectuals toward ordinary folk, but, more importantly, from the widespread refusal of black intellectuals to remain, in some visible way, organically linked with African American cultural life. The relatively high rates of exogamous marriage, the abandonment of black institutions and the preoccupation with Euro-American intellectual products are often perceived by the black community as intentional efforts to escape the negative stigma of blackness or are viewed as symptoms of self-hatred."

-The Dilemma of the Black Intellectual by Cornel West
KEEPING FAITH: Philosophy and Race in America

Often times being Black has more to do with the fear of being thought of as 'wanting to be White', the proverbial 'Oreo' as it was once called. The fear of being suspected of buying into the American dream, the idea of fairness, justice, and the reciprocal practice of equality in a country that on so many levels and at every turn is unfair, curtails the American dream to a precious few, and is often unjust—is a fear that makes every Black man and woman the overseer of his own brothers and sisters. On the plantation in slavery times the overseer made sure all the Blacks were kept in line and made it a point to humiliate the ones who were not, but today the overseer has been internalized as a paralyzing and castrating fear of being alienated from one's own and never fully accepted by the others; this is the tragic legacy of slavery, Jim crow laws, and segregation.

Often times to be Black is to believe that whatever keeps you from reaching your full potential is because of the fixed social, economic, and racist circumstances that have historically and are presently in place to keep you and others like you from ever reaching your goals. To be Black is to collectively think of ourselves as poor even though there is much evidence to the contrary; to be Black is to collectively think of ourselves as intellectually inferior even though there is much evidence to the contrary; to be Black is to believe in a limited perspective that constricts our human potential in an effort to keep a group of people unified but disenfranchised, bound together but not bonded together, hoping but not entirely optimistic. Where this limited perspective is culturally useful in allowing us to develop an art (hip-hop), a style and fashion within our communities that are distinctive and distinguished as our own, there is a down side to this limiting of perspective. I am not saying that this limited perspective works on all of us, I am only noting that it exists in the same way that many of us believe that there will never be a Black president of the United States of America.

The hypothesis here is that one of the major conditions of being Black is a limited perspective concerning our human potential that is tacitly agreed upon by others who are Black and tacitly controlled by the actions towards us (past and present) of those who are not Black. The recent catastrophe and debacle of Hurricane Katrina in its immediate aftermath solidified the perspective that Blacks had about Whites as much as it exposed how Whites really felt about their Black neighbors and citizenry. But such a limited, even confining, perspective does not nurture independent thought so much as it does to poison it and kill off the voices of would be independent African-American filmmakers who might dissent from it. If independent filmmaking in and of itself is heretical and to be truly an unsuspected member of the African-American race you must subscribe faithfully with hand over heart to the limited perspective, then being an African-American Independent filmmaker is an oxymoron. Because the nature of independent filmmaking is to explore and expose with a critical eye, not simply what is collectively known, but what is individually experienced by a—voiceless minority. To paraphrase the late French filmmaker Robert Bresson; voice what without you might not ever have been noticed. [8] Perhaps the only effective subject matter that allows a Black filmmaker to be accepted as an independent is racial subject matter- and particularly any racial subject matter that reveals the oppression and denigration of African-Americans by Whites or the system that privileges Whites over African-Americans. However valid or prescient this racial subject matter it is, *inter alia*, proof of a forced compliance to a limited perspective.

But my effort here is not to create some grand fait accompli or deliver a collective mea culpa; it is to reveal the internal overseer, the self-castrating critic inside of us that keeps us from enjoying the intellectual freedom that constitutes independent cinema. Perhaps, the best way to reveal the internal overseer is to relate it through a personal filmmaking experience. While shooting the final scenes of my film WHAT THE MAN WITH NO SHOES SAID TO THE MAN WITH NO FEET, I was confronted by one of the co-lead actors about my use of the Japanese word," seppuku," in the scene. I was told that," most Black people aren't going to know what the word seppuku means," and couldn't he use another word instead? I said," but if you and I know that it means ritual suicide by disembowelment, then there are two Black people standing right here who know exactly what it means". He went on to say that we were exceptions and again that," most Black people won't know what seppuku is." To which I answered that I refused to believe that we were the only two Black people who knew what the word 'seppuku' meant and if the context wherein which this word is spoken does not tell whoever is listening what it means, well perhaps they can look it up if they are so inclined. As Russian filmmaker Andrei Tarkovsky has said," Respect for an audience . . . can only be based on the conviction that they are no stupider than you." (Sculpting In Time, pg.173)

"I was told that most Black people aren't going to know what the word seppuku means . . ." WHAT THE MAN WITH NO SHOES SAID TO THE MAN WITH NO FEET, Wri/Dir, Andre Seewood. Nelson Jones and Doug McCray. 2005

Needless to say, we used the word, but I was struck by the notion of being "exceptions" to a rule that I had the sneaking suspicion degrades us all. This is a 'micro'-example of the internalized overseer that keeps us from exploring the boundaries, innovations, and originality that independent cinema affords its practitioners. One of the bittersweet caveats of independent filmmaking was best expressed by Canadian filmmaker David Cronenberg (THE FLY-1985, SPIDER—2004, A HISTORY OF VIOLENCE—2005) who said," in order to communicate intensely with a hundred people, you might lose a thousand on the way." [9]

Yet, it was not simply a question of dumbing the script down (this is done everyday in Hollywood to White films) but the principal upon which this dumbing down was based. By saying that," most Black people won't know," presents both the listener and the speaker with a stultifying presumption of ignorance. It is a belief in the limited perspective of an imaginary Black race that is still picking cotton and not allowed to read. It is a presumption that is ultimately unfounded and self-defeating. For even if the two of us were the only Blacks who knew what the word meant, then we would not be exceptions that prove the rule—we would have been exceptions that prove that the rule is untrue. I stand here on a certain optimism—that the glass is half full—because it is this optimism that is quickly poisoned by the pessimism of so limited a point of view.

So, many of our independent thinkers\filmmakers self-castrate their own brilliant and innovative ideas with the knife of this internalized overseer that stumps them with a constricted idea of "what most Blacks" can and cannot comprehend. As if this weren't enough, we have business, financial and cultural leaders who recapitulate this constricted idea in the language and details of marketing, demographics, and unmitigated pursuit of steep short-term profits. It is strange that so many Blacks own or have seen many innovative and original "White" independent films in private, but collectively disenfranchise themselves with the pessimism that they think makes them exceptions to the rule and not proof of the untruth of the rule.

COGNITIVE DISSONANCE and THE INTERNAL OVERSEER

We might find some evidence to support this theory of an internalized overseer in the work of sociologist, Leon Festinger and his theory of Cognitive Dissonance. We should briefly define cognitive dissonance as when a person holds two or more established beliefs or values that are inconsistent and contradictory to each other. Any person that holds these inconsistent and contradictory beliefs and values attempts to find social support from others who think like them or information that reduces the difficulty of sustaining the contradictions and inconsistencies of their positions. To use an example from Festinger," A person may think Negroes are just as good as whites, but would not want any living in his neighborhood." [10] This is a typical example of a public opinion and a private belief that causes cognitive dissonance and can only be alleviated by forging relationships with other Whites in the neighborhood who feel the same way or finding information that supports the idea that you wouldn't want them living next to you and ignoring any information to the contrary.

But my theory of the internalized overseer comes indirectly from an observation within Festinger's book about Forced Compliance. "There are circumstances in which persons will behave in a manner counter to their convictions or will publicly make statements which they do not really believe." [11] Festinger states that there are two conditions that exert an influence and cause a person to change the public expression of their beliefs while privately holding onto their original beliefs:

1) Compliance brought about through threat of punishment.
2) Compliance brought about through a special reward for complying.

The impact of Festinger's conditions of forced compliance upon my own theory of the internalized overseer is revealed in an example cited from the work of Coch and French in their book, HUMAN RELATIONS (1948). In the example a woman has her job at a factory changed to another department where after about 10 days she," increased her production above the level of the others with whom she worked. The authors state," starting on the thirteenth day when she reached standard production (60 units per hour) and exceeded the production of the other members, she became a scapegoat of the group. During this time her production decreased, toward the level of the remaining members of the group."[12] Most importantly, after the other workers were transferred the woman's production level returned to her earlier (60 units per hour) rate. So we can see that once the source of pressure, the forced compliance by the other co-workers was removed, she was able to return to her own personal standards.

I believe this is the same paradigm at work in my theory of the internalized overseer. Although one might excel individually in the development and understanding of one's own independent thought, it is when you attempt to translate or express those thoughts to a collective audience (e.g. an independent film) that you self-castrate and delude yourself with a pessimism that keeps you from pursuing those personal visions that make one an exception and prove the rule untrue. Unlike the example of forced compliance where once the influence was removed the woman went back to her own personal standards, forced compliance of the internalized overseer is 'always there' in one's own racial heredity and the myths and untruths held by ourselves and the others that surround us.

This constant pressure and influence upon African-Americans is what causes the overseer to be internalized and to exert an influence and control upon our expressed public beliefs vis-à-vis our private or personal beliefs and values. The African-American is threatened with the punishment of racial and social alienation from the members of his own race if he does not abide by the tacit edicts and pessimism of the internalized overseer. Here, we return to the fear of being called an 'Oreo', and the social and intellectual discrediting that comes with such a term. If the African-American man or woman *does* comply with this pessimism, they are rewarded with inclusiveness and social support. It is this forced compliance that is the source of the bitter resentment many Blacks hold against comedian Bill Cosby and his recent critical comments about African-American parents and their declining discipline and interest in the educational future of their children. The cure that can destroy the internalized overseer was perhaps best expressed by philosopher Charles W. Mills in his book, THE RACIAL CONTRACT, where he says," One has to overcome the internalization of sub-personhood prescribed by the racial contract and recognize one's own humanity, resisting the official category of despised aboriginal, natural slave, colonial ward. One has to learn the basic self respect that can causally be assumed by Kantian persons, those privileged by the racial contract, but which is denied to sub-persons. Particularly for blacks, ex-slaves, the importance of developing self-respect and demanding respect from whites is crucial." [13]

IN A STRANGER'S EYE

Given all that I have said about forced compliance, limited perspective and the internal overseer that circumvents and constricts the public expression of independent thought in African-American film, it is no coincidence, but certainly a great shock that four of the greatest films about being African-American were created by people who were not African-American themselves. These films are listed below in chronological order:

1) IMITATION OF LIFE, (1958) by Douglas Sirk
2) NOTHING BUT A MAN (1964) by Michael Roemer
3) THE COLOR PURPLE (1986) by Steven Spielberg
4) FRESH (1994) by Boaz Yakin

This list is by no means definitive, but rather it is substantive. It is not my intention to offend the intelligence of any reader by not mentioning the work of Oscar Micheaux, the groundbreaking comedies of Bill Cosby and Sidney Poitier, Richard Pryor, the bitter resolve of Pam Grier or the work of Spike Lee. My intent here is to focus our attention on films that explicitly say no to the status quo and subvert the 'internal overseer' to produce films whose characters and creators epitomize the true nature of independence in thought and filmmaking. Each film on this list captures African-American life at a decisive and protean stage. These films are by filmmakers who ultimately stood alone to augment the human potential for good through the heresy of what they created. We will take a brief look at each film and detail how these films express independent thought that could not otherwise have been expressed by an African-American director or writer.

IMITATION OF LIFE, a remake of an earlier 1936 film adaptation of a novel by Fannie Hurst about racial miscegenation was later given a powerful and now classic revision by a Hollywood director known primarily for his lily-White melodramas, Douglas Sirk. In IMITATION OF LIFE, class as well as race are the subject when the mixed race daughter of a Black woman attempts to "pass" as a White girl, denying her mother, but becomes humiliated at the hands of a society that has no place for her. Douglas Sirk himself gave an insightful answer as to why he made such a film to author/interviewer, Jon Halliday in 1970:

"The only interesting thing is the Negro angle: the Negro girl trying to escape her condition, sacrificing to her status in society her bonds of friendship, family, etc., and rather trying to vanish into the imitation world of vaudeville. The imitation of life is not the real life. Lana Turner's life is a very cheap imitation. The girl, (Susan Kohner) is choosing the imitation of life instead of being a Negro. The picture is a piece of social criticism—*of both white and black*. [My Emphasis] You can't escape what you are. Now the Negroes are waking up to black is beautiful. IMITATION OF LIFE is a picture about the situation of blacks before the time of the slogan 'Black is Beautiful.'

I tried to make it into a picture of social consciousness—not only of a white social consciousness, but of a Negro one, too. Both white and black are leading imitated lives . . ." [14] With IMITATION OF LIFE, Sirk's final Hollywood film, he, as a German Immigrant, tackled issues no White American director would have dared to approach in that pre-civil rights era and a subject that was still taboo in the African-American community: bi-racial children, mixed relationships and the degraded status of African-Americans in post-war American society.

It was a subject that had not been discussed openly and certainly not within the broadly appealing context of a film to a mass audience. Moreover, there was literally no Hollywood studio with an African-American director under contract who could get such a film produced due to the racism explicit in the industry at that time. It took an outsider, making what inevitably would be his "goodbye" to Hollywood, to look without the internal repression that keeps us as Blacks from seeing ourselves as human, all too human.

The second work, NOTHING BUT A MAN, is quite simply a remarkable achievement. Written and filmed right at the cusp of the civil rights movement by Robert M. Young and Michael Roemer, this film captures the external and internal frustrations of a Black man who must confront the racial prejudice of Whites as well as the docile and self-defeating spirit of Blacks. What makes this film such a remarkable achievement is the candor and honesty with which it looks at other Blacks. Through the character of Duff, a railroad section hand, who finds love with a preacher's daughter we come to understand that the Civil Rights movement (never actually mentioned in the film, but implied by the themes within the story itself) did not spring forth fully conceptualized as some would anachronistically believe. The Civil Rights movement was capitulated by the individual experiences of Black men and women who like Duff, found themselves collectively against a rock and a hard place. Blacks of the younger generation were hemmed in by the rigors of segregation and the passivity of the previous generation who as Duff says," have been stoopin' so long, you don't know how to stand up."

Again we find that because the independent filmmakers were White, they were afforded the ability to be critically distanced from their subject matter. This critical distance broadened their perspective on the subject matter, for if NOTHING BUT A MAN is a film about race then it is also a film about the resilience of an individual's potential for good and the thwarted aspirations for success that challenge all individuals in an unjust and discriminatory society; it is not a polemic, it is a portrait. This critical distance created a concise objectivity in the White independent filmmakers that is too easily discredited and discarded by African-American independent filmmakers. The internalized overseer would never have allowed so 'unvarnished' a portrait of African-American life to be recreated for the screen out of a fear of feeding into the derogatory stereotypes held by Whites and themselves. This is particularly noticeable when we hear actor Ivan Dixon, who portrayed Duff, discuss the scene where out of anger he must push his pregnant wife (Abbey Lincoln) to the floor on the videotaped interview of the DVD release of the film.

Dixon says about the role and the moment," It was like me all over again. This Duff was a guy, a roustabout kind of guy, who just kinda moved through the world. You know, making his living, doing his thing. That was me. I had lived every moment of it. You know, I had shoved my wife down like that scene . . . Although I never did shove her down when she was pregnant, but I did shove her. Moments like that were really . . . I was like reliving my own life on film and it was just the best thing I think I've ever done."[15] It was a risqué moment in the film in that it symbolized the effect of Duff's spiritual torment at the hands of his White employers and his rejection of the bourgeois ideal of marriage. This disapproved of gesture puts the audience at odds with Duff, we can see the pressure that caused the act but we disagree with the act itself. It was that gesture that left the reconciliation at the end of the film charged with emotion and redemption.

Duff, as so subtly created for the screen by actor Ivan Dixon, reveals to us the power and the pain of a Black man who dares to think and act independently against the myths, antiquated beliefs and empty values of his own race as well as the race that oppresses him. His marriage to the preacher's daughter, the source of much ridicule among his co-workers/friends is an open defiance to their moral vacancy. His attempts to unionize his co-workers led directly to his open defiance toward the White boss that wanted him to recant his convictions in front of the very co-workers he was trying to unite. And finally his acceptance of fatherhood coincides with his reconciliation with his wife and his inner compulsion to return to the town that shunned him and make a change. NOTHING BUT A MAN confronts us with the social heresy of independence (in thought and action) that makes a man turn against the general line and status quo of his circumstances to express something out loud and in public as a man in a world that treats him less than so.

Our third film is Steven Spielberg's THE COLOR PURPLE, based upon the novel by Alice Walker. More than any other film on the list, THE COLOR PURPLE gives us a powerful internal critique of African-American spiritual destruction. Celie (Whoopi Goldberg) is mistreated by her own race. Her predicament is a prejudice and a punishment meted out towards her from the hands of Black men and women, who for reasons of their own self interest have become her oppressors. Many African-Americans, during the film's release, objected to the negative portrayal of Black men in the film as either misogynistic or ineffectual. Those charges and the fact that the film was snubbed at the Oscars have tended to obscure the richness of the achievement. Here is a film that reveals to us the self-destructive effect of racial prejudice: it causes its victims to internalize their oppressors and mete out their pain upon each other. When Celie finally stands up for herself, she becomes more that just a symbol of female defiance, she is also humanized in her yearning for independence—to think and act for herself. Again, we have the eyes of a stranger, Steven Spielberg to thank for allowing us to look at ourselves unselfconsciously and without the censorship of the internalized overseer.

THE COLOR PURPLE affords us a view into the way in which we, ourselves, offend and attempt to destroy the independent spirit of our own people. Celie's early abandonment by her family into the marriage with Mister (Danny Glover) and the brutal strikes against her body and vanity (You shoal is ugly!) were all powerful gestures to 'break' her will and force her into a continuous subjugation. It is a view that perhaps only a stranger could help us to see. But it was just such an internal and self-critical view that disturbed the Black polemicists in that it takes the focus off of the eternally vilified, White Man, and critiques the self-defeating actions of the Black man against his own people. It is no question that because of this self-critical perspective THE COLOR PURPLE is by far a braver and more important film than Spielberg's later work, AMISTAD. It is this self-critical aspect that made

THE COLOR PURPLE a unique film whose blunt objectivity could not be tolerated by many African-Americans who found it indecent to criticize each other in public.

The influx of the "In The Hood" films of the late Eighties and early Nineties was as much a consequence of the formulaic approach to commercial cinema as it was a failed appeal to the legions of young African-Americans who mistakenly thought Hollywood was finally responding to the way they saw the world: as a hostile ghetto, over policed and underemployed, swarming with gangs, drug dealers, drug addicts, prostitution and senseless murder. Films like, John Singleton's BOYZ IN THE HOOD (1991), The Hughes Brothers' MENACE II SOCIETY (1993) and others seemed to liberate the voice of a young African-American generation while not so discreetly exploiting it. But with each subsequent film it became apparent that the studios were less concerned with giving a voice to the voiceless and more concerned with their steep profit margins created by using the violent stereotypes, sexual myths and the pessimism that constricts the world view of those trapped in the hood.

Very few films from this era are tolerable to watch today without a certain embarrassment that is comparable to watching some of the worst Blaxploitation films of the 1970's. Sure the films of the 1990's are technically better than the 70's blaxploitation films, but the well meaning self righteousness of BOYZ IN THE HOOD seems wooden and pedantic just as the sudden violence and 'gangbanging' dialect within MENACE II SOCIETY seems staged and overacted. How much of this dim revisionist view of those films was created by the hilarious and now classic parody of the genre, DON'T BE A MENACE TO SOUTH CENTRAL WHILE DRINKING YOUR JUICE IN THE HOOD, by the Wayans Brothers, I cannot say, but there is one film that had a certain quality that allowed it to transcend the limitations of that genre.

Boaz Yakin's FRESH (1994) was a film that was created at the very end of the genre's successful commercial run. It was during this year that the African-American audience was beginning to cool on the limited perspective presented in the 'In The Hood' films and with a knee-jerk reaction embraced films at the polar opposite: sentimental romantic or family oriented affairs like LOVE JONES (1995) or SOUL FOOD (1996). The film, FRESH, presents us with an individual caught in the vice grips of a fixed and deadly social circumstance that can only be unhinged by using the prejudice and violence of the participants against themselves. In many ways it is a continuation of the theme of individual independence discussed previously in NOTHING BUT A MAN, except that FRESH was made thirty years later and instead of an adult Black man it featured a 12 year old Black child (Sean Nelson).

The essential difference between FRESH and the other films of the In The Hood genre is that the main character (Fresh as he is called) and the filmmaker, Boaz Yakin, did not side with the so-called gangsta perspective of pessimism, ruthlessness and materialism. FRESH is a film that reveals the tragic consequences of the actions of these gangsta characters and then uses the limited perspective of these characters against themselves. The film features an elaborate revenge plot created and executed by the 12 year old boy against the elder drug dealers and gangstas that populate his world. What motivates the character to create such a scheme is found in how these gangstas were either keeping love from him (his sister, Nicole, who was strung out by a pimp-like character named, Esteban) and destroying the love he wanted before he could get it (through the sudden death of a young girl by a stray bullet from one of the gangsta's guns). His poignant meetings with his 'estranged' father (Samuel Jackson) in the park to play intense games of chess is reminiscent of Duff's meetings with his father in NOTHING BUT A MAN; these meetings are learning experiences that guide the destiny of both characters. More than anything, FRESH gave voice to a new generation living and dying of the consequences brought about by an older and misguided generation of pessimistic drug dealers and crime lords.

Again, it is a social critique of the African-American community made by an outsider just after the zenith of the gangsta rap and In The Hood film popularity that was misshaping and poisoning African-American culture. The significance of this heretical gesture should not be overlooked. Boaz Yakin made his film during an era where the only African-American films being green lit were violent drug and gang dramas. I believe it took an outsider to make this film because most of us were caught up in the glamour, the violence, and the macho illusions of the In The Hood genre. We identified too strongly with the pessimistic ghetto worldview without regard to how that pessimism was affecting the next generation after us.

So the four films I have discussed reveal the heretical nature of independent filmmaking in that it is a critique of the status quo that emphasizes the significance of the individual within the fiction (Sarah Jane, Duff, Celie, and Fresh) and the significance of the individual who creates the fiction (Douglas Sirk, Michael Roemer, Steven Spielberg, and Boaz Yakin). Although we can certainly say that both Douglas Sirk and Steven Spielberg hardly qualify as independent filmmakers, there are special conditions that account for their ability to produce 'heretical' visions in the Hollywood system. Douglas Sirk was a successful filmmaker at the very end of his career; insulated by these two conditions (success and finality) he could take the risk and make a heretical vision. On the other hand, Steven Spielberg, next to George Lucas, is quite simply the most successful American filmmaker who has adopted children, some of whom are Black. Who in Hollywood would dare say," No," to this blockbuster creating wunderkind? Yet I believe it was the strength of his source material (Alice Walker's novel) that made the film a heretical statement, as much as Spielberg's inner-sensitivity for African-Americans. Steven Spielberg was simply *the* most powerful filmmaker who could bring such a work to the forefront.

Lest we get too comfortable and believe that today it is easy for outsider Whites to make more African-American films, the recent controversy surrounding Irish filmmaker, Jim Sheridan's film, GET RICH OR DIE TRYIN', featuring rap artist 50 Cent should quell this thought. He says," Everybody keeps saying,' You know, you made a black movie.' And I keep saying,' No, I made a movie . . . I made the same movie if I were making it in Dublin or London or anywhere.' I didn't approach it like its special. I'm used to Belfast. It's the same." [16] Such comments should remind us of how privileged Whites are oblivious to their lack of racial inclusiveness in their comments that seem to berate Jim Sheridan for making one of "those" movies; Black movies that they don't really want to experience.

For African-Americans to have an important, relevant and lasting Independent Cinema we must allow ourselves the ability to think independently and to critique ourselves in public and in art. We must honor and respect personal expression in the collective art form known as cinema. What comes natural for the musician (e.g. Marvin Gaye—What's Going On? or the work of Hip-Hop artists Common and Kanye West) must be allowed to be natural for the filmmaker. If we do not lose the inhibitions of the internalized overseer, we will constantly have to have strangers (non-Blacks) to give us penetrating insight into ourselves and our culture.

We must not continue to shackle ourselves to each other with narrowly defined rhetoric and limited perspectives, but instead liberate ourselves by looking at our situation objectively in a broad context. There is more than enough blame to go around to explain our position in American society, but we do ourselves a disservice by suppressing a diversity of opinions in our arts to reveal the truths that remain hidden in plain sight. Independent cinema equals independent thought and the sooner we realize this, the broader markets our films might be able to appeal to and subsequently gain, if not the steep profits of Hollywood then at least the longevity and long term profits that characterize the classic films we enjoy and cherish.

SUMMARY

If film is both a business and an art we cannot afford to lose perspective upon either truth. If African-Americans continue to pursue films solely as a way to achieve upward class mobility (that is to get rich), then we will have effectively created a slave cinema; a cinema whose sole concern is profit and not purpose, similarity and not originality, marketability and not innovation. An independent mandate for African-American independent film would be a mandate that protects, promotes and expects daring, original, provocative, and innovative visions with an infrastructure of festivals, critics, websites, and distributors to celebrate, discuss and support these filmmakers to stand alone in their heresies that augment human potential for good. Another condition of this independent mandate would be the acceptance, encouragement and support of like-spirited collaborators who see that view as justified in its artistic integrity and do everything in their power to help get it made and shown.

Moreover, we might also have to consider the fact that the work of many independent African-American filmmakers is intentionally being suppressed by certain African-American and White cultural gatekeepers who either disagree with the content within the fiction, the race of the artist or both. These cultural gatekeepers keep large audiences from viewing the African-American independent films deliberately or 'contaminate' the selection process with disinterested or disingenuous attitudes. Historically, many of us are used to this type of cultural sabotage from Whites, but it is shocking and discouraging to receive it from other African-Americans who view the intellectual independence represented within the films as a social heresy that must be suppressed.

We should also view the private verbal attacks upon comedian Dave Chappelle, concerning his use of the "N" word and the racial content of his Comedy Central show as proof that there are cultural gatekeepers who viewed the freedom of The Chappelle Show as a form of racial heresy. Many of these gatekeepers who voiced their negative opinions of the show were African-American themselves and thus unwittingly continued to curtail the artistic freedom of African-Americans in the name of Unity. Although I cannot go so far as to believe the theory put forth that these African-American gatekeepers forced The Chappelle Show off the air, I do believe that their collective negative influence certainly exerted undue stress upon the comedian, himself.

We don't celebrate or acknowledge a large number of Independent African-American filmmakers for a variety of reasons, but the most significant reason is that we cannot tolerate the intellectual and economic heresy that is inherent to independent filmmaking and we shun filmmakers whose opinions and visions differ from the status quo or the standard pessimism of African-American life. To end our progressive descent towards a Slave Cinema we must rid ourselves of the internalized overseer that unifies us with a collective image of Black ignorance and self-defeat; only then will we have truly overcome.

NOTES

(1) Cf. Variety Magazine Jun-Aug. 2005.

(2) Charles Burnett, writer\director of KILLER OF SHEEP (1977), THE GLASS SHEILD (1995)—Julie Dash, writer\director of DAUGHTERS OF THE DUST (1991), HAILE GERIMA writer\director of SANKOFA (1993), MELVIN VAN PEEPLES, writer\director of SWEET SWEETBACK'S BADASS SONG (1971), William Greaves writer/director of SYMBIOPSYCHOTAXIPLASM: TAKE ONE (1968). My intention is not to ignore but to generate interest in these and other African-American independent filmmakers.

(3) Pg. 9, WHY ARE ALL THE BLACK KIDS SITTING TOGETHER IN THE CAFETERIA, Beverly Daniel Tatum, P.H. D., Basic Books, New York, 1997.

(4) From the article," Popular Success is Not My Area", by Lynn Hirschberg, Friday August 5th, 2005 from The Guardian Internet Magazine.

(5) Page 164, COMPANION TO THE COSMOS, by John Gribbin, Weidenfeld & Nicolson, London, 1996.

(6) Perhaps I must pause here to cite an essential difference between the way I define a heretic and a lunatic. The heretic is one who goes against religious, social or intellectual orthodoxy in an effort to increase human potential for good. A lunatic is one who goes against orthodoxy for self interest or to limit and stunt human potential for good. The contrast between my two interpretations is as broad as that of Luther placing his note on the door of the church which led to the Protestant Reformation to the Uni-bomber Ted Kaczynski placing his explosives in his letter bombs and mailing them to unsuspecting and innocent victims.

[7] Page 278, AN EMEMY OF THE PEOPLE, by Henrik Ibsen found in IBSEN The Complete Major Prose Plays, Translated and introduced by Rolf Fjelde

[8] "Make visible what, without you, might perhaps never have been seen." Page 72, NOTES ON THE CINEMATOGRAPHER, By Robert Bresson, Quartet Encounters, Great Britain, 1975.

[9] Page 105, MOVIEMAKERS' MASTER CLASS: Private Lessons from the World's Foremost Directors, by Laurent Tirard, Faber & Faber, New York, 2002.

[10] Page 1, A THEORY OF COGNITIVE DISSONANCE, by Leon Festinger, Stanford University Press, Stanford, 1957.

[11] Page 85, Ibid.

[12] Page 86-87, Ibid.

[13] Page 118, THE RACIAL CONTRACT, by Charles W. Mills, Cornell University Press, Ithaca, NEW YORK, 1997.

[14] Page 130, SIRK ON SIRK, by Jon Halliday Viking Press, Inc, 1972. For a deeper analysis of this film and a full discussion of its themes of miscegenation and the effect such efforts have on bi-racial children please read, THE UNFINISHED PERSONALITY by Andre Seewood.

[15] An excerpt that was transcribed from the 40th anniversary New Video NYC DVD release of NOTHING BUT A MAN. From the mini-documentary, Cast and Crew 40 years later by Robert M. Young.

[16] Taken from an internet article, SHERIDAN: 50 Cent film isn't a black movie, from Ireland On-Line, Thomas Crosbie Media, 2005.

www.bestdraft.org

Screenplay Consultation

"Because the only critique that matters is the one that gets you to the *best draft*."

FILMOGRAPHY

LINEAR

Works of Jean-Luc Godard
Alphaville (1965)
Pierrot Le Fou (1965)
Two or Three Things I Know About Her (1966)
Week-end (1967)
My Live To Live (1962)

Do The Right Thing (Spike Lee—1987)
The Godfather (Francis Coppola—1972)
Irreversible (Gaspar Noe 2004)

Works of Rainer Werner Fassbinder
The American Soldier (1970)
Ali Fear Eats The Soul (1973)
Mother Kursters Goes to Heaven (1975)
Fox and His Friends (1974)
Querelle (1982)

NON-LINEAR

Works of Bernardo Bertolucci
La Commare Secca (The Grim Reaper 1962)
The Last Emperor (1987)
The Conformist (1970)
Nineteen Hundred (1975)

The Godfather II (Francis Coppola—1974)
The Killing (Stanley Kubrick 1954)
Last Year at Marienbad (Alain Resnais 1961)
Slaughterhouse Five (George Roy Hill 1972)
Catch 22 (Mike Nichols 1970)
Jackie Brown (Quentin Tarantino 1995)
Amores Perros (2000) & 21 Grams (2004 Alejandro Gonzalez Inarritu)
Eternal Sunshine of the Spotless Mind (Michel Gondry—2004)

DISCOVERY NARRATIVES

Works of Roman Polanski
Repulsion (1965)
Rosemary's Baby (1967)
Chinatown (1975)
The Ninth Gate (1999)

Marnie (Alfred Hitchcock 1964)
Alien (Ridley Scott—1979)
Dead Bang (John Frankenheimer—1988)
Seven (David Fincher—1995)
The Untouchables (Brian DePalma—1987)
The Constant Gardener (Fernando Meirelles—2006)
Internal Affairs (Mike Figgis—1990)
The Pledge (Sean Penn—2001)
The Vanishing (George Sluizer—1988)

SEDUCTION NARRATIVES

Psycho (Alfred Hitchcock—1960)
Phantasm (Don Corescelli—1980)
The Sixth Sense (M. Night Shyamalan—1999)
A Beautiful Mind (Ron Howard—2001)
Spider (David Cronenberg 2004)
Mulholland Dr. (David Lynch—2001)

CONCEPTUAL NARRATIVES

Slacker (Richard Linklater—1990)
Teorema (Pier Paolo Pasolini—1968)
2001: A Space Odyssey (Stanley Kubrick—1968)
VIDEODROME (David Cronenberg—1982)
Napoleon Dynamite (Jared and Jerusha Hess—2004)
The Matrix (The Wachowski Brothers—1999)
THX 1138 (George Lucas—1970)
Close Encounters of the Third Kind (Steven Spielberg—1977)
Children of Men (Alfonso Cuaron—2006)
Le Dernier Combat (Luc Besson—1983)

ALTERNATE REALITIES

Goodfellas (Martin Scorsese—1990)
Force of Evil (Abraham Polonsky—1949)
The Big Sleep (Howard Hawks—1946)
Being John Malkovich (Spike Jones—2000)
Crash (David Cronenberg—1996)

OTHER NOTED FILMMAKERS OF INTEREST

Works of Alfred Hitchcock
Secret Agent (1935)
The Wrong Man (1956)
Vertigo (1958)
North by Northwest (1959)
Psycho (1960)
Marnie (1964)

Works of Michelangelo Antonioni
L'Avventura (1959)
La Notte (1961)
L'Eclisse (1962)
Red Desert (1964)
Blow-Up (1966)
The Passenger (1975)
Zabrieski Point (1969)

Works of Andrei Tarkovsky
My Name is Ivan (1962)
Andrei Rublev (1966)
Solaris (1972)
Mirror (1974)
Stalker (1979)

Works of Robert Bresson
Diary of a Country Priest (1950)
A Man Escaped (1956)
Pickpocket (1959)
Mouchette (1966)
Au Hasard Balthazar (1968)
A Gentle Woman (1969)
Lancelot of the Lake (1974)
The Devil, Probably (1977)
L'Argent (1983)

Works of Jacques Becker
Casque D'or (1952)
Touchez Pas Au Grisbi (1954)
Le Trou (1960)

Works of Jim Jarmusch
Stranger Than Paradise (1984)
Down By Law (1986)
Dead Man (1996)

Works of Jean-Pierre Melville
Le Samourai (1967)
Bob Le Flambeur (1955)
Un Flic (1972)
Les Doulos (1962)

Works of Sam Peckinpah
The Wild Bunch (1969)
The Getaway (1972)
Straw Dogs (1971)
Bring Me The Head of Alfredo Garcia (1974)

Works of Ingmar Bergman
The Silence (1963)
The Passion of Anna (1969)

Works of John Ford
Stagecoach (1939)
My Darling Clementine (1946)
The Searchers (1956)
Sergeant Rutledge (1960)
The Man Who Shot Liberty Valance (1962)

This is not intended to be a definitive list of works by a particular director. This filmography has been provided for the benefit of the reader as many of the films and filmmakers above are referred to throughout the contents.

Answers to the Seven Motives of Murder Scenarios

1) D: RAGE. This is a fairly obvious answer as the anger and jealousy of the husband are passions that were enraged and became the primary motivation for the murder. Everything else the Husband did after the murder were secondary motives after the fact.

2) A: DEFENSIVE. Again, this is a fairly obvious answer in the fact that the man heard someone invading his home and killed the man in defense of his property and life. Everything else the man did after the murder were secondary motives after the fact.

3) C: JUDGMENT. This is the most obscured answer because most people see two murders in this scenario where there is only one. The mother's death by accident was unintentional and therefore motivated by fate. The corrupt police who kills the other corrupt police officer for the money is not the primary motivation for the murder. It is the drug dealer who is seeking revenge for his own mother's death that is the primary motivation for the murder. The drug dealer has made a judgment against the corrupt police officer's character. He has felt a grievous loss that can only be rectified by revenge. Without his 100,000 hit being place upon the policeman's head, the intentional murder would not have occurred, unless by his own hand.

SELECTED BIBLIOGRAPHY

Alighieri, Dante. 1954. THE INFERNO. Trans. John Ciardi. New York. Mentor Books.

Allen, Jr., Eddie B., 2004. LOW ROAD: The Life and Legacy of Donald Goines. New York. St. Martin's Press.

Aristotle. 1996. POETICS. Trans. by Malcolm Heath. New York. Penguin Books.

Arraj, James and Tyra. 1998. TRACKING THE ELUSIVE HUMAN. Chiloquin. Inner Growth Books.

Bandy, Mary Lea, and Bellour, Raymond. Ed., 1992. JEAN-LUC GODARD: SON+IMAGE. New York. The Museum of Modern Art.

Barthes, Roland. 1977. IMAGE\MUSIC\TEXT. Trans, Stephen Heath. New York. Hill & Wang.

Baumeister, Ph.D., Roy F. 1997. EVIL: Inside Human Violence and Cruelty. New York. W.H. Freeman and Company.

Bazin, Andre. 1967. WHAT IS CINEMA, Vol. 1, Trans. Hugh Gray. Berkeley. University of California Press.

Bergman, Ingmar. 1987. THE MAGIC LANTERN. Trans, Joan Tate. New York. Penguin Books.

Bergson, Henri. 1911. CREATIVE EVOLUTION. Trans. Arthur Mitchell. Mineola. Dover Publications.

Bjorkman, Stig, Manns, Torsten, & Sima, Jonas. 1970. BERGMAN ON BERGMAN. Trans, Paul Britten Austin. New York. Touchstone.

Bogdanovich, Peter, and Welles, Orson. 1993. THIS IS ORSON WELLES. New York. Harper Perennial.

Bondanella, Peter. 1983. ITALIAN CINEMA: FROM NEOREALISM TO THE PRESENT. New York. Frederick Ungar Publishing Co.

Booker, Christopher. 2004. THE SEVEN BASIC PLOTS: Why We Tell Stories. London. Continuum Books.

Bordwell, David and Thompson, Kristin. 1993. FILM ART: AN INTRODUCTION. New York. McGraw-Hill Inc.

Bresson, Robert. 1975. NOTES ON THE CINEMATOGRAPHER. Trans. Johnathan Griffin. London. Quartet Books Ltd.

Burgoyne, Robert. 1991. BERTOLUCCI'S 1900: A Narrative and Historical Analysis. Detroit. Wayne State University Press.

Campbell, Joseph. 1949. THE HERO WITH A THOUSAND FACES. Princeton. Princeton University Press.

Christie, Ian, and Thompson, David. Ed., 1989. SCORSESE ON SCORSESE. London. Faber & Faber.

Coen, Joel and Coen, Ethan. 1996. COLLECTED SCREENPLAYS 1. London. Faber & Faber.

Cook, David A., 1981. A HISTORY OF NARRATIVE CINEMA. New York. W.W. Norton & Company.

Cripps, Thomas. 1973. SLOW FADE TO BLACK: THE NEGRO IN AMERICAN FILM, 1900-1942. New York. Oxford University Press.

Cronin, Paul, ed. 2002. ROMAN POLANSKI INTERVIEWS. Jackson. University of Mississippi Press.

Deleuze, Gilles. 1986. CINEMA 1: THE MOVEMENT-IMAGE. Minneapolis. The University of Minnesota Press.

—————————. 1989. CINEMA 2: THE TIME IMAGE. Minneapolis. The University of Minnesota Press.

Dick, Philip K. 1995. THE SHIFTING REALITIES OF PHILIP K. DICK. Ed. Lawrence Sutin. New York. Vintage Books.

Durgnat, Raymond. 2002. A LONG HARD LOOK AT 'PSYCHO'. London. BFI Publishing.

Eco, Umberto. 1982. THE AESTHETICS OF CHAOSMOS: THE MIDDLE AGES OF JAMES JOYCE. Cambridge. Harvard University Press.

Eisenschitz, Bernard. 1993. NICHOLAS RAY: AN AMERICAN JOURNEY. Trans, Tom Milne. London. Faber & Faber.

Eisenstein, Sergi, M. 1947. THE FILM SENSE. Jay Leyda, ed., New York. Harcourt, Brace, & World Inc.

—————————. 1949. FILM FORM. Jay Leyda, ed., New York. Harcourt, Brace, & World Inc.

Fromm, Erich. 1951. THE FORGOTTEN LANGUAGE. New York. Grove Press Inc.

Georgakas, Dan & Rubenstein, Lenny Ed. 1984. ART POLITICS CINEMA: THE CINEASTE INTERVIEWS. London. Pluto Press.

Greene, Naomi. 1990. PIER PAOLO PASOLINI: CINEMA AS HERESY. Princeton. Princeton University Press.

Gillespie, Michael Allen. 1995. NIHILISM BEFORE NIETZSCHE. Chicago. University of Chicago Press.

Haidt, Jonathan. 2006. THE HAPPINESS HYPOTHESIS. New York. Basic Books.

Halliday, Jon. 1972. SIRK On SIRK. New York. Viking Press, Inc.

Hare Ph.d, Robert D. 1999. WITHOUT CONSCIENCE: THE DISTURBING WORLD OF PSYCHOPATHS AMONG US. New York. The Guilford Press.

Hayman, Ronald. 1984. FASSBINDER: FILMMAKER. New York. Simon & Schuster.

Herr, Michael. 2000. KUBRICK. New York. Grove Press.

Herrnstein, Richard J., and Wilson, James Q. 1985. CRIME & HUMAN NATURE. New York. Simon & Schuster.

Hyde, Lewis. 1998. TRICKSTER MAKES THIS WORLD. New York. North Point Press.

Johnson, Vida T. & Petrie, Graham. 1994. THE FILMS OF ANDREI TARKOVSKY: A VISUAL FUGUE. Bloomington. Indiana University Press.

Jones, Kent. 1999. L'ARGENT. London. British Film Institute.

Kapsis, Robert E. 1992. HITCHCOCK, THE MAKING OF A REPUTATION. Chicago. The Universtiy of Chicago Press.

Kardish, Laurence and Lorenz, Juliane eds. 1997. RAINER WERNER FASSBINDER. New York. Museum of Modern Art.

Kelly, Mary Pat. 1991. MARTIN SCORSESE: A JOURNEY. New York. Thunder Mouth Press.

Kesey, Ken. 1996. ONE FLEW OVER THE CUCKOO'S NEST. New York. Penguin Books.

Kuleshov, Lev. 1974. KULESHOV ON FILM. Trans, Ronald Levaco. Berkeley. University of California Press.

Lebo, Harlan. 1997. THE GODFATHER LEGACY. New York. Fireside Books

Lenski, Gerhard E. 1966. POWER & PRIVILEGE: A THEORY OF SOCIAL STRATIFICATION. Chapel Hill. The University of North Carolina Press.

Levi-Strauss, Claude. 1979. MYTH & MEANING. New York. Schocken Books.

_____. 1966. THE SAVAGE MIND. Chicago. University of Chicago Press.

Luhr, William. 1991. RAYMOND CHANDLER & FILM 2nd Ed. Tallahassee. The Florida State University Press.

Madden, David, ed. 1968. TOUGH GUY WRITERS OF THE THIRTIES. Carbondale. Southern Illinois University Press.

MacCabe, Colin. 2003. GODARD: A Portrait of the Artist at Seventy. New York. Farrar, Straus, and Giroux.

Mills, Charles, W. 1997. THE RACIAL CONTRACT. Ithaca. Cornell University Press.

Manning, Peter, K. 1997. POLICE WORK: THE SOCIAL ORGANIZATION OF POLICING. Prospect Heights. Waveland Press Inc.

Masson, Jeffery Moussaieff. 1984. THE ASSAULT ON TRUTH: FREUD'S SUPPRESSION OF THE SEDUCTION THEORY. New York. Harper Books.

McBride, Joseph. 1982. HAWKS ON HAWKS. Berkeley. University of California Press.

Metz, Christian. 1974. FILM LANGUAGE: A SEMIOTICS OF THE CINEMA. Chicago. The University of Chicago Press.

Mills, Charles, W. 1997. THE RACIAL CONTRACT. Ithaca. Cornell University Press.

Mosley, Walter. 1990. DEVIL IN A BLUE DRESS. New York. Pocket Books.

Nichols, Bill ed., 1976. MOVIES AND METHODS Vol. 1. Berkeley. University of California Press.

Nietzsche, Friedrich. 1967. THE WILL TO POWER. Trans, Walter Kaufmann & R.J. Hollingdale. New York. Vintage Press.

Pasolini, Paolo Pier. 1988. HERETICAL EMPIRICISM. Trans, Ben Lawton & Louise K. Barnett. Bloomington and Indianapolis. Indiana University Press.

_____. 1996. POEMS. Trans, Norman MacAfee with Luciano Martinengo. New York. Noonday Press.

Pavel, Thomas G., 1985. THE POETICS OF PLOT. Minneapolis. University of Minnesota Press.

Pileggi, Nicholas and Scorsese, Martin. 1990. GOODFELLAS. London. Faber & Faber.

Polanski, Roman. 1984. ROMAN BY POLANSKI. New York. Ballantine Books.

Polti, Georges. 1921. THE THIRTY-SIX DRAMATIC SITUATIONS. Boston. The Writer's Company, Inc.

Propp, Vladimir. 1968. MORPHOLOGY OF THE FOLKTALE. Trans, Laurence Scott. Austin. University of Texas Press.

Puzo, Mario. 2002. THE GODFATHER. New York. The New American Library.

Quandt, James. Ed., 1999. BRESSON. Toronto. Toronto International Film Festival.

Rabinger, Michael. 1998. ON DIRECTING. New York. Focus Books.

Ray, Nicholas. 1993. I WAS INTERRUPTED, NICHOLAS RAY ON MAKING MOVIES. Berkeley. University of California Press.

Reichenbach, Hans. 1956. THE DIRECTION OF TIME. Berkeley. University of California Press.

Richardson, Robert. 1969. LITERATURE AND FILM. Bloomington. Indiana University Press.

Rohdie, Sam. 1990. ANTONIONI. London. British Film Institute.

_____. 1995. THE PASSION OF PIER PAOLO PASOLINI. London. British Film Institute.

Sargant, William. 1957. THE BATTLE FOR THE MIND. Cambridge. ISHK.

Saussure, Ferdinand de. 1972. COURSE IN GENERAL LINGUISTICS. Paris. Editions Pagot.

Schrader, Paul. 1972. TRANSCENDENTAL STYLE IN FILM: Ozu, Bresson, Dreyer. New York. Da Capo Press.

Schwartz, Barth David. 1992. PASOLINI: REQUIEM. New York. Pantheon Books.

Siciliano, Enzo. 1982. PASOLINI: A BIOGRAPHY. New York. Random House.

Smith, Steven C. 1991. A HEART AT FIRE'S CENTER: THE LIFE AND MUSIC OF BERNARD HERRMANN. Berkeley. University of California Press.

Stack, Oswald. 1969. PASOLINI. Bloomington and London. Indiana University Press.

Stam, Robert. 1992. REFLEXIVITY IN FILM AND LITERATURE: From Don Quixote to Jean-Luc Godard. New York. Columbia University Press.

Tarkovsky, Andrei. 1987. SCULPTING IN TIME. Trans, Kitty Hunter-Blair. Austin. University of Texas Press.

_____. 1993. TIME WITHIN TIME: THE DIARIES. Trans, Kitty Hunter-Blair. London. Verso.

Tatum Ph.D, Beverly Daniel. "WHY ARE ALL THE BLACK KIDS SITTING TOGETHER IN THE CAFETERIA?" 1997. New York. Basic Books.

Thody, Phillip. 1989. MODERN NOVELISTS: ALBERT CAMUS. London. The Macmillan Press.

Tirard, Laurent. 2002. MOVIEMAKERS' MASTER CLASS. New York. Faber & Faber.

Truffaut, Francois. 1984. HITCHCOCK, Revised Edition. New York. Touchstone Edition.

Turovskaya, Maya. 1989. TARKOVSKY, CINEMA AS POETRY. Trans, Natasha Ward. London. Faber & Faber.

Vogel, Amos. 1974. FILM AS A SUBVERSIVE ART. New York. Random House.

Weddle, David. 1994. "IF THEY MOVE . . . KILL'EM," THE LIFE AND TIMES OF SAM PECKINPAH. New York. Grove Press.

Welles, Orson. 1985. TOUCH OF EVIL. Terry Comito, ed. New Brunswick and London. Rutgers University Press.

Wilmington, Michael and McBride, Joseph. 1975. JOHN FORD. New York. Da Capo Press Inc.

Wilson, James Q. 1993. THE MORAL SENSE. New York. The Free Press.

Wollen, Peter. 1972. SIGNS AND MEANING IN THE CINEMA. Bloomington. Indiana University Press.

Wood, Robin. 1989. HITCHCOCK'S FILMS REVISITED. New York. Columbia University Press.

Wright, Will. 1975. SIX GUNS & SOCIETY. Berkeley. University of California Press.

INDEX

M r. Seewood is a multiple award winning independent writer, director, producer and educator. Mr. Seewood's reviews and articles on film and other topics of socio-political interest have appeared in Film Threat Magazine (which he co-founded with Chris Gore), The Detroit Free Press, The Metro Times Weekly, The Detroit Film Center Journal, The Michigan Vue, and the Film Dependent Website. He has taught Advanced Story Concepts and Screenwriting for Detroit's Center For Creative Studies, The Detroit Film Center, The Public Benefit Corporation and The Detroit Council of The Arts Summer Program. He is currently publishing a novel, The petti-Christ Chronicles and starting pre-production on a new feature length film to be made in Detroit.

CPSIA information can be obtained
at www.ICGtesting.com
Printed in the USA
LVHW01s2149060918
589355LV00003B/434/P